"A subtle, imaginative and brilliant work; *The Culture-Breast in Psychoanalysis* proposes an entirely new way of understanding the relationship between psychoanalysis and culture. It proposes that cultural experiences available through film, literature, music and the visual and performing arts can offer a frame, a space, and an encounter with an object, much like the 'breast' in early infantile life, so that we can, in a psychoanalytic sense, 'learn from experience'. Arguing that cultural objects can provide forms of holding and containment of unbearable thoughts and feelings, allowing for the rawness of experience to be given meaning, Noreen Giffney's profound insight helps us understand not just the transformational nature of these encounters but offers us the experience of reading the book itself as its most stunning case study. She argues with great poignancy, that we all feed at the culture-breast, and that understanding the way we psychically use cultural objects, whether as screen memories, as psychic retreats, or as containers, has the potential to open up new insights into the workings of our inner lives.

This book will become a vital point of reference for those interested in psychosocial thinking; the creative and potentially transformational area of encounter between the clinic, psychoanalytic theory, politics, arts and culture".

Lisa Baraitser, *Professor of Psychosocial Theory, Birkbeck, University of London, M. Inst. Psychoanalysis*

The Culture-Breast in Psychoanalysis

We are fed at the breast of culture, not wholly but to differing degrees. *The Culture-Breast in Psychoanalysis: Cultural Experiences and the Clinic* focuses on the formative influence of cultural objects in our lives, and the contribution such experiences make to our mental health and overall wellbeing.

The book introduces "the culture-breast", a new clinical concept, to explore the central importance played by cultural objects in the psychical lives of patients and psychoanalytic clinical practitioners inside and outside the consulting room. Bringing together clinical writings from psychoanalysis and cultural objects from the applied fields of film, art, literature and music, the book also makes an argument for the usefulness of encounters with cultural objects as "non-clinical case studies" in the training and further professional development of psychoanalysts and psychotherapists. Through its engagement with psychosocial studies, this text, furthermore, interrogates, challenges and offers a way through a hierarchical split that has become established in psychoanalysis between "clinical psychoanalysis" and "applied psychoanalysis".

Combining approaches used in clinical, academic and arts settings, *The Culture-Breast in Psychoanalysis* is an essential resource for clinical practitioners of psychoanalysis, psychotherapy, counselling, psychology and psychiatry. It will also be of interest to researchers and practitioners in the fields of psychosocial studies, sociology, social work, cultural studies and the creative and performing arts.

Noreen Giffney is a psychoanalytic psychotherapist, a psychosocial theorist, and the director of Psychoanalysis +. She works in private practice in County Donegal and is a lecturer at Ulster University, Northern Ireland.

Psychoanalysis and Popular Culture Series

Series Editors: Caroline Bainbridge and Candida Yates
Consulting Editor: Brett Kahr

This series builds on the work done since 2009 by the Media and the Inner World research network. It aims to consider the relationship between psychoanalysis and popular culture as a lived experience that is ever more emotionalised in the contemporary age. In contrast to many scholarly applications of psychoanalysis, works in this series set out to explore the creative tensions of thinking about cultural experience and its processes whilst also paying attention to observations from both the clinical and scholarly fields. The series provides space for a dialogue between these different groups with a view to evoking new perspectives on the values and pitfalls of a psychoanalytic approach to ideas of selfhood, society, politics, and popular culture. In particular, the series strives to develop a psycho-cultural approach by foregrounding the usefulness of a post-Freudian, object relations perspective for examining the importance of emotional relationships and experience. We nevertheless welcome proposals from all fields of psychoanalytic enquiry. The series is edited by Caroline Bainbridge and Candida Yates, with Brett Kahr as the Consulting Editor.

Other titles in the Psychoanalysis and Popular Culture Series:

The Inner World of Doctor Who

Psychoanalytic Reflections in Time and Space
Iain MacRury and Michael Rustin

What Holds Us Together

Popular Culture and Social Cohesion
Barry Richards

The Culture-Breast in Psychoanalysis

Cultural Experiences and the Clinic
Noreen Giffney

For more information about this series, please visit: https://www.routledge.com/The-Psychoanalysis-and-Popular-Culture-Series/book-series/KARNPSYPOP

The Culture-Breast in Psychoanalysis

Cultural Experiences and the Clinic

Noreen Giffney

Routledge
Taylor & Francis Group

LONDON AND NEW YORK

First published 2021
by Routledge
2 Park Square, Milton Park, Abingdon, Oxon OX14 4RN

and by Routledge
605 Third Avenue, New York, NY 10158

Routledge is an imprint of the Taylor & Francis Group, an informa business

British Library Cataloguing-in-Publication Data
A catalogue record for this book is available from the British Library

Library of Congress Cataloging-in-Publication Data
Names: Giffney, Noreen, author.
Title: The culture-breast in psychoanalysis : cultural experiences and the clinic / Noreen Giffney.
Description: Milton Park, Abingdon, Oxon ; New York, NY : Routledge, 2021. | Series: Psychoanalysis and popular culture | Includes bibliographical references and index.
Identifiers: LCCN 2021004845 (print) | LCCN 2021004846 (ebook) | ISBN 9781138312500 (hardback) | ISBN 9781138312517 (paperback) | ISBN 9780429458170 (ebook)
Subjects: LCSH: Psychoanalysis and culture. | Material culture—Psychological aspects.
Classification: LCC BF175.4.C84 G55 2021 (print) | LCC BF175.4.C84 (ebook) | DDC 150.19/5—dc23
LC record available at https://lccn.loc.gov/2021004845
LC ebook record available at https://lccn.loc.gov/2021004846

ISBN: 978-1-138-31250-0 (hbk)
ISBN: 978-1-138-31251-7 (pbk)
ISBN: 978-0-429-45817-0 (ebk)

Typeset in Times New Roman
by Apex CoVantage, LLC

For Nicole, who has been on this journey with me
every step of the way

Contents

Figures

About the author

Noreen Giffney is an accredited psychoanalytic psychotherapist and a psychosocial theorist. She is the Director of "Psychoanalysis +", an international, interdisciplinary initiative that brings together clinical, artistic and academic approaches to, and applications of, psychoanalysis. She has published and lectured extensively on psychoanalysis, psychosocial studies and critical theory. She works as a psychoanalytic psychotherapist in private practice in County Donegal and as a lecturer in counselling at Ulster University.

Acknowledgements

Nicole Murray read the manuscript in its entirety. She has always been my most incisive reader. I discussed every idea with her, as I do with everything I write. She is my life partner, my best friend and my most important collaborator in all things in this life. I offer this book to her with love and thanks for the experiences we have already shared, as I look forward to our continuing encounter.

I first met Aoife Kavanagh nearly thirty years ago in a secondary school classroom. So much has happened in our lives since then. I deeply value her presence in my life, and the depth and steadfastness of our friendship.

Berna O'Brien has impressed on me the importance of experience and encounter for all forms of thinking and action. Her influence on the development of my thinking and on me as a person has been life-changing, for which I feel a profound gratitude.

I feel fortunate to have a number of experienced colleagues in Ireland and the UK whose collegiality, mentorship and friendship have been vital to me as a clinician and an academic researcher as I worked on this book: Lisa Baraitser, Margaret Boyle Spelman, Rita Deegan, Ann Murphy and Toni O'Brien Johnson. They have helped me through their generosity, perhaps unbeknownst to them until now, to grow more into myself as someone who thinks and writes.

A number of people read earlier drafts of material contained within this book. Maggie Long offered me valuable suggestions upon reading Chapter 2, from the perspective of a colleague who knows my approach to teaching. Margaret Boyle Spelman and Rita Deegan brought their extensive clinical experience and expertise to bear on their reading of Chapter 3. I am so grateful for their careful reading of the text.

I remember meeting Caroline Bainbridge for lunch in London during the Summer of 2015, when she invited me to submit a book proposal to the "Psychoanalysis and Popular Culture" book series she was editing with Candida Yates. Without that invitation, I do not think this book would have come into being. I also remember that lunch as a particularly pleasant one. The experience of collegiality cannot be underestimated in the decisions we make in terms of our research: I have appreciated the ongoing interest, support, care and patience both Caroline and Candida have shown my work. My book has found a good intellectual home in their series.

This book contains a number of images: a photograph of Jennifer Rubell's sculpture, "Us" (2015), appears on the book's front cover; three photographs from Mark Gerald's ongoing photographic project, "In the shadow of Freud's couch: Portraits of psychoanalysts in their offices" (2003–), feature in Chapter 2; and Francis Danby's painting, "The Opening of the Sixth Seal" (1828), is included in Chapter 3. My sincere thanks to Jennifer Rubell, Meredith Rosen of Meredith Rosen Gallery in New York, Karon Hepburn and Holly Lord of Stephen Friedman Gallery in London, Mark Gerald and the National Gallery of Ireland for generously allowing me to reproduce the images. Each piece has been important in the development of my thinking about this book, so it is a real pleasure to have them here alongside my words.

I have given talks on subjects contained within this book to audiences at a number of events convened by professional groups or in institutional settings: the University of Roehampton; the Irish Psychoanalytic Film Festival, Dublin; Maynooth University; the Freud Museum, London; the Irish Forum for Psychoanalytic Psychotherapy; Brunel University; the Irish Poetry Therapy Network; CONFER clinical events convened in the Tavistock and Portman NHS Foundation Trust, London and at Trinity College Dublin; IMMA – The Irish Museum of Modern Art, Dublin; University College Dublin; the British Psychoanalytic Council's Psychoanalytic Psychotherapy NOW Conference at Imperial College, London; the University of Manchester; Science Gallery Dublin; the National Museum of Decorative Arts and History, Dublin; the University of Manitoba, Canada; the "New Books in Psychoanalysis" podcast series; and Birkbeck, University of London. I am grateful for these invitations and collaborations, as it is such a privilege to present material in progress and have the benefit of attendees' feedback and suggestions: Dan Anderson, Caroline Bainbridge, Sophie Byrne, Olga Cox Cameron, Janet Healy, Theresa Kelly, Philip Lance, Lisa Moran, Juliet Newbigin, Dany Nobus, Anne O'Leary, Jordan Osserman, Jane Ryan, Laurence Spurling, Jackie Stacey and Arlene Young.

I have developed and managed a number of interdisciplinary and multidisciplinary events, solely and in collaboration with colleagues, during the writing of this book. Each event has enriched my own experience and helped to open up a space for my thinking: "Melancholia" at the National Museum of Decorative Arts and History, Dublin; "Conducting Psychoanalytic Research for Publication" in the Humanities Institute at University College Dublin; "The Artist/Analyst Is Present: At the Interface between Creative Arts Practice and Clinical Psychoanalytic Practice", as part of the Irish Psychoanalytic Film Festival at IMMA – The Irish Museum of Modern Art, Dublin; "The Clinical Usefulness of Wilfred Bion's Writings for Psychotherapists" at Birkbeck, University of London; Film: In Session in Filmbase, Dublin; "Cinematic Encounters with Violent Trauma and Its Aftermath" at Science Gallery Dublin; "The Long-Term Impact of Childhood Trauma on Adult Mental and Physical Health" at the Strand Arts Centre Cinema, Belfast; "Unconscious Objects: A Series of Conversations around Art and Psychoanalysis" at IMMA – The Irish Museum of Modern Art, Dublin; "What Can We

Do with Our Vulnerability? Words to Make Meaning of Life's Experiences" at the Duncairn Centre for Culture and Arts, Belfast; "Sexuality, Identity and the State" at IMMA – The Irish Museum of Modern Art, Dublin; "Psychoanalysis and Sexuality Today: Psychosocial Influences on Transference and Countertransference" at the National Museum of Decorative Arts and History, Dublin; and "What Might Clinical Psychoanalysis Learn from Queer Theories of Sexuality? 113 Years after Freud's *Three Essays*" at the Freud Museum, London. I have worked with a number of people on initiatives and/or publications while I was writing this book: Sophie Byrne, Janet Healy, Tina Kinsella, Maggie Long, Jolene Mairs Dyer, Lisa Moran, Ann Murphy, Emma Radley and Eve Watson. It is such a pleasure to work with others in a collaborative and creative way.

I have used some of the approaches discussed in this book in my undergraduate and postgraduate teaching at University College Dublin, Trinity College Dublin, Ulster University, Independent College Dublin, the University of Limerick and Birkbeck, University of London. My thanks to the students who attended my courses for their enthusiastic engagement with the material, as well as for being open to stepping outside of their comfort zones to engage reflectively with their own personal experiences, past and present – never an easy task.

My thanks to Russell George, Ellie Duncan and Alec Selwyn at Routledge for their support and assistance: Russell signed the book, and Alec and Ellie saw the book through to publication.

I wish to acknowledge the funding I received from Ulster University while I worked on this book. My thanks, in particular, to Catrin Rhys, the Head of the School of Communication and Media, and Robert Porter, the Director of the Centre for Media Research.

A small amount of material in this book appeared in an earlier version in parts of Noreen Giffney (2015a). Sex as evacuation. *Studies in Gender & Sexuality* 16.2: 103–109; Noreen Giffney (2016a). A theory of thinking: A theory of desiring. *Studies in Gender & Sexuality* 17.3: 150–164; Noreen Giffney (2017c). Psychoanalysis in Ireland: An interview with Noreen Giffney. *Breac: A Digital Journal of Irish Studies* 7; Noreen Giffney, Eve Watson and Philip Lance (2018). Noreen Giffney and Eve Watson in discussion with Philip Lance about *Clinical Encounters in Sexuality*. *New Books in Psychoanalysis* podcast series; and Noreen Giffney (2019). The use of an object. *Studies in Gender & Sexuality* 20.4: 245–248.

Series editors' preface

The application of psychoanalytic ideas and theories to culture has a long tradition, and this is especially the case with cultural artefacts that might be considered "classical" in some way. For Sigmund Freud, the works of William Shakespeare and Johann Wolfgang von Goethe were as instrumental as those of culturally renowned poets and philosophers of classical civilisation in helping to formulate the key ideas underpinning psychoanalysis as a psychological method. In the academic fields of the humanities and social sciences, the application of psychoanalysis as a means of illuminating the complexities of identity and subjectivity is now well established. However, despite these developments, there is relatively little work that attempts to grapple with popular culture in its manifold forms, some of which, nevertheless, reveal important insights into the vicissitudes of the human condition.

The "Psychoanalysis and Popular Culture" book series builds on the work done since 2009 by the Media and the Inner World research network, which was generously funded by the UK's Arts and Humanities Research Council. It aims to offer spaces to consider the relationship between psychoanalysis in all its forms and popular culture that is ever more emotionalised in the contemporary age.

In contrast to many scholarly applications of psychoanalysis, which often focus solely on "textual analysis", this series sets out to explore the creative tension of thinking about cultural experience and its processes with attention to observations from the clinical and scholarly fields of observation. What can academic studies drawing on psychoanalysis learn from the clinical perspective, and how might the critical insights afforded by scholarly work cast new light on clinical experience? The series provides space for a dialogue between these different groups with a view to creating fresh perspectives on the values and pitfalls of a psychoanalytic approach to ideas of selfhood, society and popular culture. In particular, the series strives to develop a psycho-cultural approach to such questions by drawing attention to the usefulness of post-Freudian and object relations perspectives for examining the importance of emotional relationships and experience.

The Culture-Breast in Psychoanalysis: Cultural Experiences and the Clinic is a sensitive, bold and astute book, in which Noreen Giffney meticulously frames the complex debate that has long been raging about the relationship between psycho-analysis as a "pure" form of clinical practice and the application of psychoanalytic concepts, theories and strategies to the experiences of the cultural and social environment. Giffney persuasively builds her ideas from her own textures of experience both within the clinic and beyond – in the realms of relationality, imagination and in the context of social and cultural life, broadly defined. She showcases the power and scope of the non-clinical psychoanalytic case study to enrich not only the clinical training and practice of psychoanalysts and therapists, but also to shape an understanding of the role of cultural objects in formative experience. In offering her rich and nuanced concept of "the culture-breast", Giffney brings psychoanalytic thinking about the role of the object up to date, offering a tool with which to understand the increasing imbrication of the mind with the psychosocial environment and laying down a creative challenge to clinicians to engage with cultural experience in creative and innovative ways.

Caroline Bainbridge and Candida Yates

Foreword

Whether as babies we are wrapped in swaddling clothes to our mother's bosom – or to her back as she works in the fields – or we are sent for neoliberal isolation in our cradles for maybe fifteen hours a day, we sup from an influence of our cultures. So much do we become our culture, that the book asserts, rightly I am sure, that "[we do our] thinking with rather than about cultural objects and experiences". It is such an important distinction to make. And yet we run together, without properly orienting ourselves, the notion of thinking as a process of logic on one hand, together with on the other, an intuitive appreciation of the beauties of life. It is as if "thinking" is all of a muchness.

From the middle of his career (mid-1960s), Wilfred Bion was trying to track down this kind of difference, trying to distinguish between the evocation of an experience and the recollection of a memory. Noreen Giffney's book is putting signposts all along this journey, which ultimately questions not just the nature of holding an evocation in mind, but what the nature of psychoanalytic communication is. Though I think Bion never quite made it in the end, I think he set the goal which this book is also heading towards. Bion seemed to get lost in his difficulty in distinguishing the kind of psychotic intrusion into others that his crazy patients made, from, on the other hand, the aesthetic evocation which pervades us from cultural creations. Language itself became differentiated in order to communicate the facts of the external world and its logical processes. Intuitive intimacy is a very different kind of communicative system, based on evoking a non-sensuous experience. The latter is inherent in humans and our culture. It starts at birth. And yet we hardly know how it happens. I have mused over the years on how we have been clever enough with our technologies to create machines to simulate our cognitive functions, from the abacus to the PC, but how would we start to think about a machine that could simulate our intimate emotional connections?

We exist in something called the psychosocial, but a name does not explain. It needs exploration as we have in Chapter 1. As the cover picture shows, the experience of holding a baby, a simulated baby, a lump of glass, is altogether different from the science of the interactive homeostatic mechanisms that provoke the functions of a mother with her baby. We need to look for that connection which is not "knowledge", which is not personal, but which expands and percolates like

the scent of Bourgainvillea in summertime (or, alternatively, of course, the nox-
ious experiences pervade like dog-shit on the doormat). How can we find the
nature of that intuitive broadband that can complement our digital selves?

It is indeed the target of this book to examine the pervasions of our culture that
waft within us; what their relations are with psychoanalysis; and the ease with
which psychoanalysts can let themselves slap back into formalised and cognitive
recollections.

The book deals in its own way with this interesting problem. Its startling point
of view is that the psychoanalytic understanding of what an aesthetic object does
to its audience is quite comparable to the engagement of a psychoanalyst with his
patient. Indeed the beholder in an art gallery is essentially comparable to an analyst retrieving his countertransference for examination in an exactly parallel way.
Do not miss the important vignettes in Chapter 2 showing how an encounter with
a cultural object runs this parallel course with a clinical psychoanalytic encounter.

Equally I would say to you the reader, you must ensure you engage with the
personal enquiry of the culture-breast in Chapter 3. This is an extended reflection
on the personal meanings of the "culture-breast" – screen memory, psychic retreat
and container. It is an experiment in reaching between the heights of conceptuali-
sations, on one hand, and the depths of personal experience on the other. It is this
"reaching-between" that we need to accomplish in a much more everyday way, as
these reflections portray. We must be as well as have our experiences. And indeed,
insofar as this Foreword attempts the advice of Noreen Giffney, this book is itself
a first start on that gentle bridge between our language and our experience.

Without junking psychoanalysis as medical science, this book gently presses
for a science of the personal that can complete the "being" that is the human
being. Above all, the book is itself an iconic evocation of the breast – traversing
the dimension from the new-born to adult maturity, from academic teaching to
personal, reflective listening.

R.D. Hinshelwood,
Psychoanalyst, and Emeritus Professor of
Psychosocial and Psychoanalytic Studies,
University of Essex, UK

At the breast of culture

The image on the front cover of this book is a photograph of a sculpture by the conceptual artist Jennifer Rubell (2015b). I first became aware of her piece entitled "Us" in 2015, when I read a review of an exhibition in which "Us" appeared. In the review entitled "All about my mother: The most Freudian exhibition ever", Nell Frizell (2015) quotes Rubell as saying, "a gallery is a therapeutic space too". Rubell is interested in psychoanalysis and has made a number of artworks that can be read in connection with psychoanalysis, including "My Shrink's Couch" (2012), "Portrait of the Artist" (2013) and "Us" (2015a). "Us" appeared in a solo exhibition, *Not Alone* (2015b), shown at the Stephen Friedman Gallery in London. I was working in London at the time but was unable to visit the exhibition as I was travelling, yet the image stayed with me. The way in which her sculpture was described on the Gallery's website (2015b) also stayed with me:

> In Gallery One, "Us", a hand-blown glass sculpture of a newborn baby is passed directly from one visitor to another. The artist trusts the viewer to take personal responsibility for the sculpture, using the viewer's physical and emotional attachment to complete the work. The sculpture is more physically legible through touch than through sight.

The visitor is invited to participate in the work (Thorpe, 2015). It is the encounter between the visitor and the sculpture that "complete[s] the work". In an interview with Claire Bartleman (Rubell, 2018), in which Bartleman asks Rubell about the art objects she makes and the place of the audience, Rubell replies: "The piece *is* the interaction between the person and the object", adding that "the object is the only part of the interaction that I have any control over. I can only offer a prompt to that interaction" (p. 34).

A mixture of disappointment at having missed the exhibition and desire to hold Rubell's sculpture has remained with me over the years. Experience underpins Rubell's work in this exhibition, and experience is central to my reaction: I feel disappointment that I did not get to attend the exhibition and desire to experience holding the sculpture. This reaction and the attendant feelings are also, of course, themselves an experience. They offer me something. There is always something to be gained, even in states of loss. Thus, the experience evoked by the image impressed itself on me. I carried the experience around with me. I held it in my mind. Affect and how it underpins states of reaction and response are an important component of Rubell's work. Facilitating a space for experience is central:

> Nobody tells the viewer they can just stand in front of a painting and question how they feel. Do you feel like crying? Do you feel like laughing? Do you feel mad? And isn't that kind of the whole point of art?
>
> (Rubell, 2018, p. 36)

Encounters evoke experiences, and experiences evoke reactions, which in turn offer a space for reflection, if they can be tolerated long enough to be held in mind. Leaving a space for reflection is also a key part of the experience of engaging with an art object for Rubell. As the Stephen Friedman Gallery's (2020) profile of her work states: "When in proximity with her works viewers are encouraged to engage senses normally absent from museum and gallery contexts. Rubell's happenings prompt immediate and powerful responses from her audience. In the aftermath they invite reflection".

Jennifer Rubell gave me permission to reproduce the image of her sculpture on this book's front cover. So, while I have not had the tactile experience of holding the sculpture, I am fortunate to have the visual experience of gazing at it. Thus, my holding of "Us" is psychological rather than physical, though there is a physical component at times when I hold the book itself. I have, moreover, had the experience of associating to the image and thinking with it as an assemblage of thoughts. From a psychoanalytic perspective, the image is important to me as a cultural object that encourages me to think and to feel. Encountering it does something to me. It is, what Christopher Bollas (1992a) terms, an "evocative object": "Certain objects, like psychic 'keys', open doors to unconsciously intense – and rich – experience in which we articulate the self that we are through the elaborating character of our response" (p. 18). The cover is the first encounter a reader has with a book, and aptly Rubell's sculpture materialises the first encounter between the infant and the mother's breast. The term "breast" refers to the infant's perception of the mother as a part-object. The use of the word covers both the mother's bodily organ or bottle as well as the feeding experience. This first encounter will influence all later encounters for the rest of our lives. The introjective and projective processes played out unconsciously against the backdrop of the breast leave a lasting imprint on our psychical fabric. Rubell's image and the title she conferred on it also bring to mind Donald Winnicott's (1952) statement: "There is no such thing as a baby" (p. 99). Expanding on what he means, Winnicott continues: "if you show me a baby you certainly show me also someone caring for the baby, or at least a pram with someone's eyes and ears glued to it. One sees a 'nursing couple'" (p. 99). He is referring to "the environment-individual set-up" (p. 99), which is necessary for physical and psychological survival. Cultural objects and experiences form part of that environment.

We are fed at the breast of culture, not wholly but to differing degrees. *The Culture-Breast in Psychoanalysis: Cultural Experiences and the Clinic* makes use of this statement to explore the formative and enduring influence of cultural objects (film, art, literature, music) in our lives, and the contribution such experiences make to our mental health and overall wellbeing. The book offers readers a series of experiences to reflect upon, and provides a frame for these experiences, which require the reader to enter into an encounter with clinical writings from psychoanalysis, with cultural objects, and with themselves. The central aim of the book is to offer a space for reflection. The book advocates the need for thinking *with* rather than *about* cultural objects and experiences. Chapter 1, "Thinking clinically with the psychosocial", introduces and engages with psychosocial studies, in an effort to interrogate, challenge and offer a way through a hierarchical split that has become established in psychoanalysis between "clinical psychoanalysis" and "applied psychoanalysis". These are terms used to refer to applications of psychoanalysis that take place inside and outside the consulting room respectively. This split is affecting what gets to count as clinical writing and, by extension, what is taken into account in thinking about clinical practice. Chapter 2, "Encounters with cultural objects as case study", provides an overview of the centrality of the clinical case study and vignette in psychoanalysis and in its cultural representations. This chapter makes an argument for the clinical usefulness of incorporating encounters with cultural objects as "non-clinical case studies" in the training and further professional development of psychoanalysts and psychotherapists. Chapter 3, "The culture-breast", introduces a new clinical concept to explore the central importance played by cultural objects in the psychical lives of patients and psychoanalytic clinical practitioners inside and outside the consulting room.

The Culture-Breast in Psychoanalysis facilitates readers honing their observation, analytical and interpretative skills while at the same time developing their capacity for self-awareness, self-reflectivity and insight. This book is theoretically positioned within the Kleinian tradition of psychoanalysis, in which working with transference and countertransference experiences are central to clinical practice. This includes the non-verbal and unconscious communications of the patient, alongside the words spoken by the patient in the consulting room. This book also incorporates the insights of psychoanalysts writing in the Independent tradition, particularly with regards to the continued need for practitioners to move around in our minds between external and internal worlds. This book also brings clinical psychoanalysis into dialogue with psychosocial studies and the psycho-cultural approach to foreground the inextricability of the psychical, social and cultural realms. I provide a rationale to clinical readers as to why they should engage with the psychosocial and the psycho-cultural, as each provide opportunities to extend and deepen practitioners' clinical skills and capacities for work in the consulting room. This book is located, as I am myself, in and between the discursive spaces of the clinic, academia, and the arts and culture.

A number of psychoanalytic writers have been particularly influential in the development of my stylistic approach in this book. Firstly, reading Melanie Klein's work was a revelation to me. Her writing completely bypasses the intellectual, the logical and the rational, and goes straight for the viscera. In her refusal to engage with psychical defences like intellectualisation and rationalisation, she makes contact with parts of the reader that are usually left untouched by a piece of writing (Giffney, 2017c). Reading her work made me realise how much writing gets caught in defensive nets of intellectualisation and rationalisation, so that the thoughts remain unthought. Secondly, Wilfred Bion's writing impressed on me the key significance of experience in all reading encounters. His book, *Learning from Experience* (Bion, 1962a), made a considerable impact on my approach to reading. While reading this book, I felt "confused, disorientated, alienated, dislocated, even overwhelmed; I felt put out to sea" (Giffney, 2013b, p. 293). I came to appreciate that Bion's writing evokes an emotional experience alongside representing it in words (Bion, 1994, p. 219). His writing, therefore, cannot be read but must be felt (Giffney, 2013b, p. 289). Bion (1962a) commences *Learning from Experience* with the pronouncement: "The book is designed to be read straight through once without checking at parts that might be obscure at first" (p. ii). This produced a tangible set of experiences for reflection. As a result, this is something I have incorporated into my own book, as the reader will see later. Thirdly, Thomas Ogden's style of writing slows everything down. He advocates taking one's time. In this, he opens up a space for the reader to engage in a close, careful reading of the text, and to make it her/his own (2013b, pp. 295–296). Ogden (2012a) writes of "reading creatively" (p. 1), a process during which we as readers are changed in the process of reading. He encourages the reader to "give oneself over to the experience of reading" and to use "the experience of reading to read oneself" (p. 2). His writing prompted me to read with more than my mind, but instead with my whole self.

I have chosen to write a preface to *The Culture-Breast in Psychoanalysis*, rather than an introduction. The preface presents the overall premise of this book and provides a rationale for why I have organised the book in the way that I have. I have written something brief about the chapters, because the reader will find a detailed introduction within each chapter. I have written an afterword rather than a conclusion to the book, the reason for which will become evident upon reading its chapters. The chapters can be read in any order and independently of one another. I have divided each chapter into a number of sections to assist the reader. Each chapter includes an initial section which offers a comprehensive theoretical overview of the topic under discussion. This initial section can be read independently of the rest of the chapter. The second and subsequent sections in each chapter need to be read after the first section, because it provides context and forms part of the facilitating environment for the encounter with the chapter's theme. The chapters are long. I have done this deliberately in order to offer the reader an experience that is intensive, absorbing, immersive and which builds in momentum. I invite the reader to read whichever chapter they choose all the way through to the end, in a single sitting, the first time they read it. This makes a considerable demand on the reader, because it requires time and space, but it takes time to settle into an experience. An experience requires spending time *with*. The reader has to be prepared to wait. This is akin to the process set in motion by the psychoanalytic frame, which facilitates the slow but ultimately rewarding and worthwhile work of psychoanalysis.

Chapter 1

Thinking clinically with the psychosocial

Psychoanalysis has been employed outside the consulting room since its inception. This might be as a conceptual tool to think about culture, society or politics (Bell, 1999; Kuhn, 2013a, 2013b; Bainbridge et al., 2007; Dimen, 2011; Weintrobe, 2013; Smadja, 2015; Kohon, 2016; Morgan, 2019; Morgan, 2020; Dwairy, 2015; Akhtar, 2012), or as one of the theoretical frameworks in the development of multidisciplinary areas of study, such as the psychosocial (Frosh, 2015a) or the psychocultural (Bainbridge and Yates, 2014a). Psychoanalysis has been integrated with more established qualitative approaches to research to form new methodologies, examples being the visual matrix (Froggett, Manley and Roy, 2015), the socioanalytic interview (Long, 2018), the social dreaming matrix (Manley, 2018) or the reverie research method (Holmes, 2019). It has been incorporated as part of strategic approaches to practice-based endeavours as varied as conflict resolution (Rifkind, 2018), education (Cohen, 2007) or exhibition curating (Bartlett, 2019). Some universities include degree courses, which introduce psychoanalysis as an object of knowledge to be studied, for undergraduate and postgraduate students doing academic programmes (Yates, 2001). Journals like *The International Journal of Applied Psychoanalytic Studies* (2004–) and *Psychoanalysis, Culture & Society* (1996–), as well as book series such as "Psychoanalysis and Popular Culture" (2013–) and "The New Library of Psychoanalysis 'Beyond the Couch'" (2010–), publish articles and books by clinicians and academic researchers which adopt psychoanalysis to think about matters transpiring outside the consulting room. The terms "applied psychoanalysis" or "theoretical psychoanalysis" have been conferred on these efforts, to differentiate them from "clinical psychoanalysis" or "pure psychoanalysis" which attends to happenings that occur inside the consulting room.

The partitioning of psychoanalysis into "applied" and "clinical", depending on its functions, focus and geographical zones of practice, often has the added effect of elevating one type of psychoanalysis – "clinical" – above the other – "applied". This has resulted in the establishment of a hierarchical relationship between the two with the result that one becomes perceived as "pure" or "real", with the result that the other becomes rendered "theoretical" or "watered down". This has a knock-on effect of policing what is considered to be "clinical" writing in psychoanalytic contexts. Chapter 1 engages with one particular configuration of this issue by concentrating on the place of psychoanalysis within the developing field of psychosocial studies. Psychosocial studies concentrates on both the psychical/unconscious (Freud, 1915) and the social and cultural aspects of experience, stressing the inter-relation between individual subjectivity and the environmental context within which this is formed on an ongoing basis. The two are inextricable. It is not simply that one impacts on the other; they cannot be separated (Frosh, 2015b; Frosh and Baraitser, 2008). Psychosocial studies engages with work being produced in "clinical psychoanalysis" and "applied psychoanalysis". In doing this, psychosocial studies highlights the messiness not just between the psychical and the social, but also between that which is labelled "clinical" and that which is referred to as "applied". Psychosocial studies also challenges the privileged position of "clinical psychoanalysis" in a field that is characterised by diverse ways of continuing on work begun by Sigmund Freud. Furthermore, psychosocial studies attempts to disrupt what has traditionally been a one-way traffic of knowledge: from "clinical psychoanalysis" to "applied psychoanalysis". Psychosocial studies goes further still by integrating other theoretical approaches, for example, feminist theory, queer theory or postcolonial theory, to facilitate thinking (Baraitser, 2016; Giffney, 2017a; Vyrgioti, 2019).

Chapter 1 explores how I have put psychoanalysis into practice through my work on two different psychosocial projects. In doing this, my aim has been to facilitate clinical thinking with the psychosocial through the processes of experience and encounter in a series of interdisciplinary and multidisciplinary endeavours. I will make use of psychoanalytic concepts, such as containment (Bion, 1970c), the facilitating environment (Johns, 2005), potential space (Ogden, 2015), the evocative object (Bollas, 1992a, 1992b, 2009), the transformational object (Bollas, 1987) and the transitional object (Winnicott, 1953) to facilitate me discussing the ways in which my interdisciplinary and multidisciplinary applications of psychoanalysis enrich the capacity for symbolisation for work in the clinic. Firstly, I will describe my long-term work on gender and sexuality which includes the staging of an encounter between queer theory and a number of different traditions of psychoanalysis. This work considers the various social and cultural discourses of gender and sexuality, which emerge from inside and outside the clinic, and their impact on clinical practice. It has resulted in a number of publications and events (Giffney, 2015a, 2016a, 2019; Giffney and Watson, 2017a, 2017b, 2018; Giffney, Watson and Lance, 2018), one of which I will discuss: a book entitled *Clinical Encounters in Sexuality: Psychoanalytic Practice and Queer Theory* (Giffney and Watson, 2017a). Secondly, I will outline my development of "Psychoanalysis +" (Giffney, 2013–), an international, interdisciplinary initiative that brings together clinical, academic and artistic approaches to, and applications of, psychoanalysis. I will discuss two events I have organised as part of this initiative: "Melancholia" (Giffney et al., 2014), a multidisciplinary collaboration with colleagues, which took place in the National Museum of Decorative Arts and History in Dublin, and "Unconscious Objects" (Giffney and Moran, 2018–2019), a series of conversations around art and psychoanalysis, which I co-convened with Lisa Moran,

Curator of Engagement and Learning, at IMMA – The Irish Museum of Modern Art in Dublin.

"Applied psychoanalysis" and "clinical psychoanalysis"

While "[the] locus of psychoanalytic knowledge is in the clinical situation", according to Stephen Frosh (2010, p. 36), psychoanalysis has and continues to be employed in other settings. It is, more precisely, as Prudence Gourgue-chon (2013) remarks, the putting into practice of psychoanalytic "concepts and interventions outside the traditional clinical consulting room" (p. 192). This approach to psychoanalysis is evident in Freud's own writings, some of which feature case studies or vignettes (1905[1901], 1909b, 1918[1914]), while other pieces engage with societal concerns, everyday life, and the arts and culture to advance and illustrate psychoanalytic ideas, which in turn develops and clarifies them for their use in clinical practice (Freud, 1901b, 1907[1906], 1908[1907], 1930[1929]). Salman Akhtar and Stuart Twemlow's *Textbook of Applied Psychoanalysis* (2018a) includes thematic chapters on a vast array of subjects, including history, community psychoanalysis, sports, poverty, terror and terrorism, consultation to organisations, health policy, sculpture, photography and theatre. Thus, psychoanalysis is "applied" in a variety of settings, including in contexts relating to healthcare, policy, business, the creative and performing arts, sport and academia. Therefore, it functions both as a theoretical approach to its subject matter and a praxis in the contexts in which it is applied (Akhtar and Twemlow, 2018b, p. xxxii). Psychoanalysis has become, Frosh (2010) explains, "one of the most significant tools available to those who wish to understand the social world" (p. 5). Efforts in "[a]pplied psychoanalysis", Akhtar and Twemlow (2018b) write, "extend psychoanalytic ways of thinking to matters outside the clinical chamber" (p. xxxi). This is because, as Andrea Sabbadini (2014a) puts it, "Psychoanalysis . . . is more than what takes place within the walls of a therapist's consulting room" (p. 117). The use of psychoanalysis outside or beyond the consulting room's "walls" attends to "sociocultural phenomena" (Akhtar and Twemlow, 2018b, p. xxxi). It involves, Akhtar and Twemlow (2018b) state, the application of psychoanalytic "principles" with the aim of "deepening the understanding of cultural phenomena" (p. xiii).

Anne Erreich (2018) states the "purpose" of applied psychoanalysis as "enriching the discipline to which it is applied . . . with no expectation of altering psychoanalytic thinking itself" (p. 1066). Thus, it enhances that to which it is applied. In this scenario, psychoanalysis is also positioned as that which gives rather than receives. Erreich distinguishes "applied psychoanalysis" from, what she terms, "interdisciplinary psychoanalysis", the "goal" of which is "the consideration of data and methodology from other disciplines to improve our theory and praxis" (p. 1066). In doing so, she makes a differentiation between a psychoanalysis that gives and a psychoanalysis that receives. In tracing the development of applied psychoanalysis over the decades, Akhtar makes a distinction between "psychoanalytic anthropology" and "anthropological psychoanalysis". The former he locates in the past and the latter represents, what he calls, "the 'new' applied psychoanalysis": "The former sought to understand cultural matters using a psychoanalytic lens. The latter brings cultural matters to bear upon psychoanalytic assumptions" (p. 364). In this, Akhtar uses different terminology than Erreich does, to indicate a similar standpoint. In a plenary address to members of the American Psychoanalytic Association, Prudence Gourguechon (2011) argues for a place for, what she terms, "the citizen psychoanalyst" (p. 445). This denotes a psychoanalyst who contributes to society and in turn benefits by advancing the psychoanalytic profession's recognition to the society in which analysts are located. This "public engagement" (p. 447) takes two forms: "psychoanalytic advocacy" and "psychoanalytic social commentary" (p. 445). She defines "psychoanalytic advocacy" as "taking a principled stand on a public issue and attempting to push a resolution of that issue in a particular direction", and outlines "the psychoanalyst's offering public comment on a matter already before the public eye" as "psychoanalytic social commentary" (p. 445). She puts forward both positions as viable options for a discipline with a specialist knowledge of "human interiority" and what "lies beneath the surface" of events (p. 445).

Gourguechon's stance is potentially a controversial one, in light of the Goldwater rule, which dictates activities "unethical" that involve giving a professional opinion on people in the public arena (pp. 454–455). Gourguechon addresses this and discusses the ethical responsibility of analysts to advocate for social change in cases where human lives are being devalued, focusing on three examples: LGBT issues (pp. 458–460), the need for immigration reform (p. 460), and the need for long-term treatment for soldiers and veterans (pp. 461–462). Psychoanalysts have contributed to public discourse on other issues, such as the nuclear arms race (Segal, 1987) and climate change (Weintrobe, 2013). Akhtar and Twemlow (2018b) refer to the aforementioned as representative of "sociopolitical praxis" (p. xxxiii). They remind readers of an ethical responsibility not to employ psychoanalysis in a way that overrides, "colonises" or "imposes" on other fields in a "wild" way (p. xxxi). Sigmund Freud (1910a) decried "wild analysis" as the application of psychoanalysis without proper training or expertise in the method. It signifies an ethical breach as well as an ignorant act devoid of proper respect for the limits of one's knowledge or proficiency. Psychoanalytic technique, he says, "cannot yet be learnt from books" (p. 225). In this, "wild analysis" assumes that psychoanalysis is something that can be learned and applied, in an intellectual way, rather than something that needs to be experienced. Psychoanalytic applications need to respect the integrity and expertise of other fields, in the recognition that any psychoanalytic insights are partial and just one perspective among many possible understandings (Baudry, 1984, 1992; O'Neill, 2005, p. 126). Sylvia O'Neill (2005) takes issue with the name "applied psychoanalysis" because she believes it is "misleading". She does not think it is possible for it to be "literally *applied* outside itself because the conditions for its practice are unique" (p. 125). She prefers the word "analogy" to exemplify the activity that others refer to as "applied psychoanalysis".

"Applied psychoanalysis" clearly differs in its context, focus and aims from "clinical psychoanalysis", according to commentators. The clinic is "the crucible for its concepts and its practices" (Frosh, 2010, p. 3). The use of psychoanalysis outside the consulting room is often presented as an extension of psychoanalysis (Akhtar and Twemlow, 2018b), something that works "[i]n tandem" with "clinical psychoanalysis" (p. xxxi). In an article on method in applied psychoanalysis, Francis Baudry reminds readers that psychoanalysis "as a theory was not devised to deal with non-living subjects". Indeed, Frosh (2010) remarks that psychoanalysis centres on "a live encounter" between the analyst and the patient (p. 3). This "liveness" is "necessary" and "integral", so much so that "[a]nything else, therefore, is not psychoanalysis" (p. 3). In spite of this stark statement, Frosh believes that "the way in which psychoanalysis embodies an encounter provides a model for understanding and promoting all occasions on which 'something happens'" (p. 4). Critics of applied psycho-analysis, as discussed by Baudry (1984), "urge caution in using psychoanalysis in other than the clinical realm", pointing to the qualitative difference between a "live patient" and, by inference, a "dead" text (p. 551). He cites free association and the patient's response as two important absences in applied psychoanalysis (p. 551). The absence of the patient means, Fritz Schmidl (1972) remarks, that "the process of getting more and more information" is not possible (p. 405). "Scant evidence" and "one-sidedness" in terms of the approach to texts are also evident within "applied psychoanalysis", according to Schmidl, in his discussion of work on literature and history (p. 407).

Much discussion of "applied psychoanalysis" concentrates on methodology and "how this activity should be done" (Gehrie, 1992, p. 239) and, by implication, how it ought not to be done. This focus on the delineation between "clinical psychoanalysis" and "applied psychoanalysis" has the effect of marking out one activity as "psychoanalysis proper" (Schmidl, 1972, p. 417), with the result that the other activity is relegated to being judged against it. A split has developed within the field of psychoanalysis as a consequence of this, between those who consider "applied psychoanalysis" to be "valuable" and "legitimate", and others who take it to be "a secondary, derivative, even dubious procedure" (Esman, 1998, p. 741). This also has implications for what is considered to be "clinical writing" and "non-clinical writing", and how both are appraised. In a review of Prophecy Coles's edited collection, *Sibling Relationships* (2006), Susanna Abse (2007) expresses "concern" about the "lack of solid clinical material" in the book, which she judges to be "impoverishing" (p. 510). What does Abse mean by the term "solid clinical material"? What qualities does "material" have to have in order to be "clinical"? What elevates it to being "solid"? Simply put, it needs to be produced within the consulting room. Abse writes of "our exacting research into the human mind through the laboratory of the consulting room" (p. 510). This is crucial, according to her, as "[o]ur credibility as a profession" rests on its inclusion, because "without this, all our thoughts and premises seem thin and unconvincing" (p. 510). "It is not enough", she continues, "to use myth, literature or biographies of the lives of artists alone to fully develop and substantiate our ideas" (pp. 510–511) – cultural objects, in other words.

In including descriptors such as "solid" and "exacting" to refer to research conducted within the consulting room, and terms like "thin" and "unconvincing" to point to work published without such findings, Abse (2007) is privileging one type of work over another. In linking the consulting room with "the laboratory", and discounting work making use of cultural objects as "not enough" (p. 510), she is articulating a split that pervades psychoanalysis more generally: as to whether it is a science or an art (Slochower, 1964; Bowlby, 1979). Abse does not completely dismiss work on cultural objects. Focusing on them "alone", she says, means that "our ideas" cannot be "fully develop[ed] and substantiate[d]" (pp. 510–511). Reading Abse's words, I wonder to whom she is referring when she invokes the term "our". This "lack" of clinical material in the book leads her to "presume" that it "reflects a wider problem: that of our profession's failure to take up the challenge of a changing ethical framework that demands consent for publication of clinical material" (p. 511). In the midst of this discussion, Abse poses a question: "What is happening in our psychoanalytic world where a book can be published with almost no material in it from the consulting room?" (p. 510). This suggests a number of things, depending on how one reads the sentence, and where one places the stress. I will take up two possibilities here. Does Abse wonder "where a book can be published *with almost no material in it from the consulting room*"? In this instance, we might read this as an expression of loss or regret. Does Abse wonder "*where a book can be published* with almost no material in it from the consulting room?" In this case, we might read this as an expression of bewilderment and frustration. By extension, we might wonder whether Abse is suggesting that books "with almost no material . . . from the consulting room" ought to be published at all.

This discourse forms part of a larger debate relating to how psychoanalysis as a clinical activity is defined and understood: what *is* psychoanalysis? This is intimately connected to the question: what *is not* psychoanalysis? While being played out between "clinical psychoanalysis" and "applied psychoanalysis" at one time or "psychoanalysis" and "psychoanalytic psychotherapy" at another time (Blass, 2010), the discourse is underpinned by anxiety. This anxiety relates to a desire for respect and recognition. It is also a reaction to criticisms that psychoanalytic claims cannot be proven. While boundary setting is an element of any discipline, it is particularly prominent when the discipline is trying to establish itself initially or in different domains, and/or perceives itself to be under attack. This might be from within (there are many different traditions of psychoanalysis competing for prominence; for example, King and Steiner, 1991) or from without (other disciplines, such as psychiatry and psychology, also compete for dominance). Psychoanalytic clinicians have responded in a variety of ways. For example, some clinicians have attempted to meet the concrete demand for evidence by arguing for the efficacy of psychoanalytic treatment in clinical journals (Fonagy et al., 2015; Leichsenring and Klein, 2014; Shedler, 2010). Psychoanalysis works because it has beneficial outcomes that can be "objectively" observed. A number of clinicians have drawn on and adapted psychoanalytic theories to develop manualised and/or shorter-term or fixed-term treatments, examples of which include Transference-Focused Psychotherapy (Yeomans, Clarkin and Kernberg, 2015), Mentalization-Based Treatment (Bateman and Fonagy, 2016), and Dynamic Interpersonal Therapy (Lemma, Target and Fonagy, 2011). These approaches bring psychoanalytic concepts together with theories of development, attachment and psychopathology and more direct, cognitive-styled interventions in the consulting room. Psychoanalysis is something that is useful, with practices and material effects which can be measured. This has a knock-on effect of privileging particular methodologies for conducting research – qualitative and quantitative – above theoretical and textual approaches to research. In other instances, clinicians find an object ("applied psychoanalysis" or "psychoanalytic psychotherapy") and use it as a toilet-breast (Meltzer, 1967, p. 20) to hold the criticisms that have been levelled at psychoanalysis as something that is "ineffective", "fake", "outmoded", "improper". This also has to do with the psychoanalytic process itself, which requires holding a position of not knowing on the part of the analyst, which is incredibly demanding on the psyche. A need for certainty is often projected into other aspects of the analyst's life, including into the psychoanalytic group and the discipline itself (Giffney, 2019).

All of this impacts on the writing of psychoanalysis: stated and unstated rules dictate the "proper" way to write *about* psychoanalysis, particularly when it comes to clinical practice. The "proper" way often becomes the "only" way, as established conventions governing *how* to write a clinical paper determine where (in which journal, in which section of the journal) and whether it is published. The underlying assumption is that "clinical" papers include case material: case material is defined as information collected from being inside the consulting room. Papers usually follow a similar format, which includes a brief introduction to the patient and the context within which s/he presents, accompanied by a series of vignettes from the analyst's own clinic or from the work of her/his colleagues or supervisees. This material is sandwiched between a theoretical overview of whatever concept or theme the author is considering, and a discussion of the clinical material and its implications for practice. A tradition of doing things a certain way has become instituted as a normative ideal within the field, with the consequence that *one* way is held up as an exemplar of *the* way. All efforts are then evaluated with this in mind. This results in a rather formulaic way of presenting clinical insights: "A" + "B" + "C", with "B" standing in for material from the consulting room. "B" represents the example that is introduced and discussed. It is the point at which readers can see how someone else does it, while leaving space for the reader to imagine how s/he might learn from the writer or how s/he might do things differently in her/his own practice.

What insights can be gleaned from the clinic that eclipse those that might be learned from "applied" contexts? Aaron Esman (1998) explores the distinction between "real" psychoanalysis and "applied" psychoanalysis, and the "borders" that "allegedly separate" the two (p. 742). It is, he tells readers, the "presence" or "absence" of the patient that is "the most frequently cited distinction" between a psychoanalysis that is "clinical" and one that is "applied" (p. 745). His article "question[s] the primacy of the clinical situation as the source of some of our essential propositions" (p. 745), concluding that "there are no principled distinctions between the application of psychoanalysis to the products of culture and its application to the treatment of patients" (p. 749). His choice of the qualifier "principled" is significant; it is not that there are no differences between a clinical and an applied approach, but one is not superior to the other. As he puts it, "Each may be done well, wisely, judiciously . . . or it may be done poorly, wildly, carelessly" (p. 749). In this, he is framing psychoanalysis as a methodology that is applied to a "subject" (p. 749), which might be a patient or a text, and which may take place inside or outside the consulting room. Esman draws attention to how Freud made reference to societal and cultural objects to develop, illustrate and support his "nascent ideas" (p. 742). Freud's theories were underpinned by his interest in the social and the cultural, together with his clinical work, from the beginning. Esman also highlights the difficulty of relying on clinical accounts alone because of the inexactness of the retrospective reporting of "facts" from sessions. He makes reference to André Green's observation that a discussion at a psychoanalytic symposium revealed "a total lack of consensus as to what constitutes a 'clinical fact' in psychoanalysis" (p. 746). Esman adds the gloss that "it appears increasingly that such 'facts' are to be seen, by many at least, as will o' the wisps, constantly changing, ever elusive, intersubjectively or socially constructed" (p. 746).

It is not just the presence of a patient that distinguishes clinical psychoanalysis from applied psychoanalysis; it is the *experience* of sitting with a patient. Wilfred Bion (1970a) points to the distinctiveness of psychoanalysis as it is practised in the clinical setting, something that is unique and that must be experienced. He commences the introduction to *Attention and Interpretation* with the comment:

> I doubt if anyone but a practising psycho-analyst can understand this book although I have done my best to make it simple. Any psycho-analyst who is *practising* can grasp my meaning because he, unlike those who only read or hear *about* psycho-analysis, has the opportunity to experience for himself what I in this book can only represent by words and verbal formulations designed for a different task.
>
> (p. 1)

This pays homage to the kernel of psychoanalytic practice: the encounter between a patient and a clinician, in the controlled setting of the consulting room. While highlighting what psychoanalytic clinicians share, Bion (1965) identifies the simple reality that "no one can ever know what happens in the analytic session, the thing-in-itself, O" (p. 33); indeed, "the clinical experience affords a mass of detail that cannot be communicated in print" (Bion, 1965, p. 22). Thus, there is something incommunicable about the analytic experience. The talking cure cannot migrate outside the walls of the clinic by means of the vehicle that frames its practice – words – and remain intact. There is something that can be communicated only through experiencing it. This does not dampen the desire to get inside someone else's session, to try to see how others *really* do it, to have it explained in minute detail. While words might not be capable of "represent[ing]" what goes on in the consulting room, according to Bion (1994, p. 219), they can, when used effectively, "recreate" an experience. This is, Bion comments, key to psychoanalytic writing:

> the criteria for a psycho-analytic paper are that it should stimulate in the reader the emotional experience that the writer intends, that is power to stimulate should be durable, and that the emotional experience thus stimulated should be an accurate representation of the psycho-analytic experience (Oa) that stimulated the writer in the first place.
>
> (Bion, 1965, p. 32)

Given this, it seems possible that an example could be chosen from outside the consulting room to communicate, through a process of evocation, an experience that transpired inside the consulting room.

In addition, Lynne Layton (2020a) has argued for a "social psychoanalysis", which exhibits a "commitment to a psychosocial and psychoanalytic way of understanding history, culture, and subjectivity" (p. xxxiii). This is an approach that integrates the social, cultural and psychical aspects of the patient's and analyst's experiences as integral to the work that takes place in the consulting room. Layton points to the "psychic conflict caused by cultural demands to split off part of our humanity . . . and struggles between resistant and conformist unconscious forces" (p. xxiv). This work directly speaks to, and develops out of, Sigmund Freud's (1930[1929]) writing in "Civilization and its discontents". A great deal of psychical demands are placed on us as human beings who must live in a world populated by others. This has consequences both for us as individuals and on the societies in which we make our lives. One of the "central elements" of social psychoanalysis includes examining, Layton (2020b) says, "the way identity categories are lived" (p. 1). Clinically speaking, Layton (2012) believes that "unconscious enactments are often psychosocial in nature" (p. 58). This suggests that psychical conflicts get acted out in the clinic in terms of the social and the cultural. This occurs because these "enactments" result from the "denial" of the inter-relationship between "the psychic and the social" (p. 62). They are split off and often become projected into the transference-countertransference dynamic. They are, moreover, "repetition compulsions that sustain rather than challenge the culturally created inequalities and traumas that have caused psychic distress" (p. 62). Layton (2020a, 2020b, 2020c) introduces a new concept, "normative unconscious processes", for a phenomenon that occurs in the consulting room when "interactions between patient and therapist . . . produce racism, sexism, and classism" (2020b, p. 1). These "processes" are "enactments" that are the "lived effects . . . of unequal power arrangements", which, if they continue to lie outside of the analyst's awareness, "reproduce traumatic experience" (Layton, 2020a, p. xxx; see also Leavy-Sperounis, 2020). Layton (2020c) draws on Wilfred Bion's work to look at the schism enacted between the psychical and the social in clinical practice, which is wrought through an environmental context subject to "dominant ideologies" (p. 43). Layton insists that psychoanalytic clinicians need to engage with theory and practice to find ways through this split "to re-establish the links between the psychic and the social" (p. 43). The psychosocial as it is conceptualised and operationalised in psychosocial studies is well placed to facilitate thinking on this matter, given its focus on the inter-relation between insides and outsides.

The psychosocial

"Psychosocial studies" is an umbrella term used to represent an area of research and teaching in development since the 1990s (Hollway, 2008; Association for Psychosocial Studies, 2013–; Frosh, 2019b, p. 1), with a commitment to theoretical rigour and reflective practice, together with a strong emphasis on methodological innovation. It interacts with and draws upon the insights of a number of disciplines, including but not limited to psychoanalysis, psychotherapy, psychology, sociology, anthropology, literary studies, the creative and performing arts, philosophy, cultural and media studies, social work and social care. It signifies, for some, a field of study in itself, while others resist this move towards categorisation, instead stressing the interdisciplinary, cross-disciplinary, multidisciplinary, transdisciplinary, anti-disciplinary or non-disciplinary nature of their pursuits. There are three discrete yet overlapping spaces in and between psychosocial studies. They are concerned with the place of theories, practices and objects (Figure 1.1).

There have been a number of attempts to tentatively map out the concerns of psychosocial studies without closing down additional or future possibilities. Liz

Figure 1.1 The spaces in and between psychosocial studies

Frost and David Jones (2019) describe a number of "distinguishing characteristics" which they insist "are definitely not rules":

- Various forms of psychoanalytic theory are often used as tools that might provide insight into the psychological realm.
- There is a tendency towards the use of qualitative rather than the quantitative methodologies.
- Very often there is interest in practice rather than simple theorisation or critique.
- There is frequently a commitment to crossing disciplinary boundaries (p. 4).

In his overview of the establishment of the Centre for Psychosocial Studies at Birkbeck, University of London in 2000 (now the Department of Psychosocial Studies), Stephen Frosh (2003) includes a number of "principles" underpinning the Centre:

- concern with the human subject as a social entity;
- interest in the emergence of subjectivity in the social domain;
- interest in critique, defined as a concern with ideological issues in psychology;
- methodological pluralism, including an active assertion of the value of qualitative and theoretical research as well as more traditional quantitative research;
- theoretical pluralism, including interest in discourses traditionally marginalized in academic psychology (e.g. psychoanalysis, systems theory, feminist theory, phenomenology);
- interest in inter- and transdisciplinary approaches to psychological theory and research;
- interest in personal and social change, including psychotherapy (p. 1551).

Writers are resistant to curtailing the way in which others define psychosocial studies for themselves. Self-definition is key. As Frost and Jones (2019) comment, "there is no hegemonic version of psychosocial studies" (p. 4).

My own teaching, research and practice have contributed towards my understanding of psychosocial studies as exhibiting a number of features (Figure 1.2). These features are intertwined to the extent that it can be difficult to introduce one without the others, or to decide which one to describe first:

1   An interest in how people develop identities and form relationships, consciously and unconsciously.
2   A curiosity about the world and why situations are the way they are, rather than accepting phenomena as self-evident or without question. A concentration on the micro (everyday life) is balanced by an attendance to the macro (social and cultural discourses and institutions).

the psychical and
the social

ethics and
social justice

the micro and the
macro

**Psychosocial
Studies**

reflective practice

ambivalent
relations with
disciplinarity

the centrality of
psychoanalysis
among other
theories

Figure 1.2 Features of psychosocial studies

3   An ability to be flexible with regards to following enquiries where they might
    take one, so not restricting one's researches to one discipline, theory or way
    of working.
4   A capacity to sit with uncertainty without foreclosing explorations prema-
    turely, coupled with an appreciation for the importance of theory, especially
    psychoanalysis, for opening up a space for thinking.
5   A desire to engage in thinking about oneself and how one relates to the
    world around oneself, evidenced by the prioritising of self-awareness and
    self-reflectivity.
6   A commitment to reflexive ethical decision-making practices and social
    justice.

"Psychosocial" is, according to Katherine Johnson (2015), "widely used
in health studies to indicate an interaction between certain psychological and
social factors" (p. 5). Rhodri Hayward (2012) traces the first appearance of

"psychosocial", a "compound word", to the 1890s, locating its early development within the fields of social work, psychiatry and psychology in the inter-war years (p. 4). The term has, Kath Woodward (2015) informs readers, "been around for some time, especially in the context of practical application, for example, in health care, in dealing with the 'whole person' rather than the presenting symptom and its associated anatomical part" (p. 7; see also Redman, 2016, p. 78). Understood in this way, psychosocial offers, in other words, a holistic approach to the individual and the situation they find themselves in. The individual is thus seen as a whole person with a mind as well as a body and with a lifetime of experiences; not just a symptom or presenting part-object to be treated or cured. The context within which someone presents is crucial. Thus, the word "psychosocial" has migrated from practice-based settings, with the result that practice and practice-based applications continue to be held in high regard within psychosocial studies. Frost and Lucey (2010), for example, refer to "the bridges between thought and practice that characterises much psycho-social work" (p. 2). The "psychosocial" as it features in "psychosocial studies" is distinct from the "bio-psycho-social", which is, Hollway (2006) writes, an "atheoretical" approach in the health sciences that describes "the additive treatment of different levels of analysis in the same research framework" (p. 467). Stephen Frosh (2010) remarks that the "bio-psycho-social" model is "not distinctive or theoretically innovative" with "its components" remaining "more or less untouched" (p. 195). Hollway and Tony Jefferson (2013) are keen to point out that their understanding of the psychosocial "is very different from the conventional, atheoretical usage of the term psychosocial, often in medical and health studies, that rolls together the two terms without attention to the problems created by individual-social dualism" (pp. xii–xiii).

These characterisations of the "psychosocial" pit it "[i]n contrast" (Johnson, 2015, p. 5) to the "bio-psycho-social". They, furthermore, serve to differentiate the "psychosocial" from the "bio-psycho-social" while also serving, by implication, to mark out the "psychosocial", as it appears in "psychosocial studies", as something that is theoretically grounded and methodologically innovative in its approach to the disciplines it moves within and between. Frosh (2019b) remarks that "contemporary psychosocial studies is rather different from the more traditional 'psycho-social' of psychiatry and social work" (p. 7). This, in effect, locates the "more traditional" "psycho-social" in the past and with other disciplines, while championing "contemporary psychosocial studies" as something new and current. Some writers make use of the term "psycho-societal" rather than psychosocial (Wengraf, 2018, p. 234; Froggett, Manley and Roy, 2015, p. 21). Hollway (2008) describes the emergence of the International Research Group for Psycho-Societal Analysis (2001–) out of an interest in qualitative empirical research that brings together "social/societal" and "psychological/psychoanalytic" perspectives on "real-world questions" (p. 200). The Group is Europe-based and concerned with "small group in-depth analysis of data" collected by members, with "psychoanalytic principles" offering a framework (p. 200). From Hollway's overview, psycho-societal appears to be a more specific term, and activity, than psychosocial. It is important to note that Hollway and Froggett were inspired by their attendance at a psycho-societal event to approach colleagues in the United Kingdom about the possibility of organising an event for colleagues interested in a psychosocial approach, with a view to establishing a network (pp. 199–200).

The way in which the word "psychosocial" and its attendant term "studies" appear is also notable, because discourses have material effects on practices and more broadly on people's lives. The term "psychosocial studies" generally appears in written form with a lower case "p" and "s" to emphasise the refusal to cohere into a formal discipline that has, by extension, the potential to discipline the activities of those who work within the area. The word "psychosocial" is punctuated, at times, by a hyphen, "psycho-social". Some writers use "psychosocial", while others use "psycho-social" (Woodward, 2015, pp. 7–8), at the same time that certain authors employ both versions within a single paper (Figlio, 2014). Sasha Roseneil (2014a) refers to both versions of the term as "twins" (p. 119), when pointing to the existence of "a long standing debate in the field about the ontological and epistemological implications of hyphenating, or not" (p. 119, n. 10). When discussing the outcome of a Google Scholar search for "psychosocial studies", Roseneil includes the following text in parentheses: "which includes its hyphenated twin" (p. 119). This intimates that it is "psychosocial" that is the more common rendering of the term, but also the more expansive, because it "includes" "psycho-social" within it. The debate about the hyphen is foregrounded in Lynne Layton's (2008) use of parentheses to highlight the place of the hyphen, in her editorial to a special issue of the journal *Psychoanalysis, Culture & Society* entitled "British psycho(-)social studies" (p. 339). For those who adopt it, the hyphen serves a strategic purpose. As Anne-Marie Cummins and Nigel Williams (2018) explain, the appearance of the hyphen is not an "accident or mere preference" (p. xv). Paul Hoggett (2008) employs the hyphen to underline the "difference" between "psycho" and "social" (p. 382). This act of "preservation" is, Hoggett believes, "crucial" because "[r]espect for difference" includes the need to "resist the temptation to blur, assimilate and merge" (p. 382). His inclusion of the hyphen also gestures towards the need, in his view, to maintain "distinctions" in other arenas, for example, between public and private and between inside and outside (p. 383). The hyphen operates, in this instance, as that which links as well as that which illuminates difference. It is "a transitional space" (p. 383). It accentuates, via the hyphen, the psychosocial interest in what happens in-between, in the gap or "middle", and in "liminal" spaces more generally (Woodward, 2015, p. 5). Cummins and Williams (2018) "retain" the hyphen because, for them, "the presence of the hyphen signifies a different and more complex duality than *just* the psycho and the social" (p. xv). The hyphen is "a place" which is " 'both-and' as well as 'neither-nor' " (p. xv; quoting Hoggett, 2008, p. 384). In this iteration, the hyphen is a space of hope and for desire: "a place where interrelations that form the reality we encounter and want to happen and are worth holding on to for that precise reason" (p. xv).

Frosh and Lisa Baraitser (2008) assert that the "unhyphenated psychosocial" conjures the image of the Moebius strip, in which

> underside and topside, inside and outside flow together as one, and the choice of how to see them is purely tactical, just like the decision as to whether to look at the subject from a "social" or a "psychological" perspective.
>
> (p. 349)

It is, it seems, an impossibility to look for one without seeing the other. They are entangled. While Hoggett stresses difference and distinction, accented by the hyphen, Frosh and Baraitser underline enmeshment. Woodward (2015) chooses to write "psychosocial" as "a single word", stating that this "is not ideological" (p. 7); rather it is, she says, "for pragmatic reasons", because of its familiarity as something that "embraces a range of different approaches" (p. 8). Woodward's employment of "ideological" suggests a context that implies a tension in the way in which the word is spelled. This tension is alluded to by Liz Frost and Helen Lucey (2010) as an "area of contestation", as they note "divisions within the psychosocial 'community' about what the hyphen and its lack signifies" (p. 1). They refer to it as "the presence or absence of a hyphen in the spelling of 'psychosocial'" (p. 1), pointing to how it manifests in the very title of the publication for which they are writing an editorial: "Welcome to the newly launched *Journal for Psycho-Social Studies*, also referred to as the *Journal for Psychosocial Studies*" (p. 1). The editors express their ambivalence about the hyphen, stating that "[e]ven though the journal name is currently registered with a hyphen, the current editors prefer it without, so that is something that may change in the future" (p. 1). The journal, which had previously appeared exclusively online, is now published in print and online by Policy Press (Frost and Jones, 2019, p. 3). The hyphen has disappeared from the "relaunch edition" (Frost and Jones, 2019, p. 3), as has the "for" in the title of the journal, as it appeared in Frost and Lucey's (2010) editorial: *The Journal for Psycho-Social Studies* is now *The Journal of Psychosocial Studies* (Frost and Jones, 2019).

This debate around a hyphen might at first appear to be pedantic; however, it illuminates important aspects of the psychosocial: Everything is available for thinking. Nothing is considered already known. Meaning is provisional and subject to revision. Context is important. The power of discourse cannot be underestimated. Each researcher and/or practitioner must take responsibility for thinking things through in relation to their approach to a topic. What might at first appear to be obvious, unimportant or a minor detail can point to an underlying philosophy, rationale or strategic approach to the subject at hand. I have chosen to write "psychosocial" thus. If I were to speak the word "psychosocial" aloud, my choice would not be discernible. A listener might assume that I spelled it one way or the other, and note it accordingly. Readers, however, will notice that a hyphen does not appear in "psychosocial" as I have written it, but how do I articulate what

I have done? There are a number of ways I might account for the action I have taken, including, for example:

- I have chosen not to use a hyphen
- I have decided not to hyphenate
- I have not included a hyphen
- The hyphen is absent
- The word is lacking a hyphen
- The hyphen has been excluded
- The word appears without a hyphen
- I have included an/the unhyphenated version of the word
- I have represented the term as one word rather than two

While I might choose to write "psychosocial" in the way that I do for a whole array of reasons, conscious and unconscious, my action takes place within a discursive context; one in which the way in which the word appears matters. The hyphen matters, whether it appears in print or not. This reminds me that "hyphen" is itself a word and not simply a sign that confers meaning on a word or words. How I choose to frame my decision tells readers something about my choice and its motivation, and whether I position myself in line with one side or the other in a debate. I might not intend it, but my decision tells the reader something about me, even if that something constitutes an assumption that the reader confers on me, because of the way in which I write the word "psychosocial". My decision also tells me something about myself, though it might not be available to me what that something is. My decision offers me an opportunity to reflect, if I choose or have the capacity to do so. The hyphen is thus present in, what might at first appear to be, its absence. Importantly, psychosocial studies notes and attends to absences and silences.

Psychosocial approaches are invested in making an active intervention in how we live our lives and the ways in which we relate to ourselves and the world around us. This aspect of psychosocial studies concentrates on the self, subjectivity and identity within the context of the social. The "relationship between the social and the personal" is "central" (Bullard, 2017, p. 84). We are both subjects of and subjects to the social, cultural and historical discourses within which we make our lives (Ryan, 2017, pp. 14–16; Wolfreys, 2004, pp. 232–239). Our sense of self and identity emerge within these contexts; framed, facilitated and constrained by them. "In different contexts", Barry Richards (2019b) reminds us, "different parts of our selves come into play" (p. 5), which is why the individual needs to be considered within the broader context of the environmental. While we are all individuals (separate, different, with a subjectivity of our own), we are also always part of a group (Volkan, 2018). As such, we identify and disidentify, consciously and unconsciously, with and from certain attributes in order to experience a sense of belonging and recognition. A number of demands are made on us by society, and those demands have an impact on our sense of self and agency (Freud,

1930[1929]). There is a "tension" between the individual and the social, one that is "necessary and inevitable", according to Erica Burman (2008, p. 376). We position ourselves at the same time that we are positioned by other people. Identity is understood as something that is individual but also collective (Volkan, 2020). As Joanna Ryan (2017) remarks when writing about class, "we are both subject to the workings of power and of society, and also experience and see ourselves as subjects (albeit divided ones) with desires and agency" (p. 14). Thus, research in psychosocial studies focuses on how our subjectivity, sense of self and identity are formed through the interaction of internal (psychical, unconscious) and external (social, environmental) factors. Critical thinking about social and cultural systems of power plays an important role.

Psychosocial studies engages with a range of multidisciplinary areas of research that focus on identification, interpellation, performativity and identity with reference to, for example, sex, gender, sexuality, race, ethnicity, class, dis/ability, age and religion. Introjective and projective processes are important for examining the unconscious underpinnings operating in large-group prejudicial attitudes and exclusionary practices, and manifesting societally as racism, misogyny, homophobia, classism, ableism, biphobia, transphobia and so on (Frosh, 2005; Goodley, 2011; Auestad, 2012; Keval, 2016; Giffney and Watson, 2017a; Auestad and Treacher Kabesh, 2017; Hansbury, 2017; Sklar, 2019). "'Both . . . and . . . and' thinking is, for me, a *sine quo non* of the psycho-social", writes Hollway (2014, p. 141). This "'[b]oth . . . and . . . and' thinking" is often characterised by researchers drawing on the insights of more than one theory in their explorations, in a concerted effort to see things from a variety of perspectives: postmodernism and poststructuralism; psychoanalysis; feminism, masculinity studies and gender studies; queer theory and LGBTI studies; postcolonial theory and critical race and ethnicity studies; and disability studies, to name but a few. Research attends to the micro and the macro (Woodward, 2015, p. 5): exploring how day-to-day happenings and encounters are affected by, while also impacting on, institutional structures and discourses that govern our place in the wider world. There is an emphasis on self-awareness and self-reflectivity about one's personal experiences and interactions, examined against the backdrop of societal discourses and structures. Writers show an attendance to, and an appreciation of, the minutiae of everyday life and their impact on the psyche of the individual, while recognising that life happens within the boundaries of the mind's capacity to process what one is experiencing (Baraitser, 2008; Roseneil, 2014b, 2019a; Lewis, 2009, 2012; Lance, 2019; Davids, 2011; Ryan, 2017). There is an emphasis on encounter and experience in psychosocial studies and an attempt to make connections and evoke responses that are more than simply intellectual. An example of this is Myna Trustram's (2016) performative essay which highlights the role of the experiential in her use of performance as a way to explore the psychosocial.

So, while the personal takes centre stage, it is the interconnection between the unconscious and the conscious that becomes a particular focus. Psychosocial studies is grounded in an appreciation of relationality, within ourselves (intrapsychic aspects) and between ourselves and others (interpsychic aspects). As Woodward (2015) expresses it, "[t]he dialectic between inside and outside at all levels is a distinctive feature of the psychosocial" (p. 140). In other words, the belief is that as we become informed about ourselves and the world around us, we can enact change (Johnson, 2015). Psychosocial studies attends to the inter-relation between conscious and unconscious aspects of experience and how they get played out within social and cultural contexts: "how the 'out-there' gets 'in-here' and vice versa" (Frosh and Baraitser, 2008, p. 347). The relationship between the psychical and the social is crucial for thinking about the formation and continued development of subjectivities, selves, identifications and identities (Woodward, 2015, pp. 58–77; Frost and McClean, 2014, pp. 41–61). The emphasis is on tracing "the interplay", Frosh and Baraitser (2008) write, between what is "external" and that which is understood to be "internal" (p. 347). These "psychic formations" relate to the mind and its functions, more particularly, to the operations of the unconscious (p. 347). This serves to help us grasp why people behave in certain ways in particular situations, and why there is not necessarily a clear correlation between a situation and an action.

Action is determined, in other words, not just by a situation and conscious factors, but also by that which lies outside of awareness. Frost and McClean (2014) remark,

> it is not possible to really understand how people negotiate their lives without understanding that both the unconscious and conscious elements of their personalities, their relationships with other people and the social and cultural environments in which these transactions and understandings take place entwine.
>
> (p. 5)

While the psychical and the social are linked, their interactions differ, depending on the context and the person. According to Woodward (2015),

> [i]t is not a matter of adding on the social to a psychological approach or one that explores the social with an added psychological perspective. Psychosocial studies are innovative because both elements are always in play, though not always in the same ways.
>
> (p. 5)

Psychosocial studies understands the psychical and the social in a way that is particular and distinctive. Frosh and Baraitser (2008) position the psychosocial "as a critical approach interested in articulating a place of 'suture' between elements whose contribution to the production of the human subject is normally theorized separately" (p. 348). This bringing together of that which is "normally theorized separately" is one of the defining features of the psychosocial.

It is a "stance" (Frost and Jones, 2019, p. 4) that demands the development of, what Barry Richards (2019a) terms, "a kind of binocular vision" (p. 171).

Richards conjures up literal acts of seeing in his references to binocular and monocular vision, in an effort to represent the insight that becomes possible via a psychosocial approach. He describes the "theoretical base" of psychosocial studies as "a relatively broad church" (p. 171). Binocular vision is, as Richards articulates it, distinctively interdisciplinary and the "unifying feature" of psychosocial studies (p. 171). He differentiates between "the monocle of any single discipline" and the "sharper and richer" "picture" facilitated by "binocular vision" (p. 171). Binocular vision brings together "some insights from both psychology and the social sciences" so that they are "held in mind at the same time" (p. 171). This simultaneous holding together of different ways of understanding the world "at the same time" is necessary if "the integration of the two perspectives is [to be] successful" (p. 171). Sasha Roseneil (2019b) argues that among the commitments of psychosocial studies is "an explicit project to undo the 19th century distinction between psychology and sociology" (p. 495). This is not achieved by collapsing one discipline into another, reading one through the other or making one a sub-discipline of the other. The psychosocial is neither "social psychology" nor "sociological analyses of psychological topics", Richards (2019b, p. 171) points out. Instead, psychosocial studies brings into concert disciplines, theories and methodologies usually more aligned with either the psychological or the sociological, to concentrate on aspects of experience linked to both. In Frost and McClean's (2014) words, "a psychosocial approach involves integrating what are traditionally seen as psychological and sociological paradigms" (p. 5). Psychoanalytic concepts are also often incorporated in an attempt to bridge the divide between the two. Research focuses on issues relating to the self, subjectivity and identity, and is concerned with investigating the ways in which the environment in which we grow and make our lives influences who we think and feel we are, and vice versa. Our environment is a product of our experiences of, interactions with, and representations of, it. This is because "our subjective experiences" and the "social structures" within which we have to build our lives are "interwoven" (Frost and Jones, 2019, p. 4). Thus, it is necessary to develop the "capacity" to think them both together, at the same time (p. 4). This is no easy task. For Hollway (2006), a psychosocial approach seeks to "understand subjectivity and agency in a way that transcends individual-social dualism and draws on psychoanalysis for this purpose" (p. 468).

While psychosocial attention often rests squarely on the relation between the psychical and the social, writers sometimes take cultural objects into account, often in terms of a triangulated approach, bringing the cultural into dialogue with the psychical and the social (Woodward, 2015, pp. 47–50; Baraitser, 2017, p. 10; Bennett, Froggett and Muller, 2019; Gross, 2020). In an essay on psychosocial curating, Vanessa Bartlett (2019) makes the comment that "psychosocial studies works towards a state of transdisciplinarity that offers an intertwining between the mind and cultural context" (Bartlett, 2019, p. 2). Bartlett's approach to curating brings together the psychical, the cultural and the social in her psychosocial consideration of curators as "care-driven facilitators" in "a cultural moment" with, what she terms, "an increasing focus on socially orientated perspectives that complicate definitions of illness" (p. 1). Psychosocial research has engaged in particular with visual culture: art, film and television (Bainbridge, Ward and Yates, 2014a; Jacobs, 2015). Jill Bennett, Lynn Froggett and Lizzie Muller (2019) conceive of a new term, "[a]rts-based, psychosocial" to indicate "projects that work *from and with* lived experience, examining the subjective aspects of that experience in dynamic relation to social, material and institutional settings" (p. 186). They are writing here with reference to a number of projects with an aesthetic component (p. 186). The visual matrix, for example, is a psychosocial methodology developed by Lynn Froggett, Julian Manley and Alastair Roy (Froggett and the Creative and Credible Project Team, 2015; Froggett, Manley and Roy, 2015; Manley and Roy, 2016) to "elicit" and reflect upon "aesthetic, social and emotional responses" to an external "stimulus" (Froggett and the Creative and Credible Project Team, 2015, p. 1). The matrix focuses particularly on considering "shared experience, stimulated by sensory material" (Froggett, Manley and Roy, 2015, p. 1). It is designed as a group experience, with an emphasis on associating to whatever material is presented by speaking thoughts aloud to the group, after which space is given to reflect and think analytically about what emerged during the group experience. The emphasis is on facilitating a more holistic response, including integrating affective experiences which might not make it to awareness in environments where there is a focus on the intellectual. The visual matrix has been applied in a variety of settings and to explore a number of topics (Manley and Roy, 2016; Roy and Manley, 2017; Clarke, 2017; Ramvi et al., 2018; Haga Gripsrud et al., 2018).

Explorations of the cultural within the context of the psychosocial generally take place within a psychoanalytic framework; however, as Caroline Bainbridge and Candida Yates (2011) point out, "in the psychosocial context, psychoanalysis is used mainly to illuminate the relationship between politics and society" (p. ii). In response to this, Bainbridge and Yates have been developing the idea of the "psycho-cultural", which they present as an "approach" (Bainbridge and Yates, 2012, p. 113), a "project" (p. 116), a "terrain of enquiry" (p. 117), a "model" (Bainbridge, 2011, p. 33) and a "mode of . . . analysis" (Bainbridge and Yates, 2014b, p. 14). "A key characteristic" of the approach, according to Bainbridge and Yates (2011), involves bringing together "theories and methods from the disciplines of psychoanalytic and psychosocial studies with those from the fields of media and cultural studies" (pp. i–ii). Thus, while related to the psychosocial, the psycho-cultural is positioned by Bainbridge and Yates (2014b) as something "new" (p. 1) and "distinctive" (Bainbridge and Yates, 2012, p. 113), which is neither identical nor reducible to the psychosocial. The psycho-cultural privileges a commitment to reflective thinking about cultural objects and experiences (Bainbridge and Yates, 2011, p. v, 2012, p. 116, 2014b, p. 2). The psycho-cultural is underpinned by psychoanalysis, specifically object relations (Yates, 2018, p. 54; Bainbridge, 2019b, p. 65), with an emphasis on experience (Bainbridge, 2019a, 2019b, p. 78), encounter (Bainbridge and Yates, 2014b, p. 6), process (Bainbridge and Yates, 2012, p. 113) and dialogue (p. 117). Psychoanalysis forms part of a range of cultural studies methods employed by the psycho-cultural project, including textual and contextual analysis, critical semiotics, reception and audience studies, and feminist theory (Bainbridge and Yates, 2012, 2014a; Bainbridge, Ward and Yates, 2014a). Psychoanalytic writers, such as Donald Winnicott, Wilfred Bion and Christopher Bollas, are particularly important for the psycho-cultural (Yates, 2019; Bainbridge, 2020; Bainbridge and Yates, 2014a; Bainbridge, Ward and Yates, 2014a). The psycho-cultural has emerged from Bainbridge and Yates's collaborative work on the Media and the Inner World (MiW) research network, which invites academics, clinicians and media professionals to speak and write together about the relations between the cultural, the psychical and the social, as well as how the cultural is used within the latter contexts (Yates, 2008, p. 408; Bainbridge and Yates, 2011, p. i, 2014b, p. 1). The psycho-cultural makes the cultural central to these considerations, particularly with regards to "affective", "irrational" and "emotional" aspects of experience that might be at the edges or lie outside conscious awareness (Bainbridge and Yates, 2014b, p. 1).

As with the psycho-cultural, work in psychosocial studies is often underpinned by psychoanalysis as a methodological and theoretical framework, in its attendance to the psychical/unconscious and the social and cultural facets of life. Its presence is "key" to psychosocial studies for many (Hollway, 2008, p. 386; Figlio, 2014, pp. 175–176). In Peter Redman's (2016) assessment, "There can be little doubt that psychoanalysis is a – probably *the* – major intellectual resource for psychosocial study" (p. 79). This is because, in Frosh and Belinda Mandelbaum's (2019) words, psychoanalysis makes "a vocabulary and set of concepts" available (p. 2). These are "an especially powerful and well-worked-out set" (Frosh, 2019a, pp. 104–105) for interrogating psychical machinations. Psychosocial accounts regularly employ psychoanalytic concepts, such as the unconscious, object relations, projection, introjection, identification, projective identification, containment, holding, reverie, free association, to name but a small selection. Arguments have been presented as to which traditions of psychoanalysis work well with psychosocial studies and which aspects of those traditions prove beneficial and problematic (Frosh, 2010, pp. 204–209; Frosh and Baraitser, 2008; Hollway, 2008; Jefferson, 2008). The insights of group analysts serve an important function, alongside those of clinical practitioners who work with individuals and couples (Burman, 2008; Roseneil, 2019b; Anderson, 2019). According to Frost and Jones (2019), "psychoanalysis is methodologically the natural ally to those who believe that the psychological realm cannot be fenced off and measured in any objective way as though it is separate from the surrounding social world" (p. 5).

There is also a long tradition in psychoanalysis, extending from Freud, which considers the psychical within the context of the social and the influence of social factors on psychical processes, as discussed earlier with regards to applied psychoanalysis (Morgan, 2019, 2020; Thomas, 2018). While not always the grounding theory underpinning psychosocial accounts (Frost and Jones, 2019, p. 5), psychoanalysis is central to many, so much so that Frosh remarks (2019), "there have been times when psychosocial studies and psychoanalytic studies have been used as almost interchangeable terms" (p. 104; see also Frosh, 2018). Elsewhere, Frosh and Mandelbaum (2019) underscore the enmeshment between the two to the extent that the psychosocial is "sometimes even confused with psychoanalytic studies" (p. 2). While psychoanalysis is vital to the work of psychosocial studies, Frost and Jones (2019) impress on readers the fact that the psychosocial takes in a broad spectrum of themes including "debates on ethics, politics, culture, racism, extremism, activism and climate change" (p. 5). This is prefigured by Frost and Lucey's (2010) question nearly a decade earlier: "Does 'psycho' only mean psychoanalytic, or more broadly psychological?" They pose this question after stating that the "range" of different approaches, topics and perspectives is "extremely broad" (p. 4). The prefix "psycho" can gesture towards an array of other words: psychotherapy, psychoeducation, psychodynamic, psychocultural, psychological or more particularly psychology – while all relating to psychoanalysis, these words point to other approaches and theories of the mind.

A number of people have raised concerns about the position which psychoanalysis has come to occupy in psychosocial studies. Frosh (2019a) remarks that "psychoanalysis . . . has to be warded off from becoming definitional of psychosocial studies" (p. 111). He stresses that "it is important to retain a sense of difference" between the psychoanalytic and the psychosocial (p. 104). Frosh is drawing attention to the dominant influence of psychoanalysis and the need to differentiate between the two so that the relationship does not become one of subsumption or subordination. Similarly, Peter Redman (2016) comments that many "view psychosocial studies as an applied form of psychoanalysis" (p. 74). In this instance, rather than psychoanalysis being one of a number of theoretical approaches used by psychosocial studies, psychosocial studies has been reduced to being one of the applications of psychoanalysis. Psychosocial studies thus functions in this scenario as applied psychoanalysis, rather than a separate, vibrant, independent entity in its own right. Psychoanalysis has, in the process, begun functioning as a "'master' discourse" (Redman, 2016, p. 79) that closes down rather than opens up spaces for thinking (Frosh, 2019a, p. 106). Redman (2016) also reminds readers that "not all psychosocial researchers are psychoanalytically orientated" (p. 87), something that is obscured in discourses that posit psychoanalysis equals psychosocial studies. Independence in terms of thinking is crucial, according to Frosh (2016), who says that he is "opposed to this psychoanalytic saturation", stating that "it is precious to have the freedom to move around intellectually" (p. 479). Without the "freedom to move around intellectually", psychosocial studies can take on the feeling of being like a mono-discipline, providing holding yet limiting at the same time.

Psychosocial studies has an ambivalent relationship with disciplinarity. "A discipline is", in Stephen Frosh's (2015b) words,

> a field of study that is organized according to accepted principles, so the community of scholars who work in it know what its interests are . . . and agree on the range of practices that can be drawn on to explore these problems or apply knowledge that this exploration produces.
>
> (p. 2)

Disciplinarity offers, in other words, clarity around foci, priorities and practices. It provides a recognised space within which to position oneself. It also makes demands on those who work within it to adhere to the boundaries set down by the discipline. Many people will be unaware of these boundaries, as they usually only become visible when they are challenged or traversed, or when one's work is deemed – usually by critical others – not to fit. Frosh (2014) has experienced the repercussions of challenging disciplinarity, as someone who was originally based in the discipline of psychology: "For Wendy Hollway and me, it was the very material sense of being marginalised in the discipline of psychology that led to becoming a kind of 'refugee' looking for a new intellectual home" (p. 162; see also Figlio, 2014, pp. 170–171). I have experienced a gamut of reactions to my own academic work from academics firmly located within, and identified with, the parameters and priorities of a single academic discipline: curiosity, confusion, dismissal, admonishment, derision.

Having completed a doctoral research project (Giffney, 2003, 2004, 2012), which brought together historical and literary research methods, underpinned by critical theory, in a department of history, I found myself fielding questions at academic interviews that assumed I was one discipline or another – usually "the other" of whatever discipline I was being interviewed for. Interviewers were concerned whether I would "fit" with "their" department, because my work seemed to be something else. I later completed clinical training in psychoanalytic psychotherapy in a department of psychiatry in a school of medicine, which accentuated the response I received from academic panels wondering what it was I "really" worked on. Was I more of a researcher or a practitioner or a lecturer? The focus had now moved from what discipline I identified with to what activity or identity marker I prioritised. Interviewers looked unconvinced when I answered that I considered myself to be all three. The concern then became whether I would commit myself to academic work or if I was "really" a clinician moonlighting as an academic, with the result that I would not give my academic work proper attention. While explicitly asking about the focus of my work, interviewers seemed to be trying to figure out which discipline I aligned myself with and if I would work with or against (these questions were often set up in terms of a binary opposition) "their" discipline. Over the course of my career, I have worked and taught in a range of different mono-disciplinary, interdisciplinary and multidisciplinary environments, including departments, centres and institutes of history, English literature and film, women's and gender studies, sociology, psychotherapy and psychoanalysis, psychology, psychiatry, psychoanalytic psychotherapy, humanities, psychosocial studies, and communication and media with an emphasis on counselling studies.

Given my experience, I can understand why psychosocial studies has such an ambivalent relation with disciplinarity. This "are you in or out?" thinking oftentimes demanded by mono-disciplines has been written about by feminist academic and activist Ailbhe Smyth (2013), while reflecting on her experience of navigating disciplinary thinking and structures when establishing Women's Studies in an Irish academic context:

> It has taken literally years to extract myself from "my discipline of origin" . . . and I most certainly do not intend to return there. . . . Of course, long years of (any) discipline leave their mark and I am constantly irritated and dismayed to discover my narrow habits of thought, my one-track perspective, the gross limitations of my understanding of what we need and might want to know and how we can come to know it. But the point is that I actively and positively do not want to be locked into disciplinary/disciplined narrowness.
>
> (pp. 9–10)

Psychosocial studies has been described variously as an interdisciplinary, multidisciplinary, transdisciplinary, non-disciplinary or anti-disciplinary endeavour (Frosh, 2013; Baraitser, 2015). It is portrayed, by different writers and in different contexts, as a field of knowledge (Roseneil, 2014a; Association for Psychosocial Studies, 2013–) and as an assortment of activities that challenge, resist or disrupt the disciplining effects of mono-disciplinary approaches to knowledge. Frosh (2015b) argues for psychosocial studies as a transdisciplinary space that "call[s]" disciplines "into question", that "provoke[s] or undermine[s]" them (p. 2). This is a psychosocial studies that refuses to play the game of the dominant mono-disciplinary system, which functions as a blunt instrument that constrains and limits thinking. A transdisciplinary psychosocial studies, Frosh insists, operates from inter- and multidisciplinary approaches because "it is not just a meeting ground for other disciplines" (p. 2). He wonders if it is "moving towards being an 'anti-discipline' in the sense of being opposed to disciplinarity" (p. 1). Psychosocial studies is also positioned as a "non-disciplinary space" (Baraitser, 2015, p. 209), "opposed" to "a fetish of methodological and disciplinary purity" (Frosh, 2013, p. 11). Baraitser (2015) posits the view that "the appeal to the non-disciplinary is perhaps a rather romantic attempt to side with the marginal, fluid and nomadic practice of thinking across (or even hovering above), rather than between, pre-existing disciplines" (p. 209).

Travelling alongside this "romantic" (Baraitser, 2015, p. 209), or potentially idealistic, trajectory for psychosocial studies is a realistic and practical attitude to the context within which people have to work, which requires some form of disciplinary-like activity. Roseneil (2012) articulates the strategic functions of psychosocial studies when she writes: "there comes a time when decisions are made consciously to build a new field of endeavour, to consolidate what has emerged thus far, to 'go public', and seek recognition and draw in others, beyond the already-committed" (p. 1). This requires a balancing act between identifying oneself as allied with something while keeping the contours of that something fluid enough to allow for what cannot yet be known, thought or understood. Frosh and Baraitser (2008) have drawn attention to the fact that "psychosocial studies is always at risk of being reappropriated by its more conventional, 'foundational' disciplines", due to its being "an ill-defined entity" (p. 350). Various writers have written about the development of a field, area, space, territory or tradition of psychosocial studies, particularly within the context of the United Kingdom (Frosh, 2003; Hollway, 2008, p. 203; Walkerdine, 2008; Hollway and Jefferson, 2013, pp. xii–xiii; Richards, 2018, p. xvii), which includes the setting up of the Psychosocial Studies Network in 2007 (Roseneil, 2012, p. 1), the establishment of the Mapping Maternal Subjectivities, Identities and Ethics (MAMSIE) Network in 2007 (Baraitser and Spigel, 2009), the formation of the Sociology, Psychoanalysis and Psychosocial Study Group in the British Sociological Association in 2011 (Hollway and Jefferson, 2013, p. xii; Frosh, 2019b, p. 2), and the launch of the Association for Psychosocial Studies in 2013 (Roseneil, 2012; Roseneil, 2014a). The Association for Psychosocial Studies (2013–), for example, cites the following as one of its four objectives: "the promotion of the field of Psychosocial Studies as an academic discipline and the dissemination of knowledge concerning Psychosocial Studies". There are a number of undergraduate and postgraduate degree courses as well as research groups currently operating at universities, such as the University of Essex, the University of the West of England, the University of East London, Anglia Ruskin University, the Open University, and Birkbeck and Goldsmiths at the University of London, to name a few. Frosh, Hollway and Redman established and have acted as the series editors for "Studies in the Psychosocial" book series at Palgrave Macmillan since 2013 (Frosh, 2014), while Liz Frost and David Jones have been the general editors of *The Journal of Psychosocial Studies*, which was re-launched as a print and electronic journal by Policy Press in 2019.

The previous developments signify a move towards more recognisable acts in terms of disciplinarity: a space for meeting and strategising (organisations), learning and researching (university courses and research groups), and publishing (international, peer-reviewed book series and journal). In spite of these "solidifying moves" towards "a more aspirational discipline" or "disciplinary space" (Frosh, 2019b, p. 2), descriptions posit psychosocial studies as being in its "infancy" (Bullard, 2017, p. 84), "emergent" (Clarke and Hoggett, 2009, p. 2) or "emerging" (Baraitser, 2015, p. 207), "embryonic" (Clarke and Hoggett, 2009, p. 1), and still "in the throes of definition" (Manley, 2010, p. 86). The word "psychosocial" is often employed by writers as a label to identify their own writing. The psychosocial "embraces a diversity of disciplinary backgrounds" (Hollway and Jefferson, 2013, p. xiii). Indeed, variations of the word "diversity" are prominent among descriptions of the psychosocial (Frosh, 2003, p. 1562; Hollway and

Jefferson, 2013, p. xiii): Frost and Lucey (2010) allude to "the broad dimensions of psychosocial studies" (p. 2), while Frosh (2019b) points out that it "draws on a very wide range of influences" and "is a very varied area of work" (p. 3). It is presented as a "project" (Roseneil, 2012, p. 2, 2019b, p. 495), "an emergent psychosocial current" (Froggett and Hollway, 2010, p. 281), an "attitude" (Manley, 2010, p. 65), an "approach" (Frost and McClean, 2014, p. 7; Woodward, 2015, p. 3), a "stance" (Frost and Jones, 2019, p. 4), a "framework" (Frost and McClean, 2014, p. 7), a "paradigm" (Clarke and Hoggett, 2009, p. 1), or a "mode of inquiry" (Woodward, 2015, p. 4). Hollway (2014) refers to the "psycho-social imagination" (p. 140; see also Roseneil, 2014a, p. 133), while Frost and McClean (2014) posit that "[p]sychosocial theory is in process" (p. 10). So, it is clear that the definitional parameters of psychosocial studies continue to be dynamic and open to revision. It cannot, Sasha Roseneil (2014a) articulates, be "the property or product of any single mind" (p. 134).

Writers continue to ask what psychosocial studies is and does (Bullard, 2017, p. 86). Rather than seeing this as an obligatory exercise in definition for the benefit of the uninitiated, I understand this as generative of new perspectives and as representing an extension of the self-reflective attitude underpinning much psychosocial work. Psychosocial studies is, after all, a praxis, one in which being and doing inform the other. While "many differences . . . animate" psychosocial studies, in Roseneil's (2014a) view, researchers "share an impulse to historicize, contextualize, specify, and criticize" (p. 106). Roseneil emphasises acts of doing that bring researchers together, while motivating people to undertake research on particular themes. Psychosocial studies has made a particular intervention in formulating new qualitative research methodologies (Clarke and Hoggett, 2009; Cummins and Williams, 2018). With that in mind, Simon Clarke and Paul Hoggett (2009) refer to psychosocial research as "a cluster of methodologies which point towards a distinct position, that of researching beneath the surface and beyond the purely discursive" (p. 2). They are gesturing here towards the place of psychoanalysis, which underpins many of these new methodologies, which have developed out of more traditional social science methods, such as interviews and focus groups (pp. 2–3). Thus, these methodological innovations have been particularly visible in the social sciences, and there is considerable overlap between an expressly psychosocial approach and a psychoanalytic one (Stamenova and Hinshelwood, 2018; Rustin, 2019, pp. 251–267). The unconscious is central in the collection and analysis of data, and the researcher's self-reflexive attitude forms a vital part of both. There is a rejection of the idea of a neutral or objective researcher, who simply records what appears to be there and writes a reflective statement about one's motivation for, and experience of, doing the research. In line with this, psychosocial studies puts forward the idea of a reflexive researcher; one who co-creates the data, rather than discovering or witnessing it, as if it preceded the research process. "Reflexivity", Frosh (2010) comments, "challenges the claim that there can ever be a 'truth' that is separate from the practices that give rise to it" (p. 209).

The methodologies forming part of psychosocial studies include processes relating to observation, fieldwork, individual interviewing and group responses. Observational methods draw on those derived from naturalised psychoanalytic infant observation (Sternberg, 2005; Thomson-Salo, 2014) and adapt them for observational research conducted either in a controlled environment (Skodstad, 2018; Elfer, 2018) or in everyday life (Roseneil, 2014b). Interviews privilege the unconscious in the relational encounter as well as in the findings or data in, for example, the reverie research method (Holmes, 2019), the biographic-narrative interpretative method (Wengraf, 2018), the socioanalytic interview (Long, 2018) and the free associative narrative interview (Hollway and Jefferson, 2013). Group experiences of visual material are conducted as encounters and reflected upon to facilitate participants becoming aware of the multitude of reactions they have to an experience. The social dreaming matrix (Manley, 2018), the social photo-matrix (Redding Mersky and Sievers, 2018), social dream-drawing (Redding Mersky and Sievers, 2018) and the visual matrix (Froggett, Manley and Roy, 2015) are all designed to expand group members' capacity to reflect on aspects of experience that might be outside of language and conscious awareness, using an adapted form of free association and reflective interpretation. Clarke and Hoggett (2009) foreground the "reflexive researcher's role" in "sustained self-reflection on our methods and practice, on our emotional involvement in the research, and on the affective relationship between ourselves and the researched" (p. 3; see also Jervis, 2009; Crociani-Windland, 2018). Thus, auto-ethnography and autobiography also form an important role in the research process, as well as operating as approaches in and of themselves (Petrov, 2009; Lewis, 2009; Roseneil, 2019a). All of these research methodologies privilege the experience of the research process, including the encounter between the researcher and the participant. The emphasis is on immersing oneself (Frosh, 2019b, p. 10) in an experience that can then be reflected upon, and is an integral part of the research and its outcomes.

If reflective thinking is central to psychosocial studies, so too is ethics (Frosh, 2019b, p. 10). While ethical considerations are essential to any research process, it is particularly important to consider possible risk and ethical issues pertaining to research that actively invites participants to engage in a research process that focuses on unconscious mechanisms and defences (Clarke and Hoggett, 2009, pp. 20–22). Given the emphasis on psychosocial studies as a praxis, people involved are sometimes also clinical practitioners of psychoanalysis, psychodynamic psychotherapy and/or group analysis, or working as practitioners in related fields, such as social work, social care, social policy, organisational consultancy, psychiatry, or clinical, counselling or organisational psychology (Association for Psychosocial Studies, 2013–). Frosh cautions against equating the clinical situation with applications of psychoanalysis outside the consulting room (Frosh, 2008, p. 419). He believes this creates "problems" if "careful attention" is not paid to how the theory is applied in different contexts (p. 418). Derek Hook (2008) concurs with this view in adumbrating "the difficulties inherent in the attempt to replicate the clinical technology of psychoanalysis in non-clinical environments", in what can amount to "overstretching the clinic" (p. 398). Cautionary comments like the aforementioned, which echo concerns expressed in relation to applied psychoanalysis, have prompted academics to reflect on the way in which they employ psychoanalysis in the development of psychosocial research methodologies. Holloway and Jefferson (2013), for example, offer this reflection on their earlier work:

> Perhaps we should refer to "psychoanalytically informed" methods and concepts rather than "psychoanalytic", in an effort to make clear that our use of terms, such as free association, interpretation, transference and countertransference, projective identification, and the idea of unconscious processes, is not identical to their use in clinical psychoanalysis?
>
> (p. 150)

Many involved in psychosocial studies occupy dual roles as researchers within the university and practitioners outside academic settings. Their practice-based experiences, in turn, inform their work within academia. Psychosocial studies researchers operate more generally as practitioners in social justice terms, in being invested in making material interventions in the world outside the classroom, clinic or publishing venue, with the aim of challenging intolerant discourses and oppressive acts, by offering an insight into the workings of these social and cultural manifestations of psychical processes. This forms part of an attempt to interrupt the cycle of exclusion that results from prejudicial attitudes and structural inequalities (Woodward, 2015, pp. 127–130). This often entails an analytical engagement with the discourses of politics (Richards, 2018; Volkan, 2020), in a concerted effort to examine the inter-relation between the psychical, social and cultural elements that operate within individual and group contexts, with reference to their material impact on people's lives. Lisa Baraitser and Laura Salisbury (2020) undertake a close textual analysis of "containment, delay, mitigation", titular terms used by the British government to signpost their response to the COVID-19 pandemic. These terms serve to mark out three phases and the public health strategies attendant to each phase. They also contain a raft of discourses within each one. Drawing on psychoanalysis, the work of philosopher Adriana Cavarero (2009) on "horrorism", and the challenges posed by World War II, Baraitser and Salisbury track the temporal dimensions of waiting and care embedded within the government's strategy. They argue that in order to remain grounded in the ethics of care, all actions must be underpinned by thinking; thinking referring here to the work of Bion (1962b) on alpha-function or thoughts needing a thinker to think them. Baraitser and Salisbury (2020) include an appeal near the close of their article:

> [A]ny future mitigation must not throw aside all attempts to stay with practices of care that seek to contain and delay cases of COVID-19, if it is not to inflict "horrorism" and abandonment at the moment when care is still needed.
>
> (p. 10)

This entails "care-ful attention" (p. 3), as well as a "commitment" (p. 12) to retain a capacity for thinking as an integral part of any actions that might be taken. Baraitser and Salisbury make reference earlier in their piece to the "mantra" that emerged during the pandemic: "stay at home; protect the NHS; save lives" (p. 3). This "mantra" represents a call to action that has been repeated again and again by the British Prime Minister, Members of Parliament and public health officials. As Baraitser and Salisbury write with reference to Wilfred Bion, "the call to action that Bion suggested in 1940 was implicitly a call to thoughtful action rather than something that might be used as an evasion of thinking" (p. 10).

Thinking clinically with the psychosocial

Laurence Spurling (2019) commences his article entitled "Mapping the field of psychoanalytic psychosocial practice" with a memory: during a conversation with a colleague about how to "better incorporate the impact of social reality on psychoanalytic practice" (p. 175) in their clinical training of psychodynamic psychotherapists, Spurling's colleague remarked:

> she understood how teaching students ideas, concepts and theoretical frameworks from disciplines other than psychoanalysis . . . would provide a better social, historical and cultural context to enable our students to establish a clearer and more robust link between psychic and social reality. "But", she said, "I still don't understand how all of this translates into clinical practice".
>
> (p. 176)

Spurling comments that he has found her question "surprisingly difficult to answer" (p. 176). This question, which he terms "a simple question" (p. 175), motivated him to write his piece, in order to consider the efforts of clinicians who claim to have integrated these elements into their practice. His article constitutes, in his words, "a partial or preliminary answer to my colleague's question" (p. 176). His researches have led him to formulate a further question of his own: "Can translating psychosocial thinking and ideas into clinical practice be done using existing psychoanalytic theoretical and clinical frameworks . . . or does something more substantial and radical need to be taught about how we theorise and practise psychoanalysis?" (p. 176). Spurling is writing here about the place and function of a psychosocial intervention: can it be incorporated into an existing psychoanalytic framework for practice, or will it materially impact on the frame itself? In an effort to "find a more satisfactory way of answering" his colleague's question, he sought out writings in clinical psychoanalysis that identified themselves as writing from "broadly speaking", according to Spurling, "a psychosocial perspective" (p. 176). The "psychosocial perspective" taken by these clinicians is evidenced by their "actively and thoughtfully" making links between "psychic and social reality", while considering issues relating to gender, sexuality, race, class and culture (p. 176). Spurling also equates "working psychosocially" with "working with difference" or "working in a way that values equality and diversity" (p. 176).

After carefully reading pieces by Katie Gentile (pp. 178–180), Lynne Layton (pp. 180–184), Fakhry Davids (pp. 184–188) and Danielle Knafo (pp. 188–191), Spurling is left wondering "precisely *how* this work could or should be done" (p. 176). He identifies this "small sample" as examples of "psychoanalytic psychosocial work" (p. 177). He differentiates between two ways of approaching clinical work from a psychosocial perspective: firstly, "those that claim to be operating within existing psychoanalytic frameworks", and secondly, "those that explicitly claim that new ways of thinking and working are needed" (p. 177). He situates work by Gentile and Layton with the first statement and writing by Davids and Knafo with the second. He reaches three conclusions. Firstly, he finds differences in "how the term 'psychosocial' is understood" (p. 192) and how that impacts on how clinicians approach their practice: whether they feel they incorporate a psychosocial approach within an existing psychoanalytic framework or if a psychosocial approach makes a material intervention in how a psychoanalytic framework is conceptualised and implemented. Secondly, he discovers differences in the way transference and countertransference are understood and worked with clinically (p. 193). This can also be dependent on the psychoanalytic tradition within which the clinician practises. Thirdly, he observes differences in how the clinicians understand and work with analytic neutrality (p. 194). A clinician drawing attention in the consulting room to social and cultural differences and inequalities within the context of their analytic relationship with a patient could, Spurling says, be interpreted by critics as "confusing analysing with moralising" (p. 194). He is highlighting the relation between theory and technique in his article; how one informs and affects the other. He is also exploring the nature of the link between what goes on inside and outside the clinical setting.

Spurling's piece has prompted me to think further about my own psychosocial interventions in the training and further professional development of psychoanalytic clinicians. I will begin by considering the work I have done with cultural discourses of sexuality with reference to a number of publications and events that have emerged from it, after which I will discuss my work with cultural objects within the context of an international, interdisciplinary initiative I founded and direct. In this way, I will employ Spurling's piece as an object to think *with*. In her meditation on objects as "things to think with", Sherry Turkle (2007) remarks that

> [o]ne role of theory . . . is to defamiliarize [familiar objects]. . . . Theory enables us, for example, to explore how everyday objects become part of our inner life: how we use them to extend the reach of our sympathies by bringing the world within.
>
> (p. 307)

Turkle is writing with reference to everyday objects, such as laptops, teddies, radios, keyboards and so on. Theory, in Turkle's estimation, helps us to see and think about objects in new ways, particularly the psychical function performed by objects. Using my clinical writings on cultural discourses of sexuality ("Grappling with uncertainty") and my interdisciplinary initiative using cultural objects ("Interdisciplinary by design"), I will use Spurling's piece to "defamiliarize" my own psychosocial "objects" (writings and events) to engage with, and reflect upon, the motivation for, and function of, these interventions in terms of clinical practice. For me, the question is not about whether the psychoanalytic frame as it is currently conceptualised can accommodate a psychosocial intervention or whether it needs to change. The question for me relates to how the clinician changes as a result of an encounter with the psychosocial, in terms of developing and honing their capacity for self-awareness, self-reflectivity and insight, which in turn gives them more space to reflect on what is already going on in the transference-countertransference dynamic in their consulting room. It is not a question, in other words, of bringing something into the clinic; rather it is about being able to accommodate within oneself – the analytic frame or setting is, after all, psychical as well as physical – what is already there. I see this less as a "new field of psychoanalytic psychosocial practice" (Spurling, 2019, p. 195) and more as thinking clinically with the psychosocial.

Grappling with uncertainty

I will focus on the theme of grappling with uncertainty and the place of reaction and response in the psychoanalytic consulting room, within the context of working with issues relating to gender and sexuality. I will consider my psychosocial intervention in this regard, by concentrating on countertransference, the experience evoked in the psychoanalytic clinician while working with a patient. Before moving to consider countertransference as it relates to gender and sexuality, I will provide an overview of some of the writings about countertransference, particularly with regards to the analyst's struggle to maintain analytic neutrality. I am trained in the Kleinian tradition of psychoanalysis, and practise as a psychoanalytic psychotherapist in that tradition. When we invoke the term "psychoanalysis", it is not singular. There are many different traditions of psychoanalysis: Kleinian, Contemporary Freudian, Independent, Relational, Jungian, Lacanian and so on. This is important because when psychoanalytic practitioners talk about clinical concepts, we might either use different concepts or have very different understandings of the same concept. I draw attention to this because there are very different ways of understanding and working with countertransference across the traditions (e.g. Fink, 2007, pp. 126–188; Raphael-Leff, 2012, pp. 125–128). Countertransference has become a fundamental clinical concept in Kleinian psychoanalysis, particularly with regards to working with the countertransference as a key aspect of clinical technique. This is with regards to the patient's internal world and making interpretations (Hinshelwood, 1991; Bott Spillius et al., 2011a). This has not always been the case (King, 1989, pp. 5–9). Sigmund Freud (1910b) describes "counter-transference" as among a number of "innovations in technique" with respect to the clinician, citing it as "aris[ing] in him as a result of the patient's influence on his unconscious feelings" (p. 144). While recognising the involvement of the patient in this process, Freud writes that "we are almost inclined to insist that he shall recognize his counter-transference in himself and overcome it", because "no psycho-analyst goes further than his own complexes and internal resistances permit" (pp. 144–145; see also Freud, 1913, p. 112). Freud recommends the importance of self-analysis and the need to "continually carry it deeper" to facilitate her/his work with the patient (p. 145). Elsewhere Freud (1915[1914]) advises the necessity of "keeping the counter-transference in check", as a way to maintain an attitude of analytic neutrality towards the patient (p. 164). He refers to the "problem of counter-transference" in a letter to Ludwig Binswanger, commenting that "technically" it is among "the most intricate of psychoanalysis" (Freud, 1913, p. 112).

Melanie Klein (1957, p. 226, 1961, p. 19) remained close to Freud's position on countertransference, acknowledging its existence while being wary of it. Elizabeth Bott Spillius et al. (2011h) write that Freud and Klein shared the view that countertransference was "a misperception of the patient caused by the analyst's psychopathology" (p. 288). The countertransference uncovers more, in other words, about the analyst than the patient. In discussing the ways in which contemporary Kleinian analysts depart from Klein's thinking, Elizabeth Bott Spillius (2012) states that "all Kleinian analysts now assume that the analyst's counter-transference . . . is at least in part a response to the patient's projective identification and can be a useful source of information about the patient" (p. 50). This situation has arisen for a number of reasons, not least from the pioneering work of Paula Heimann's writing in this area, which was considered "heresy" by many at the time (King, 1989, p. 6). Heimann (1949/50) wrote an influential piece about countertransference, in which she argues that "the analyst's emotional response to his patient within the analytic situation represents one of the most important tools for his work. The analyst's counter-transference is an instrument of research into the patient's unconscious" (p. 74). It is "a key" (p. 78) or "a significant pointer" (p. 77) to the psychical world of the patient. The countertransference registers, through the feelings roused in the analyst, aspects of the patient's unconscious, which "guides him towards fuller understanding" (p. 77). Heimann insists that it "is the most dynamic way in which the patient's voice reaches him" (p. 75), further cautioning that in the event that the analyst "tries to work without consulting his feelings, his interpretations are poor" (p. 74). The countertransference is, as Heimann articulates it here, an essential part of the analytic process that needs careful attention, and not simply "a source of trouble" (p. 73) as she had been hearing from her analytic trainees. In revisiting her paper in a second piece published a decade later, Heimann (1959/60) drew attention again to the fundamental importance played by countertransference in analytic work, highlighting the centrality of the analytic "relationship" and what makes it different from other relationships in the patient's life: it is the "degree" and "use" made of her/his feelings by the analyst (p. 152). This does not mean that analysts simply interpret out of their feelings, but rather they examine their feelings within the context of "the actual data" available in the session (p. 153). The analyst's countertransference is thus a significant part rather than constituting the entirety of her/his technique.

Writing around the same time as Heimann, Heinrich Racker (1953, 1957, 1968) argues that the countertransference is a "tool for understanding the mental processes of the patient (including especially his transference reactions)" (1957, p. 306). This "tool" can be employed to assist the analyst in terms of knowing "what" and "when" to interpret (p. 306). He engages with Heimann's work, commenting that countertransference experiences "of great intensity, even pathological ones" are useful (p. 305). Racker (1953) refers to these "pathological" aspects as "countertransference neurosis", which "perturbs the analyst's work" (p. 313) and which require analysis by the analyst (p. 314). Racker (1957) also makes reference to the "total countertransference", to bring "clarity", as well as to "separate and differentiate" the various aspects of the countertransference (p. 310). This is also, he claims, to emphasise

> the importance of paying attention not only to what has existed and is repeated but also to what has never existed (or has existed only as a hope), – that is to say, to the new and specifically analytic factors in the situations of analysand and analyst.
>
> (p. 330)

Wilfred Bion (1962a, 1962b, 1970c, 1970e) significantly developed Heimann's work on countertransference and Klein's concept of projective identification in his writings on unconscious communication, reverie, thinking and containment. Many other analysts have written about countertransference over the decades, especially in relation to self-observation of countertransference; containing and bringing meaning to projections as unconscious communications rather than acting them out; making use of countertransference when framing and timing the delivery of interpretations to the patient; and the inter-relation between patients' transference and analysts' countertransference reactions (Brenman Pick, 1985a, 2018; Joseph, 1985, 2015; Ogden, 1999; Mitrani, 2001; Cooper, 2013; Oelsner, 2013; Waska, 2015).

In lauding the way in which developments have been made in relation to understanding and using countertransference as "an important technical advance", Roger Money-Kyrle (1956) warns that "the discovery that counter-transference can be usefully employed does not imply that it has ceased ever to be a serious impediment" (p. 330). He frames this phenomenon as "disturbances" or "deviations" in "normal counter-transference" (p. 330). Irma Brenman Pick (1985a) writes of the fine line between the "use" of the countertransference as a "tool" and its "pathological" counterpart (p. 34). She insists that there is no "absolute separation" between them; rather it is something that the analyst has to work through continuously in her/his work with patients (p. 34). In referring to "how problematic the clinical reality is" (p. 34), Brenman Pick appears to be implicitly referencing the stark difference between the clarity that might be available in a piece of theory and the lived reality of working with psychical processes that do not go according to a pre-ordained plan in the consulting room. Indeed, Heimann (1949/50) sounds a cautionary note herself in her discussion of countertransference, in saying that its employment "is not without danger", while reminding readers that "[i]t does not represent a screen for the analyst's shortcomings" (p. 77). The countertransference is thus not there for the purpose of absolving the analyst from having to think. This places a huge strain on her/him with patients who unconsciously attack that capacity via projective identification. There might also be areas within the analyst her/himself that might resist thinking or which have not been submitted to thinking. These can present considerable difficulties for an analysis, if the analyst does not attend to them within her/his own personal analysis and in the supervisory context. Even with the aforementioned in mind, the "predisposition" to "neurotic reactions" in the countertransference are "continuous", according to Racker (1953, p. 316).

In fact, the term "reaction" is utilised frequently by clinical writers when discussing the analyst's countertransference (Racker, 1953, p. 316; Money-Kyrle, 1956, p. 341; Brenman Pick, 1985a, p. 40; Cooper, 2013, p. 174). Heimann (1949/50) includes the word "response" when referring to the countertransference. For example, "This rapport on the deep level comes to the surface in the form of feelings which the analyst notices in response to his patient in his 'counter-transference'" (p. 75), or the analyst "must use his emotional response as a key to the patient's unconscious" (p. 78). I believe this is more than simply semantics. I think Heimann's employment of "response" suggests that psychical work has taken place within the analyst which facilitates the countertransference becoming available as a tool (p. 74). What does it mean to respond? To respond is to act, to react, but it is something different, something more. To respond is to react plus something else. An analyst must find within her/himself a response before s/he considers making an interpretation to a patient. Otherwise, however technically accurate an interpretation delivered out of a reaction might appear, it will be registered as a reaction rather than a response in the patient's unconscious. I encounter an object, I enter into an experience, I have a reaction as a consequence of that experience, at which point I might act, I might react. Or I might wait. This is not a choice that I can consciously make. It is a capacity that is or is not present. This is what I have referred to elsewhere as "waiting in time" (Giffney, 2016a, p. 155), what Bion (1962b) names the no-breast or no-thing (pp. 111–112), what Klein (1952c) calls the bad breast (p. 63). It is this space that provokes frustration, which Bion (1962b) explains can be evaded and evacuated into the object via a process of projective identification or modified and transformed into a thought. This is no simple task. Time must be "endured" (Baraitser, 2017). This is part of the work of alpha-function, the thinking mechanism described by Bion (1962a, pp. 15–16), which facilitates the process of thinking thoughts through. This is also, I would argue, what constitutes the demarcation between a reaction and a response. A response requires considerable work on the part of the psyche. It is not simply a *fait accompli* if a capacity for alpha-function exists in the subject's mind.

In his paper entitled "The use of an object and relating through identifications", Donald Winnicott (1969) makes a distinction between "object-relating" and "object-usage" (p. 117). A reaction corresponds to the former; a response to the latter. He is referring to the psychical use of an object, specifically to what happens to an external object in the subject's internal world. The difference for the object is that in object-relating the object is subjectively perceived, while in object-usage it is objectively perceived (p. 121). Object-relating involves a relationship with the object that is based on "a bundle of projections" (p. 118). The object is therefore a narcissistic extension of the subject, to the extent that the object is not seen for itself but only as it exists as a reflective surface for the subject's projections. The subject is encountering, in this instance, themselves rather than another, though they remain unaware of this. Object-usage involves a relation to the object "as a thing in itself" (p. 118), outside the subject's "omnipotent control" (p. 120). It demands an "acceptance" on the part of the subject that the object has an "independent existence" and has "been there all the time" (p. 119). It is necessary to develop, Winnicott tells readers, "a capacity" to use an object (p. 116). This capacity must not be assumed in the adult. The transformation from object-relating to object-usage turns on the subject's psychical destruction of the object (p. 121), the survival of the actual object in a non-retaliatory way (p. 122), at which point the subject recognises the object as part of a shared external reality (p. 126). In this, there develops an appreciation for "object-constancy" (p. 126). Winnicott's (1953) description of the transitional object operates in the "intermediate" (p. 2) space between object-relating and object-usage. It is neither an "internal" nor an "external" object, though it contains elements of both (p. 13), while being distinctive in its difference (p. 19). It helps to mediate the process of accepting "difference and similarity" (p. 8), "me" and "not-me" (p. 2).

Alpha-function and object-usage underpin the analyst's work in the countertransference, especially when it comes to experiences of certainty and uncertainty. Psychoanalysis deals with one of the fundamental facets of life: We must find a way to live with uncertainty. No-one knows what will happen in the future, however hard we try to hypothesise or plan ahead. Life has a way of surprising us. This fact evokes great anxiety in us. We often grasp after certainty as a way to manage it. Each of us does this to greater or lesser extents, consciously and unconsciously. Psychoanalytic practitioners are not immune to this. It becomes a difficulty, however, if clinicians grasp onto certain thoughts to the extent that it prevents them from thinking about a patient or aspects of a patient's experience. There is a difference between having thoughts and thinking them through; one does not equate to the other. Some of this existential anxiety regarding certainty and uncertainty gets played out broadly against the backdrop of gender and sexuality. In other words, clinically speaking, thoughts can sometimes exist about gender and sexuality in the absence of a capacity for thinking them. These thoughts might be assumptions or stereotypes the clinician holds about gender and sexuality, particularly when confronted with experiences that diverge from their own. When this is the case, an individual patient's experience can become reduced in the clinician's mind to a category or diagnosis, already known and understood. In this instance, the clinician has latched onto certainty, with the result that thinking falls away. There is no need for thinking because the clinician already knows.

Existential anxieties regarding certainty and uncertainty get played out a lot against the backdrop of gender and sexuality (Giffney and Watson, 2017a; Hansbury, 2017; Roseneil, 2019a). It is one of the reasons I approached Eve Watson, a psychoanalytic colleague in Dublin in Ireland, in 2008 to ask her if she would be interested in collaborating with me on an interdisciplinary psychosocial research project on clinical psychoanalysis and theories of gender and sexuality (Giffney and Watson, 2017a, 2017b). I had noticed that psychoanalytic clinicians, who displayed a real curiosity and impressive thoughtfulness about the minutiae of psychic life, tended to speak in reified terms when it came to gender and sexuality (Giffney, 2017a, 2019). This was not true of everyone, but it was a noticeable occurrence. I was wondering how clinicians could think in such a nuanced way about a whole manner of things yet talk in stereotypes when it came to gender and sexuality. I was interested to see how we might explore and challenge this phenomenon of reification as it related to gender and sexuality. When I use the word "reification", I am referring to a situation in which thoughts about gender and sexuality are present but there is no evidence of thinking (Figure 1.3). By "thinking", I do not mean an intellectual, rational or conscious process; I am talking about the capacity to process or symbolise experiences in the unconscious, so that they become psychically meaningful (Bion, 1962a, 1962b; Giffney, 2016a). In reification, in place of thinking are words that have been picked up from books and articles, clinicians who have taught the practitioner during their clinical training, training analysts and supervisors, other individuals in the practitioner's life, and the social and cultural milieu generally.

These words are products of concretisation: ideas that have been identified with but that remain beta-elements (Bion, 1962a, pp. 13–14) or thoughts in search of a thinker (Lopez-Corvo, 2006), to use Wilfred Bion's terminology (Bion, 1997). Bion (1967a) writes of "the importance of doubting that a thinker is necessary for thoughts to exist" (p. 165). He is referring to the patient's attacks on linking (p. 165; see also Bion, 1959). It is useful to hold Bion's idea of "thoughts without a thinker" in mind when discussing the lack of thinking evident in how clinicians sometimes talk about gender and sexuality. The words that deliver these unintegrated fragments may present as intellectually meaningful or rationally reasonable discourse, but they are psychically meaningless to the subject who utters them. They are, in other words, reactions rather than responses. Objects are being used in a concrete way, incorporated to the point that it looks as if they have been taken in, but it soon becomes apparent that they might have been ingested but not absorbed

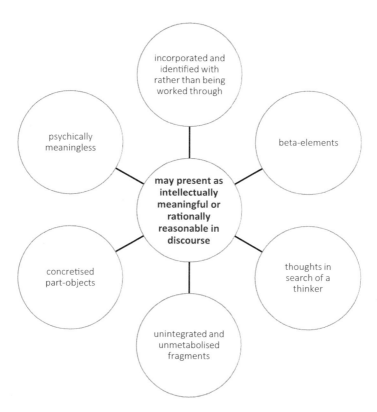

Figure 1.3 Unconscious mechanisms underpinning acts of reification

or digested, so that they are reproduced at a later date in an unmetabolised way. What presents in place of a considered response is an amalgam of part-objects, stray words and phrases passing as "facts" or "informed opinion", coupled with societal and cultural assumptions and stuck together with unprocessed reactions, displaced from a whole variety of prior experiences. This can be observed in a clinician's absolute certainty. There is no space for the patient's experience.

Why might this happen psychically for the clinician? When we enter the consulting room to meet a patient, we endeavour to open ourselves up for an encounter with the other. This is easy to say but, as anyone who works clinically is aware, it is very difficult to do. It is incredibly difficult to remain open to the other and the other's experience. This experience of difference has profound and far-reaching effects for all of us as individuals and as a group of psychoanalytic clinicians. The turbulence engendered in us as a result of sitting with the uncertainty of encountering a different subjectivity leads us to seek certainty in other aspects of our experience. We can get stuck on certain ideas, so that particular things become concrete and definite. We are the ones who know. For some of us it might be gender and/or sexuality, or it might be something else. We are not immune to the seductions of certainty and the charms of omnipotence. Gender and sexuality can become convenient depositories for some of these concretised, unmetabolised and unthinkable thoughts, because they are such intimate and difficult aspects of experience for most, if not all, of us. Gender and/or sexuality can function as a "toilet-breast", Donald Meltzer's (Meltzer and Harris, 1974) term of the use of an object as "a receptacle in order to unburden oneself" (p. 140), a container for persecutory projections, too much for the subject's mind to bear (Meltzer, 1967, p. 20). When this happens, the patient or an aspect of the patient becomes a receptacle for the projections of the clinician, because the experience has become too much – for whatever reason.

Clinical Encounters in Sexuality (Giffney and Watson, 2017a) has been designed to engage with this aspect of experience. Education can only go so far in terms of clinical practice: One can tell people about diversity and how to work with diversity. I firmly believe, however, that the experience is unlikely to make it deep into the mind, especially if there is resistance, because it is quite intellectual in its approach. Instead, it is necessary to offer someone an experience and an encounter. *Clinical Encounters in Sexuality* resulted from an eight-year clinical and interdisciplinary research project between Eve Watson and myself (2017a). The book includes thirty chapters by thirty-two invited contributors. The contributors include academic theorists working in sexuality studies and clinical practitioners from a number of psychoanalytic traditions: Freudian, Independent, Kleinian, Jungian, Lacanian and Relational. The clinical contributors work with adults and/or children and adolescents. The book stages an encounter between queer theory and clinical psychoanalysis, but it also facilitates an encounter between a variety of different psychoanalytic traditions *about* sexuality. In this way, the book operationalises queer theory as an interlocutor for these different psychoanalytic traditions to come together, because queer theory is one of the leading theoretical discourses about sexuality. Queer theorists are also wary of psychoanalysis as a clinical practice because of the history of psychoanalysis and its treatment of lesbian, gay, bisexual and transgender individuals. The book is organised in a particular way that is not usual. We used a number of structuring devices to foster a self-reflective attitude in readers about sexuality, which has tended towards reification, including in psychoanalysis and particularly in psychoanalysis as it appears in the clinic.

Firstly, the book is organised around four questions that are literally posed for the readers by me in the introduction and which the reader is asked to keep in mind as they read. These questions are as follows:

• What are the discourses of sexuality underpinning psychoanalysis, and how do they impact on clinical practice?
• In what ways does sexuality get played out for and between the psychoanalytic practitioner and the patient?

- How do social, cultural and historical attitudes towards sexuality impact on the transference and countertransference, consciously and unconsciously?
- Why is sexuality so prone to reification? (Giffney, 2017a, p. 20).

Secondly, the book is arranged into three sections, each of which facilitates the reader engaging a series of encounters with a variety of discourses, and ultimately with their own views about sexuality. Thirdly, the book is framed by an introduction by myself (Giffney, 2017a) and an afterword by Watson (2017). These both function as the facilitating environment for the reader's interaction with the text and with themselves. It might be usual for an afterword like Watson's to be the introduction, but in this book the function of the introduction is to provide a frame to open up a space for the reader to find their own way, and then to experience some containment provided by the afterword. Thus, the book is performative in style. In other words, the book's set-up creates the conditions it describes. The book literally as well as discursively opens up a space for clinical readers to engage in encounters with their transferences to sexuality and think about how they might be bringing assumptions into the consulting room, unbeknownst to themselves.

This is accomplished by means of the different functions performed by each of the three sections in the book (Giffney and Watson, 2017a), as well as by the fact that authors do not get to respond to other authors who have responded to their work. Authors also got to see the entirety of the book for the first time upon its publication, because the book also provides a series of encounters for each of them. They are perceived by some readers as a group perhaps, but they are in reality a number of individuals who each have a unique way of relating to sexuality and the discourses included in the book. Section one includes six chapters on queer theory by academic theorists of gender and sexuality. They write on theoretical concepts that are of interest to queer theory and clinical psychoanalysis: identity, desire, pleasure, perversion, ethics and discourse. They write from their own theoretical expertise, keeping in mind the influence that psychoanalysis has had on queer theory, as well as addressing clinical readers who might not be familiar with the field. Section two features fourteen clinical chapters by psychoanalysts and psychoanalytic psychotherapists, who offer responses to the chapters in section one, while reflecting on whether they believe queer theory might be useful for clinical thinking about practice. Section three presents seven chapters by authors who are familiar with both psychoanalysis and queer theory. They write about their encounters with the various encounters enacted by the book. The book also includes a chapter by a psychoanalytic practitioner and art critic on the book's cover image, "There Can Be No Arguments" by the artist Karla Black (2011), in recognition of the fact that the first encounter that the reader will have is a visual one with the book's cover image.

As described earlier, the central structuring devices underpinning *Clinical Encounters in Sexuality* (Giffney and Watson, 2017a) are threefold: encounter, reaction, response. This triangular dialectic does not work along linear or developmental lines. Rather, it is a frame that facilitates the reader having an experience.

What readers do with that experience is specific to each individual reader and so cannot be predetermined, controlled or replicated. Every encounter with a book produces an experience that is unique to each reader. What distinguishes *Clinical Encounters in Sexuality* (Giffney and Watson, 2017a) in this regard is the attention paid to the particularity of the experience, so that experience itself becomes an object to be wondered about. It is central to the book and to the work we do as psychoanalytic clinicians. Indeed, all acts of reacting and responding take an object. They are, by their very nature, reactions or responses *to* something. The preposition *to* gestures towards a relation, a link. Even when the intention is to sunder the link, or attack it, a link nevertheless persists for the moment during which the object is encountered. And so there is, by extension, a temporal element to reacting and responding. How I react or respond to something in this moment will differ from how I react or respond to it at another moment. Context is key. Context in this case is both the psychical and environmental factors that make reacting and responding possible in the first place.

The aim of *Clinical Encounters in Sexuality* (Giffney and Watson, 2017a), for me, is not to teach or admonish, to manipulate or to coax. Rather, it invites the reader into an array of potential experiences from cover to cover, including the cover. It is up to the reader whether to engage, and how much. As I set forth in my introduction to the volume:

> This book is above all an opportunity for readers to engage in an experience with their own views on sexuality and how they might be bringing predetermined beliefs into the consulting room unbeknownst to themselves, if they work in clinical practice.
>
> (Giffney, 2017a, p. 38)

That is, for me, the book's primary intervention, though not its only intervention. Readers will make use of the book in a multitude of ways, and indeed have done so already (Baraitser, 2019; Roseneil, 2019a; Lance, 2019; Cavanagh, 2019; Richards, 2019; Nigianni and Voela, 2019; Anderson, 2019; Watson, 2019; Giffney and Watson, 2017b; British Psychoanalytic Council, 2017; Giffney and Watson, 2018; Anderson and Stacey, 2018; Giffney, Watson and Lance, 2018). I see the strands of the book as akin to Donald Winnicott's squiggles (Dethiville, 2019): They are offers to play *with* and, in doing so, to risk learning something about oneself. While readers will learn something about psychoanalysis and queer theory and gender and sexuality among other matters from *Clinical Encounters in Sexuality* (Giffney and Watson, 2017b), I hope they will risk learning something about themselves. As Money-Kyrle (1956) puts in in relation to countertransference reactions: "[T]he analyst, by silently analysing his own reactions, can increase his insight, decrease his difficulties, and learn more about his patient" (p. 341).

To revisit the question posed by Spurling (2019) in his piece on "psychoanalytic psychosocial practice": "Can translating psychosocial thinking and ideas into clinical practice be done using existing psychoanalytic theoretical and clinical frameworks . . . or does something more substantial and radical need to be taught about how we theorise and practise psychoanalysis?" (p. 176). The point of the aforementioned work is not to bring something into the clinic – it is not about changing what we do, but rather is about changing who we are. Any change takes place within the clinician, in a subjective way, which in turn facilitates her/him noticing more of what is already in her/his clinic and, in effect, being more open to what the patient is communicating.

Interdisciplinary by design

I will concentrate on the theme of interdisciplinary by design, which is the tag-line for "Psychoanalysis +", an international, interdisciplinary initiative that I founded and direct. I will consider my work on this initiative with reference to how it brings psychoanalysis into dialogue with the psychosocial and the psycho-cultural. I will preface this discussion with an overview of transference, as this concept is central to clinical practice in the Kleinian tradition of psychoanalysis. Facilitating the development of clinical practitioners' capacity for bringing awareness to and reflecting on transferences is a key feature of the events forming part of the Psychoanalysis + initiative. Psychoanalysis offers the patient a very particular experience (Freud, 1914, p. 40). This experience is facilitated by means of a "live encounter" (Frosh, 2010, p. 3). It will be unlike anything the patient has experienced before, yet it will feel, at times, as if it is all too familiar. This is because of the workings of transference, which constitutes, according to Ralph Greenson (1967),

> a special kind of relationship toward a person; it is a distinctive type of object relationship. The main characteristic is the experience of feelings to a person which do not befit that person and which actually apply to another. Essentially, a person in the present is reacted to as though he were a person in the past. Transference is a repetition, a new edition of an old object relationship. . . . It is an anachronism, an error in time. A displacement has taken place; impulses, feelings, and defences pertaining to a person in the past have been shifted onto a person in the present. It is primarily an unconscious phenomenon, and the person reacting with transference feelings is in the main unaware of the distortion.
>
> (pp. 152–153)

Transference is "the central focus" of psychoanalysis (Curtis, 2015, p. 91). While transference facilitates the process of analysis, it also constitutes a resistance to treatment (Freud, 1912b). Transference is a repetition; a repetition that is transferred from the past onto the present and produced unconsciously again and again. Instead of remembering, the patient "*acts it out*" (Freud, 1914, p. 36). These repetitions are not just enacted in the consulting room but in "all other areas of the patient's current situation" (p. 37).

Melanie Klein (1952b) developed Freud's writings on transference, broadening and honing clinicians' understanding of it in her thinking about "total situations" transferred from the past, as well as "emotions, defences, and object-relations" (p. 55). She expanded the focus from "direct references to the analyst" to "the whole material presented" (p. 55). All material introduced by the patient has some bearing on the transference, whether or not the analyst is explicitly mentioned. Betty Joseph (1985) advanced Klein's idea of the total situation to "include everything that the patient brings into the relationship", more precisely "what is going on within the relationship, how he is using the analyst, alongside and beyond what he is saying" (p. 157). Joseph writes of the "whole situation" that is "lived out in the transference" (p. 157). The transference is "a living relationship", a site where object relationships are acted out (p. 158). To concentrate only on what is being articulated verbally misses out on that. It is necessary to get a sense of the feel of the transference, because patients communicate "beyond their individual associations and beyond their words" (p. 167). This getting a feel for the transference is made possible via the analyst's countertransference (p. 167). For her, the transference is a "framework", something dynamic where "something is always going on" (p. 156). Joseph (2015) emphasises the necessity of tuning into the "here and now" in the session, in which she "follow[s] the movement" (p. 2) or the moment-to-moment shifts in the transference. The here and now is privileged by psychoanalysts because it is "the level at which our technique is most transformative" (Civitarese, 2013, p. 161).

The analyst's attendance to the here and now draws on what Wilfred Bion (1967b) has to say about psychoanalytic observation, which "is concerned neither with what has happened, nor with what is going to happen, but with what is happening" (p. 380). Psychoanalytic observation is connected with Bion's (1967, 1970d) writings on memory and desire, which he believes are intrusions and "harmful to [the analyst's] mental fitness" (Bion, 1970d, p. 42), as they take the analyst's attention away from what is happening in the here and now (Giffney, 2013a). Bion's ideas develop on from Freud's (1912a) "evenly-suspended attention" and Heimann's (1949/50) "freely roused sensibility" (p. 75). "Every session attended to by the psychoanalyst must", Bion (1967) writes, "have no history and no future" (p. 381). Memory and desire must be excluded (Bion, 1970d, p. 48), to make space for O, which cannot be known, only experienced (Bion, 1970d, p. 52). O is "the ultimate reality, absolute truth, the godhead, the infinite, the thing-in-itself" (Bion, 1970b, p. 26). The analyst "intuits" (Bion, 1967a, p. 134), a verb used to refer to a non-sensory registering of the experience within oneself. Reverie is the term given by Bion to the "state of mind . . . open to the receipt of any 'objects' from the loved object" (Bion, 1962b, p. 36). These objects, beta-elements or projections, are transformed into alpha-elements through the analyst's capacity for alpha-function. The analyst brings meaning to these split-off evacuated beta-elements, so that experiences that were previously intolerable for the patient become more manageable when they are offered back to the patient via an interpretation, at which point they can be re-introjected (Giffney, 2016a). Bion (1970c) describes this process, which contains intrapsychic and interpsychic aspects, as "containment"; the patient is contained by the analyst as container. All of this psychic work takes place in the countertransference. The analyst thus becomes the instrument for this psychic work, a crucible for transformation (Brenman Pick, 1985a).

Developing a capacity to be open to receiving and working with patients' transferences is needed for analytic work. This requires more than an intellectual engagement. It is one of the reasons the trainee analyst undertakes an analysis with a training analyst. This enables the developing analyst to have an experience of transference, as well as to arrive at an understanding of its intensity, durability and power. It is also to gain an appreciation for what patients might be communicating in their transferences. "The best proof that one has correctly grasped something about the history of the patient", insists Giuseppe Civitarese (2013), "comes from the emotional truth of the analytic relationship lived in the here-and-now of the session. An intellectual understanding of the patient's past and present is useful, but it is not enough" (p. 172). How the analyst understands the terms "past" and "present", as they operate in the clinic, is an important consideration. When writing about the psychoanalytic consultation, Thomas Ogden (2012b) remarks that there are two "forms of history" being brought into the session by the patient: "the consciously symbolized past", which can be articulated verbally and organised into a narrative, and "the unconscious living past", which is consciously unknown to the patient and lived out in the experience of the analysis (p. 186). The latter, "the patient's 'living past'", is "of central analytic interest" (p. 186). It is constituted by object relations embedded since early life and which provide unconscious psychological framing for the patient since then (p. 186).

In "The dynamics of transference", Freud (1912b) wonders "why transference is so much more intense with neurotic subjects in analysis than it is with other such people who are not being analysed" (p. 101). There are a number of reasons for this, including the regression of the patient (Eichler, 2010, pp. 17–19), the analyst's interpreting of the transference (Steiner, 1993, pp. 131–146), and the fact that object relations are "vivified" and "lived/relived" in the treatment (Zeavin, 2018, p. 61). The intensity of the experience offered by psychoanalysis is made possible by means of the analytic setting. According to Dana Birksted-Breen (2010–2011):

> The setting is more than a reference to the physical layout and the practical arrangements. The analyst's attitude is part of the setting. This attitude includes an openness to the patient and whatever the patient is bringing, refraining from action, judgment and retaliation, a desire to understand the patient's point of view, actions and phantasies within the context of what that person has experienced and the ways in which the patient has had to deal

with those experiences, as well as the recognition that all emotions, however abhorrent, exist in all of us, including the psychoanalyst.

(p. 56)

The analytic setting begins, in other words, in the mind of the analyst. Anything outside of the analyst's mind constitutes an action. So, the analytic setting provides framing for the session; this is practical, material and psychical. The analyst is, as Lynne Zeavin (2018) articulates it, "always part of the frame", with the frame being "inextricable from transference meanings ascribed to the analyst" (p. 58). The analyst is both an "observer" and a "participant" within the analytic space (Civitarese, 2013, p. 172). The "internal setting", which refers to the interiority of the analyst and is a pre-requisite for analytic action to establish and maintain the setting in other respects, makes significant demands on the analyst to create "a dream space, a stage set or a play area" within her/himself (p. 172). This requires a fair amount of psychical flexibility, an ability to be able to play and to play *with* (Winnicott, 1971b).

Psychoanalysis + is located within Donald Winnicott's (1971b) idea of playing as "a thing in itself" (p. 54) and "an experience, always a creative experience" (p. 67). Psychoanalysis + (2013–) is an international, interdisciplinary initiative that foregrounds psychoanalysis as a clinical practice and a theoretical tool for tracing the unconscious dynamics underpinning occurrences in cultural, societal, and political contexts. It also takes psychoanalysis itself as a signifier or object to be wondered about and questioned. It has a commitment to psychosocial and psycho-cultural work, and seeks to serve a bridging function between the clinic, the academic institution, and the arts and cultural sphere. And so, Psychoanalysis + brings together individuals interested in clinical, theoretical and artistic approaches to, and applications of, psychoanalysis. This is because psychoanalysis exists in an interdependent and mutually enriching relationship with the cultures and societies within which we as clinical and theoretical practitioners find ourselves. The "+" in the title gestures towards the fact that psychoanalysis is always more than itself. In other words, psychoanalytic practitioners have always drawn on and incorporated insights from other clinical and non-clinical fields into our work, for example, literature, psychiatry, music, neuroscience, art, psychology, mathematics, medicine, philosophy, nursing, classics, social work, film, theatre and so on. Psychoanalysis is thus always, can only be, interdisciplinary. The space between "Psychoanalysis" and "+" also recognises the gap needed for productive things to happen which cannot be known in advance. The "+" also symbolises an openness to new possibilities and collaborations, which also cannot be predetermined.

My aim has been to create a space where clinicians, artists and curators, academics and anyone interested in psychoanalysis can come together to have an experience together, after which they can be facilitated to talk and reflect on that experience. Thus far, Psychoanalysis + has included a series of collaborative and interdisciplinary projects, publications, events and podcasts in Irish and international locations, including "Film: In Session – A Series of Screenings about Psychoanalysis and Film" in Filmbase, Dublin (Giffney, 2013–2014); "Melancholia" at the National Museum of Decorative Arts and History, Dublin (Giffney et al., 2014); "Conducting Psychoanalytic Research for Publication" at University College Dublin (Giffney, 2015b); "The Clinical Usefulness of Wilfred Bion's Writings for Psychotherapists" at Birkbeck, University of London (Giffney, 2015c); "Cinematic Encounters with Violent Trauma and Its Aftermath" in the Science Gallery Dublin (Giffney, 2016b); "Sexuality, Identity and the State" at IMMA – The Irish Museum of Modern Art, Dublin (Giffney and Byrne, 2016); "The Artist/Analyst Is Present: At the Interface between Creative Arts Practice and Clinical Psychoanalytic Practice" at IMMA – The Irish Museum of Modern Art, Dublin (Giffney, 2017b); "Psychoanalysis and Sexuality Today: Psychosocial Influences on Transference and Countertransference" at the National Museum of Decorative Arts and History, Dublin (Giffney and Watson, 2017b); "What Might Clinical Psychoanalysis Learn from Queer Theories of Sexuality? 113 Years after Freud's 'Three Essays'" at the Freud Museum, London (Giffney and Watson, 2018); and "Unconscious Objects: A Series of Conversations around Art and Psychoanalysis" at IMMA – The Irish Museum of Decorative Arts and History, Dublin (Giffney and Moran, 2018–2019).

Hundreds of people have taken part as speakers or delegates in events, some of which were organised by me solely while others were convened in collaboration with other people from clinical, academic and/or artistic spheres. I have used a variety of formats for different events and sometimes within a single event: seminar, workshop, lecture, informal response, conference, open discussion, structured discussion, art performance, roundtable discussion, installation, symposium, screening, reading group discussion, art exhibition visit, and public conversation. The events have engaged with a broad range of clinical and non-clinical disciplines and art forms, including psychoanalysis, psychotherapy, film studies, literary theory and criticism, philosophy, history, gender and sexuality studies, art history and visual culture, creative arts practice, drama studies, curatorship, sociology, creative writing, race and ethnicity studies, forensic psychotherapy, neuroscience, horror studies, and clinical, counselling and social psychology. I sometimes ask speakers or respondents to speak from their position of expertise, while other times I invite them to take a risk and step outside of what they know to engage with a topic or a discourse that is unfamiliar to them. The objective of Psychoanalysis + is to challenge orthodoxies, expand horizons and foster a collaborative approach to thinking. It endeavours to facilitate this open, collaborative and creative attitude in ourselves so that we can, in turn, facilitate our patients in their analyses. Psychoanalytic clinical practitioners learn so much from the experience of working with patients, undergoing analysis, attending clinical supervision and courses, and reading and discussing psychoanalytic theory and so on, but we also learn from those who do not practise psychoanalytically and those who do not practise clinically at all but who have skills and expertise in other areas.

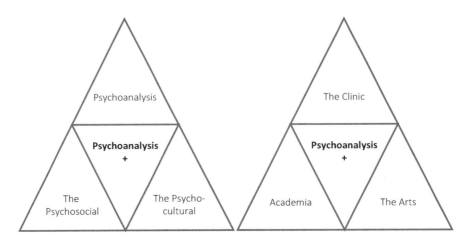

Figure 1.4 The triangulations of Psychoanalysis +

Psychoanalysis + is located in and between psychoanalysis, the psychosocial and the psycho-cultural on the one hand; the clinic, academia and the arts on the other. Psychoanalysis + is, like the psycho-cultural approach, "triadic" (Bainbridge and Yates, 2011, p. i) in its investments. This is both in terms of its focus and positioning (Figure 1.4). Psychoanalysis + attends to the overlaps and disjunctions between the aforementioned discourses and spaces, as well as making productive use of the spaces between each of them. These spaces are material, discursive and psychical. Psychoanalysis + occupies a transitional space. It shares an affinity with the concerns of psychosocial studies and the psycho-cultural approach, particularly with regards to the inter-relation between the psychical, cultural and social, as well their emphasis on experience and reflection. Bainbridge and Yates (2014b) comment that the psycho-cultural approach attends to "the emotional processes involved in mediating cultural experience" (Bainbridge and Yates, 2014b, p. 1), while "highlighting the importance of process" (Bainbridge and Yates, 2012, p. 113). Frosh (2003) remarks that psychosocial studies "testifies repeatedly to the pervasiveness of complexity, ambiguity and uncertainty" (p. 1565). In this, Psychoanalysis + does not present a product or ready-made meal. Participants need to invest in the process, to be willing to work and also to be prepared to wait for meaning to emerge.

A number of psychoanalytic ideas provide the theoretical frame for Psychoanalysis + (Figure 1.5), namely learning from experience (Bion, 1962a), the facilitating environment (Johns, 2005), potential space (Ogden, 2015), containment (Bion, 1970c), the use of an object (Winnicott, 1969), the evocative object (Bollas, 1992a, 1992b, 2009), the transitional object (Winnicott, 1953) and the transformational object (Bollas, 1987). I will consider how Psychoanalysis + functions as a frame, a space

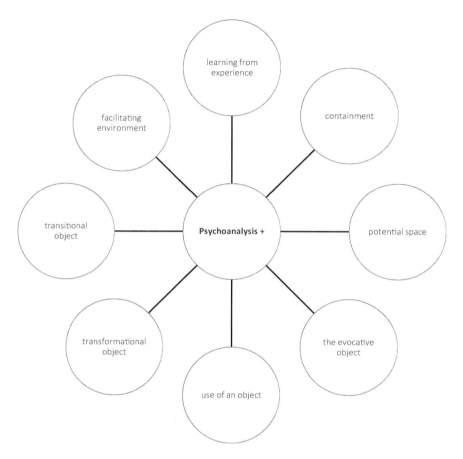

Figure 1.5 Theoretical underpinnings of Psychoanalysis +

and an object that offers participants an experience by means of a live encounter in a group setting, while also inviting them to reflect on what is evoked in them. In this, Psychoanalysis + offers an experience and, through that, evokes another experience, all the while inviting participants to reflect, which is, of course, a further experience. This layering of experiences is designed to generate something that is intensive, immersive, absorbing and interactive. Participants are invited to give themselves over to the experience while also retaining an ability to think, reflect and relate. Thus, they are invited to be in and out of the experience at the same time. The Psychoanalysis + initiative works with ideas of learning from experience (Bion, 1962a) and the use of an object (Winnicott, 1969), which are terms used to describe a more symbolic way of relating to one's experiences and objects. This requires participants to navigate potential space. Potential space is a term used by Winnicott and described by Ogden (2015) as

> an intermediate area of experiencing that lies between fantasy and reality. Specific forms of potential space include the play space, the area of the transitional object and phenomena, the analytic space, the area of cultural experience, and the area of creativity.
>
> (p. 121)

Graham Lee (2015) describes Winnicott's approach to creativity as "a fundamental and psychologically skilful response to the gap between self and the environment" (p. 273). It is an intermediate or transitional space where something spontaneous can happen. It is a space for playing (Winnicott, 1971c). Potential space is "the place" where cultural experience is located (Winnicott, 1967, p. 135).

I co-organised "Melancholia" (Giffney et al., 2014), a two-day, multidisciplinary event at the National Museum of Decorative Arts and History in Dublin, Ireland in 2014. The event presented the term "Melancholia" as an object for consideration, beginning with Freud's (1917[1915]) work on mourning and melancholia through to contemporary understandings in clinical, theoretical and creative arts contexts. It describes an experience, one that is very difficult to manage. This word has an abundance of associations, including to other terms such as "depression", "the sublime" and "affect". The event centred around a question that was posed to delegates: "What does 'melancholia' mean and how is it understood, worked with and represented in different contexts?" The verb "understood" was used broadly to refer to conscious and unconscious processes. The event included over eighty delegates, including invited clinicians, artists and academics. The programme included a range of formal talks, brief responses, facilitated and open discussions, as well as a film screening, an art installation, an art video screening and an art performance. Invitees specialised in the areas of clinical psychoanalysis, psychotherapy and psychology, visual arts practice and curatorship, and the academic fields of philosophy, film studies, literary theory and criticism, history, art history and visual culture, and gender and sexuality studies. The emphasis was on group experience and reflective discussion. The different formats at "Melancholia" were designed to stimulate and heighten affective and somatic reactions to material on the theme of the event, in order to help participants to integrate the rawness of these experiences with more intellectual understandings. Some of the material had the potential to elicit visceral reactions. This was especially true of Lars von Trier's film, *Melancholia* (2011), Cecily Brennan's (2005) art video, "Melancholia", and Amanda Coogan's (2014) art performance, "Oh Chocolate".

In order to provide holding and containment, the intensity of these experiences was carefully mediated by formal talks (by Caroline Bainbridge, Judy Gammelgaard and Bice Benvenuto in response to the film *Melancholia*; see Bainbridge, 2019a), short responses (by Ann Murphy, Emma Radley, Lisa Moran, Medb Ruane and Marie Walshe to the video "Melancholia"), and facilitated discussions with the artists Cecily Brennan (by Tina Kinsella) and Amanda Coogan (by Noreen Giffney). This was to provide space for reflection and to facilitate meaning-making through containment. The aforementioned also form part of Winnicott's idea of the facilitating environment, which is "not only physical care, in all its varieties, but the emotional climate provided by – most often, but not always – the mother" (Johns, 2005, p. 81). Jennifer Johns (2005) outlines some of the components of the facilitating environment (washing, changing, bathing, feeding and so on), which is underpinned by the mother's "attunement" in her consistency, regularity and "repeated" acts of physical care (p. 87). This is part of the mother's task of "holding" the infant (Winnicott, 1960a, pp. 49–50). Holding was provided at this event in other ways, for example, through the choice of room with its high ceiling and large windows; the arrangement of participants' chairs in concentric circles; the spacing and length of the breaks; the refreshments provided upon arrival, at the breaks and during lunch; the provision of reading material on the theme of the seminar in advance; and the inclusion of all delegates' names and brief professional biographical statements in the event brochure. These aspects that are at the edges of the event constitute a part of its frame and, as such, they are instrumental rather than incidental. If a good-enough facilitating environment is provided, it will not be noticed. This makes way for the experience itself.

I co-convened "Unconscious Objects" (Giffney and Moran, 2018–2019), an inter-disciplinary series of conversations around art and psychoanalysis, with Lisa Moran, Curator of Engagement and Learning at IMMA – The Irish Museum of Modern Art in Dublin, Ireland in 2018–2019. I developed the series in discussion with Lisa and co-convened the sessions with her. The programme brought together arts practice and clinical psychoanalysis in an effort to consider what they might have to offer each other, as both fields emphasise experience, encounter and creativity. The series comprised five sessions on different themes: "Art and Psychoanalysis" (October 2018), "Objects" (November 2018), "Spaces" (January 2019), "Practices" (February 2019) and "Encounters" (March 2019). The initial session provided an opportunity for the group to begin thinking together about art and psychoanalysis. Sessions two to five were programmed alongside exhibitions showing at IMMA, to facilitate a sustained engagement with the work of particular artists and curators. Sessions two to five began with an hour-long visit to a different exhibition each time, framed by introductory talks by Lisa. The exhibitions included work by Monir Shah-roudy Farmanfarmaian (2018; November session), Mary Swanzy (2018–2019; January session), Wolfgang Tillmans (2018–2019; February session), and the IMMA Collection: Freud Project (2018–2019; March session). After a tea and coffee break, the session continued in an art studio at IMMA with a ninety-minute discussion of the exhibition, together with two or three articles by psychoanalysts on the theme of the session facilitated by Noreen, which group members were sent in advance. The group was limited to twenty-two members, including the conveners, and members had to commit to attending all five sessions. The group brought together professionals from the arts and curatorship, as well as clinical practitioners with backgrounds in psychoanalysis, psychotherapy, psychology, psychiatry, art therapy and nursing.

I entitled the series "Unconscious Objects" to reference the art objects we would be considering, as well as to signpost the theoretical framework of the series which was psychoanalysis, specifically object relations. Object relations, Jay Greenberg and Stephen Mitchell (1983) explain, makes reference to the fact that "people live simultaneously in an external world and an internal world, and . . . the relationship between the two ranges from the most fluid intermingling to the most rigid separation" (p. 12). Object relations stresses the link, the relationship, the encounter between external and internal objects and experiences. Object relations, Lavinia Gomez (2017) says, "is not the same as interpersonal thinking: unconscious processes are central" (p. 4). Thus, object relations also denotes relationships between internal objects, which are set down in early childhood and provide a psychical frame for the person's relation with her/himself and other people. "Unconscious Objects" also alluded to three particular clinical concepts, "the transitional object" (Winnicott, 1953), "the evocative object" (Bollas, 1992a, 1992b, 2009) and "the transformational object" (Bollas, 1987). Winnicott (1953) refers to the transitional object as "the first 'not-me' possession" (p. 2), which helps the child to mediate her/his mother's absence and the experience of separation from her. The transitional object also occupies "the intermediate area between the subjective and that which is objectively perceived" (p. 4), so it is an object in the external world, yet it is not perceived fully as such by the infant. Christopher Bollas (1987) names the transformational object "the first object" (p. 28), in which "the mother is experienced as a process of transformation" (p. 14). The transformational object is sought again and again in the environment in the hopes that it will "transform the self" (p. 14). It represents an "existential" rather than a "representational knowing" (p. 14). It is sensed, in other words, through the affective experiencing of it rather than at a rational or intellectual level.

Evocative objects are objects in the world, according to Bollas (1992b), which "bring to mind latent concepts" (p. 32). These objects are stimulating in a variety of ways, including "sensationally", "structurally", "conceptually", "symbolically", "mnemically" and "projectively" (p. 32). Therefore, "[w]e experience them" (Bollas, 2009, p. 80). Our choice of objects is a form of "expression" (Bollas, 1992b, p. 34). Objects "provide a syntax for self experience" (p. 35). All three concepts deal with how external objects are sought and harnessed unconsciously as ways to negotiate our experience of the world. These external objects occupy a third space, in-between psychical and external reality. We partly see them for themselves, yet they are not wholly independent of our projections. Our investments in these objects tell us something about ourselves. The objects also refer to experiences. The object is often a means to an experience that is desired and/ or needed, yet the reasons usually prove unknown to our conscious mind. These objects provide opportunities for reflection. "Unconscious Objects" presented participants with a variety of objects: the art objects in the exhibitions, the psychoanalytic reading material sent in advance of each session, the introductory talks to the exhibitions, the refreshments at the break, the gallery and studio spaces, and the comments of participants during facilitated discussions. This is not to mention that we as people also operate as objects in the unconscious for others. The facilitating environment, which was framed and held by Lisa and myself in different ways, invited participants to join us in these encounters between art and psychoanalysis, with one another, as well as with aspects of themselves. The series offered participants, above all, a chance to sit and talk and think together; to symbolise.

To return to Spurling's (2019) colleague's question, which prompted him to write his article about "psychoanalytic psychosocial practice" (p. 176):

> she understood how teaching students ideas, concepts and theoretical frameworks from disciplines other than psychoanalysis . . . would provide a better social, historical and cultural context to enable our students to establish a clearer and more robust link between psychic and social reality. "But", she said, "I still don't understand how all of this translates into clinical practice".
>
> (p. 176)

This issue regarding translation from theory to practice is not necessarily one that entails the mapping of skills or techniques, which would impact concretely on how one manages the frame and conducts the analysis. The influence of a psychosocial and psycho-cultural initiative like Psychoanalysis + is to contribute towards increasing one's capacity to work with the patient's transferences, particularly as regards registering what is being evoked in oneself. Thus, the effect on practice is symbolic. It is to enable us to receive what is already there, rather than hanging on to what we think we already know, unbeknownst to ourselves (Giffney, 2013a). It is to keep space available for, what Bion (1977) names, "the excluded part", which is different for each one of us:

> I would like to be on the side of any of these things which have been excluded whether it is the diaphragm which separates the top from the bottom, or whatever it is. Later I shall hope to talk about the excluded part of psychoanalysis, or what will be excluded from your consulting room tomorrow, when you and your analysand meet. The excluded part plays a large part and may not even yet have emerged into psychoanalytic theory.
>
> (p. 14)

Chapter 1 has introduced psychosocial studies in an effort to find a way through an unhelpful hierarchical split that has developed in the field of psychoanalysis. This is a split between "applied psychoanalysis" and "clinical psychoanalysis", terms used to denote applications of psychoanalysis that take place outside and inside the consulting room respectively. While not arguing that these two applications are the same or that one is reducible to the other, there is an overlap between them, especially when it comes to psychoanalytic writing. The continued carving up of the field into these discursive categories serves to limit what gets to count as clinical writing and, by extension, taken into account in considerations of clinical practice. The borders between clinical and applied discourses are not as rigid in psychosocial studies. There is room to move around. I have advocated thinking clinically with the psychosocial, which does not mean making any material changes to how we work in clinical practice. Rather, it challenges our assumptions and expands our horizons. Change is subjective; it happens inside us. I have argued that thinking clinically with the psychosocial facilitates us becoming more open and available to what is already happening in our consulting rooms, which in turn will facilitate us working in increased analytic depth with our patients.

Chapter 2

Encounters with cultural objects as case study

Clinical case studies, vignettes and process notes are essential in the clinical training and ongoing professional development of psychoanalysts and psychotherapists. One or other of these might appear in books or articles or be brought to the teaching situation by the clinical lecturer or trainee or the supervisory meeting by the supervisee or supervisor. The case study, in particular, is the pre-eminent teaching tool in psychoanalysis. While providing some brief but necessary details about the history and current situation of a patient, the case study also functions as a text that facilitates the clinical writer contextualising clinical concepts and displaying the workings and impact of clinical technique on the patient's unconscious. In this, the case study is one of the ways through which otherwise abstract theoretical ideas can be transmitted. Its use in the training room encourages the growth of psychoanalytic knowledge and understanding. The case study has also been, since the beginning of psychoanalysis, the literary exemplar of the method's therapeutic attendance to the singularity of each patient and the particularity of every individual's unique analytic experience. Trainees learn the importance of the written word for documenting experiences in the consulting room, honing observation and analytical skills, developing the capacity for self-reflection and insight, and containing thoughts and feelings without acting out of them. Each psychoanalytic trainee is required to undergo her/his own training analysis through which s/he becomes, through experience, the literal embodiment of a psychoanalytic case study. And so the case study is imbedded in the formation and development of the psychoanalytic clinician's professional identity and sense of self.

Chapter 2 integrates my clinical experience as a psychoanalytic psychotherapist with my earlier background in the arts and humanities to think about how we might utilise examples drawn from culture as case studies and vignettes. I use the terms "non-clinical case study" and "non-clinical case vignette" to refer to cultural objects emerging from the applied fields of film, literature, music and the visual and performing arts. I will discuss the ways in which I have put culture to work in my clinical teaching to create an opportunity for a sustained engagement with psychoanalysis in its clinical and theoretical forms. Non-clinical case studies and vignettes are useful for explaining and illustrating clinical concepts to trainees, while providing a space for discussions with experienced practitioners on clinical themes, with an emphasis on broadening and deepening the conversation. I will attend specifically to how encounters with culture can open up a space for clinical thinking around transference and countertransference phenomena as they emerge in work with patients in the consulting room. Encounters with culture offer each of us an opportunity to be with our thoughts and feelings while immersed in the experience, after which we can tease out the intricacies of that experience in order to hone our capacity for receptivity, reflectivity and insight, as well as our observation, analytical and interpretative skills for our work in the clinic. I will outline why I think working with non-clinical case studies and vignettes is best done in a group setting. I will argue that working with non-clinical case studies and vignettes can enable trainees and fully-qualified clinicians to become more receptive to patients' transferences and enhance reflectivity about the countertransference experience, including its usefulness for thinking about how, when and why we make interpretations to patients. I will outline my utilisation of non-clinical case studies and vignettes as part of a developing pedagogical approach to clinical teaching and continuing professional development training what I term, the "Cultural Encounters Case Study Method".

The clinical case study and vignette

Candidates undertaking clinical psychoanalytic training engage in a number of experiences that contribute to their development as clinicians (Kernberg, 2016): a personal analysis, an infant observation, a psychiatric placement, an analytic group experience, theoretical and clinical lectures and seminars, written assignments and a research project, clinical work with training patients and clinical supervision with an experienced clinician. Part of the trainee's task is to integrate these many different experiences into her/his evolving professional identity as a psychoanalytic practitioner. All of these experiences serve particular functions necessary for psychoanalytic work. One of the most important tasks undertaken by the trainee is to develop a capacity to sit with a patient. This also requires the trainee to be able to sit with her/himself. In answer to a question relating to the qualities she thinks are most important for a psychoanalyst, Betty Joseph (2011) replies:

> To have a sense for the truth, have a real sense for the truth in relation to yourself, and be prepared to know or to try to find out what is going on and how things are hitting you, because only that is going to enable you, really, to face what is going on for other people (See also *Encounters through Generations*, 2011).

Each of the elements of clinical training impresses on the trainee the centrality of the unconscious in the life of the patient and in analytic work, particularly the unconscious dynamics underpinning the therapeutic relationship: transference and countertransference. The trainee also develops an experiential knowledge of the intractability of the symptom and the enduring influence of early life experiences in the psychic life of the adult. The trainee furthermore comes to appreciate the rationale behind psychoanalytic treatment's focus on facilitating the patient developing long-term insight rather than on the clinician attempting to enact a short-term cure. The case study and vignette are fundamental to imparting the theoretical aspects of the previous material, particularly as they relate to clinical technique (Spurling, 2015, pp. 113–182; Eichler, 2010, pp. 67–111; Lemma, 2016; Waska, 2013).

The case study is a description of a treatment, an overview of a process. It imparts something that has been learned from a clinical experience. It might come to the recipient by way of speech or writing, and there is a desire evident on the part of the speaker or writer to show something. And so the case study assumes an audience. In this, it has a pedagogical function. It seeks to impart something that has been learned about technique or theory, a particular presentation or a state of mind. It tends to include an overview of the patient's history and current situation, which serve as necessary precursors to the clinician's discussion of something specific and, moreover, a sudden shift or gradual change in the nature of a treatment. The case study is written retrospectively about insights that have been gained over time, including in cases that are ongoing. It is reflective in style and, in this, it is an invitation to the recipient to reflect on their own work in the consulting room. The inclusion of "verbatim" or "raw material" is deemed to be of importance for providing recipients with a "less contaminated" though "not free of selection bias" insight into happenings in the consulting room, so that recipients might be able to help a presenter to think about material in alternative ways that might not currently be available to her/him (Blass, 2013, p. 1139). The presentation of a case can thus facilitate a clinician to understand material in a new way or process experiences that have not yet been worked through, in an effort to facilitate deepening the treatment (Ackerman, 2018, p. 72). The vignette is briefer than the case study. Where the case study provides an evolving sense of a patient's situation over a period of time, the vignette concentrates on a moment in a session. Vignettes work best when outlining a specific occurrence or a particular insight that has been learned. The vignette is used for the purpose of illustrating and supporting a point that a clinician has just made or is about to make. It provides the evidence for a speculation. Where a case study is a frame, a vignette is a prop. A case study might contain several vignettes, each of which will be utilised in an endeavour to develop the presenter's points and advance her/his argument.

Introductions to psychoanalytic approaches to therapeutic work by, for example, Denise Cullington (2019), Hannah Curtis (2015) and Daniel Pick (2015), incorporate a blend of clinical case studies and vignettes as well as anecdotes from everyday life to introduce psychoanalytic concepts and to suggest how they might work in practice. The way in which the case study and vignette are operationalised reveals something about the presenter's way of thinking and style of working. As Ivan Ward (1997) puts it, "the therapist writes *himself* up. He becomes a psychotherapist-for-others" (p. 8). Ward discusses the tradition of presenting case studies in psychoanalysis, focusing especially on the triangular relational dynamic enacted between the presenter, her/his audience and the patient as s/he is presented. In the intermingling of the presenter's words and those of her/his patient, s/he "creates something new" (p. 6). While the content of the case study or vignette is important, the way in which it is delivered also gives the audience an impression of how the work itself might have unfolded in the consulting room (Michels, 2000, pp. 365–366). Writing of Sigmund Freud's case studies, John Forrester (2016) remarks, "the transmission of psychoanalysis via Freud's clinical writing implies the repetition – or at the very least the remobilization – of the original relations of transference and countertransference evident in the relation between patient and analyst" (p. 107). In this, the presenting of clinical material has a performative effect in its presentation (Mulligan, 2017), and so also evokes an affective reaction in its audience (Spurling, 1997, pp. 71–73). It does not just impart something but *does* something. It stirs in its audience reactions, and in this it is also an invitation to each audience member to reflect on why s/he might be reacting in particular ways to the material itself and its presentation (Giffney, 2017a, p. 38). It is designed to move the audience to think. As a piece of clinical documentation, the presenter, Ward tells us, seeks to "paint a realistic clinical picture and understand it in theoretical terms" (p. 5). Ward highlights the importance of utilising a vignette, in particular, "to make the theory come alive in the real situation" (p. 7). This focus on the "aliveness" of the material is also attested to by Elias Mallet Rocha Barros (2013), who writes of the need to both "keep the experience alive" for the analyst as well as communicate a "live experience" with a patient who will be encountered only through the case material (p. 94). Dale Boesky (2013) stresses the need, from his perspective, for a balance between process notes or what he terms "samples of actual clinical interactions" with statements that contextualise process material for the recipient (p. 1141).

For Susan Budd (1997), case material is a facet of psychoanalytic theory, though one that is understood "in a different way from the way we understand the rest of psychoanalytic theory" (p. 30). It can only be understood, she says, "through a kind of intuitive identification with both the patient and the analyst" (p. 30). Melanie Klein (1961) cautions against taking notes during sessions as it would "disturb the patient considerably" as well as "divert the analyst's attention", while she disagrees with recording sessions because it "is absolutely against the fundamental principles on which psycho-analysis rests, namely the exclusion of any audience during an analytic session" (p. 11). Even if the audience is privy to a session via written notes or an audio or video recording, such devices cannot capture the "essence of the situation", according to David Tuckett (1994, p. 866). The patient presented outside the consulting room, in supervision for example, is, Thomas Ogden (2009b) comments, "not the living, breathing person" but "a fiction" created by the presenter (p. 34). As Sigmund Freud (1916[1915]) writes, "you cannot be present as an audience at a psychoanalytic treatment. You can only be told about it; and, in the strictest sense of the word, it is only by hearsay that you will get to know psychoanalysis" (p. 18). Thus, the clinical case study and vignette record experiences that have transpired. They are written after the fact and thus are the products of memory rather than of experience, as it happens, in the here and now. Wilfred Bion (1965) expresses reservations about the retrospective reporting of such examples because, for him, "the clinical experience affords a mass of detail that cannot be communicated in print" (p. 22). This difficulty in communicating experience is not limited to the reporting of it. Thomas Ogden (2018) comments on the work of the analyst and the patient as it unfolds in the consulting room: "Patient and analyst in every moment of their work together bump up against the fact that the immediacy of their lived experience is incommunicable" (p. 400). So, there is something incomplete about the vignette certainly but also the case study. This sense of incompleteness arises partly from the fact that analysts "select from the infinitely numbered moments of an analysis and weave a narrative" (Mulligan, 2017, p. 811), as well as from the impossibility of being able to put everything into words. This includes in the clinic itself. The invitation to the patient to free-associate, Freud's (1940, p. 202) "fundamental rule", impresses on both the patient and analyst the "impossibility of saying everything" (Parker, 2018, pp. 11–12).

The context within which a case study or vignette appears can also impact on how it is presented and what material is necessary to change or edit, in order to take into account confidentiality and to ensure that the patient remains unidentifiable. The analyst's first responsibility is to the patient and her/his treatment. Catherine Chabert (2013) addresses the ethical demands of presenting case material, making the differentiation between the relative privacy afforded by supervision and how the need to maintain confidentiality becomes of paramount importance when presenting one's work to a group, so that certain details in a case study or vignette might need to be altered (pp. 94–95). This ethical imperative is explored by Sarah Ackerman (2018) who looks at the ethical dilemma underpinning the "disguise versus consent" debate and its attendant impact on a patient's treatment (pp. 65–72). Should the writer, for example, disguise the patient by including minimal details, make amendments, or bring together a number of different treatments in the form of an imaginary patient? Should the analyst ask the patient's permission to include material from their work together? Even when pseudonyms are used and confidentiality is maintained through including minimal details about the patient's life, there are times when patients' identities become known retrospectively, as happened in the cases of, for example, Joseph Breuer's (1895) patient "Anna O" (Bertha Pappenheim) and Sigmund Freud's (1918[1914]) patient "The Wolf Man" (Sergei Pankejeff), to name just two well-known examples. Whatever way a clinician approaches the presentation of a case study or vignette, especially in writing, will impact on the transference-countertransference dynamic (Stein, 1988). Ackerman (2018) delivers a stark warning to any analyst who chooses to write about a patient. The analyst "should", she maintains, experience "conflict and doubt" about this act, which carries "risks": "She should imagine her patient's responses to each word, and ask herself again and again what she might leave out" (p. 78). The appearance of the word "should" in Ackerman's discourse is a function of the superego, but also a reminder that any writing about patients always includes a narcissistic investment on the part of the writer (p. 75); one that needs to be carefully reflected upon.

Psychoanalysis is, Michael Rustin (2019) reminds readers, "a practice-driven field of knowledge" with the case study "the primary source of psychoanalytic knowledge" (p. 109). As psychoanalysis has come under increasing pressure to display its scientific value and efficacy with self-professed "evidenced-based methods", imported from other disciplines, such as psychology, the case study has been perceived as lacking in rigour and usefulness as an objectively-verifiable method of assessment (pp. 100–103). Some clinicians have engaged in the discourse of "evidence-based practice", undertaking their own research into the effectiveness of psychoanalytic treatment and presenting their findings in clinical journals in the fields of psychiatry, psychology and psychotherapy (Fonagy et al., 2015; Leichsenring and Klein, 2014; Shedler, 2010; Yakeley, 2014, 2018). Others, such as Robert Hinshelwood (2013, pp. 68–72), have argued for the usefulness of the case study as a method of "research on the couch" and its very particular contribution to knowledge: "a psychoanalytical treatment is not like a course of penicillin. It is not a probability exercise, it is about finding all the hidden variables, different but discoverable in each individual case" (p. 70). Subjectivity, in other words, cannot be measured using standardised tools; rather, the human subject's experience requires individual attention. The Single Case Archive Project (2013–), a collaboration between researchers at Ghent University, the University of Leuven and the University of Essex, is a growing online archive composed of single case studies in psychotherapy, with an emphasis on psychoanalytic work. It is organised systemically for use by clinicians, researchers and students. The Archive responds to the dismissal of single case studies, in particular, as overly subjective and thus unscientific by some critics. In the face of such criticism, the Archive collects together a wide variety of cases that have been important in the development of clinical practice over the decades. The "human psyche", the project directors inform us, "is far too lively and (re-)active to be captured by standardized tests". According to the Single Case Archive Project's leaders, "more and more scholars" agree that the pursuit of "objectivity" via standardised tests has not brought them any closer to the object they seek. The Archive includes a searchable database with a number of descriptive categories, including topic, title, author, journal, diagnosis, publication year, theoretical orientation, gender patient, age patient, ethnicity patient, gender therapist, age therapist, duration therapy, outcome therapy, length of case and type of study.

Sigmund Freud's case histories, particularly of "Dora" (1905[1901]), "Little Hans" (1909a), "The Wolf Man" (1918[1914]), "The Rat Man" (1909b) and "Judge Daniel Schreber" (1911), have been pored over for decades by clinicians and academics as archetypes of the psychoanalytic method and taken as invitations to analyse Freud as a thinker, a clinician, a writer and a man (Matthis and Szecsödy, 1998; Fuss, 1995; Dalzell, 2011). Whether as required reading for trainees in advance of seeing their first training patient or literary texts for theoretical analysis, Freud's case studies offer the reader an insight into his clinical formulations and approach to treatment. While describing his protagonists – some patients (1905[1901], 1909b, 1918[1914]), some not (1909a, 1911) – Freud offers his readers examples of some of his evolving clinical concepts in practice. Inter-weaving a discussion of clinical technique, a keen aptitude for aetiology and a penchant for storytelling, Freud sets out to challenge the work of others and some of his own earlier theories while outlining the complexities of unconscious processes and their response to clinical intervention. The reader will find many psychoanalytic concepts and theories mentioned, inferred or considered in detail. These are sometimes included to help Freud to deepen his understanding and reflect on his approach, while at other times the individual's material is used to explicate or support a theory being put forward: transference, projection, dreams, negation, hysteria, repression, the symptom, the primal scene, phantasy, the Oed-ipus Complex, *nachträglichkeit*, the screen memory, the compulsion to repeat, identification, psychosis, obsessional neurosis and sublimation to name but a few. Freud also takes the opportunity to educate his readers about the practical arrange-ments necessary for psychoanalytic work and his rationale for same: for example, taking the patient's "whole story of his life and illness" (1905[1901], p. 16) and not taking notes during sessions (1909b, p. 159, n. 2).

There has been, since Freud's death, a sustained interest in clinical case studies and accounts of work in the consulting room (Matthis and Szecsödy, 1998). This might be from the point of view of the therapist or the patient. Stephen Grosz (2014) reflects on his career of twenty-five years as a psychoanalyst in his book, *The Examined Life: How We Lose and Find Ourselves*, while Barbara Taylor (2015) documents her long analysis in *The Last Asylum: A Memoir of Madness in Our Times*. There are also reflections by psychoanalysts on their own personal analyses, such as Margaret Little's (1985) discussion of her time as a patient with Dr. X (pp. 11–13), Ella Freeman Sharpe (pp. 14–18) and Donald Winnicott (pp. 19–37). Little writes her piece in an effort to illustrate the development of some of Winnicott's theories as they arose and were developed in the process of live encounters in the consulting room from her "unique position" (p. 10) as a patient. A.H. Brafman (2018) collates a number of clinical vignettes to present written "portraits" of patients from his clinical work in a series of thematic chapters in *Life in the Consulting Room*, while psychoanalyst and photographer Mark Gerald (2003–, 2011, 2016) presents literal portraits of his subjects, practising psychoanalysts, in their consulting rooms in his ongoing photographic project, "In the shadow of Freud's couch: Portraits of psychoanalysts in their offices" (2003–). Virginia Hunter's (1994a) *Psychoanalysts Talk* is a particularly impressive exam-ple of how the case study can be used for clinical thinking and expanding one's capacity to reflect on one's work with patients. Hunter gives a case study from her own practice (pp. 14–18) to a number of eminent psychoanalysts and asks them to comment on the case from the position of their own expertise, as well as interviewing each one in turn about their life and approach to clinical work. The resulting eleven interviews and case discussions with, for example, Hanna Segal (pp. 41–80), Frances Tustin (pp. 81–110) and John Bowlby (pp. 111–139), become important case studies of psychoanalytic conceptualisation, formulation and technique in themselves, with Virginia Hunter functioning as the container holding all the different perspectives together in one place.

Melanie Klein's (1961) *Narrative of a Child Analysis* is an especially important case study. It details, in Klein's words, her work with 10-year-old "Richard", who attended ninety-three sessions over a four-month period during the Second World War. Richard presented to her with hypochondria, a fear of children and depression (p. 15). Over the course of his treatment, Klein facilitated the boy in partially working through his depressive anxiety and Oedipal difficulties (p. 466). What at first appears to be a plodding introduction and re-introduction of part-objects by Klein in her interpretations gradually facilitates Richard's delving into his feelings towards his parents, his brother, random children and adults in the area, and Klein herself. This continuous repeating of material is tantamount to working through for Klein: "working-through – a process which Freud found so fundamental for analysis – makes it necessary to go repeatedly over similar material, using the new details which come up and make a fuller analysis of the emotional situation possible" (p. 192; see also p. 249). Interpretations facilitate the patient "going deeper" into her/his unconscious, transforming the repetition of material into insight (Klein, 1932b, p. 27, n. 3). Klein's invoking of Oedipal configurations opens Richard up to exploring the love, hatred, fear, guilt and sadness he feels towards his primary objects. The reader witnesses Richard working through these feelings vividly and painstakingly in his play, his drawings and his interactions with Klein. The case study results from Klein's "extensive" notes and gives the reader a sense of the "day-to-day movement in the analysis and the continuity running through it" (p. 11). Among her aims, Klein endeavours to "illustrate [her] technique in greater detail" and show readers "how interpretations find confirmation in the material following them" (p. 11). Each entry includes a description of the session's happenings, as well as Klein's reflection on her technique and how it relates to theory. Elliott Jaques (1961) says that the case study is significant because it "reveals new ideas at the point of their emergence, ideas intuitively conceived, but not yet developed or conceptualised" (p. 6). Thus, the presentation of the case study gives the clinical writer space in which to allow new ideas to breathe, to test out hypotheses before refining them into theoretical statements and incorporating them into larger theoretical paradigms.

The case studies presented by clinicians are sometimes composites of a number of patients or scenarios, or fictional accounts designed specifically by the clinician to illustrate points s/he is making. Claudia Luiz (2018), for example, brings together "facets of people" she has known "in real life" and examples from her "imagination" to give readers an introduction to what it is like to work as a psychoanalyst and, in particular, a sense of the "emotional experiences" encountered in the consulting room (p. xii) in her pedagogical book, *The Making of a Psychoanalyst: Studies in Emotional Education*. There have also been a number of fictional representations of therapeutic processes (Huskinson and Waddell, 2014; Hopson, 2019), an example being the television show *In Treatment* (2008–2010), which makes use of the case study approach to present an imaginary account of what it might be like to practise or attend therapy. *In Treatment*, an American re-make of the Israeli-produced *Be'Tipul* (2005–2008), follows the life and work of therapist Paul Weston over three seasons. Each episode is framed as a session with the use of shot reverse shot to give the viewer an impression of therapist-patient interactions. The series charts the developing therapeutic relationship between Paul and his patients over time, with a number of patients attending for weekly sessions during the course of a single season. The show features dramatic plot sequences that are troubling to some critics; as Brett Kahr (2011a) puts it: "For those in the mental health field keen to damn all heretics who do not practise exactly as we do, *In Treatment* offers a field day of boundary violations that one can lambast" (p. 1056). While the clinical case study includes the clinician's thoughts and feelings about her/his work with a patient, *In Treatment* "goes further", Caroline Bainbridge (2014) writes, "by providing us with the voyeuristic opportunity to look in on the supervisory relationship" between Paul and his supervisors (p. 56). This voyeurism elicited by the framing of the programme gives viewers, Bainbridge argues, an illusion of being "all-seeing" and "omnipotent" (p. 56). This encourages the fantasy that the viewer is an integral part of the case study and not an excluded bystander with some but never all of the information. This invitation "into the feel of what occurs" (Orbach, 2016, p. ix) in the therapeutic space underpins Susie Orbach's radio programme, *In Therapy* (2016–2017). Described on the British Broadcasting Corporation's website as an opportunity for listeners to "get to hear the therapist at work, experiencing what it's like to eavesdrop on the most intimate of exchanges", *In Therapy* features a series of unscripted and improvised sessions with actors "to give a sense of the taste and flavour of an encounter" (Orbach, 2016, p. ix). Transcripts from the radio series, together with Orbach's (2016, 2018) reflections on each session, were published first, in 2016, as *In Therapy: How Conversations with Psychotherapists Really Work*, and later re-issued as an expanded volume with additional sessions, an appendix and a new introduction, in 2018, as *In Therapy: The Unfolding Story*. While Orbach (2018) gives the actors some basic background details including why the client has presented for therapy (pp. 290–291), the sessions are unscripted and designed to "give a range of a therapist's working day" (p. 291) and "to get as near to the experience of the consulting room" as she could (p. 289).

This desire to give the reader, listener or viewer a feel for the emotional experience of what goes on in the consulting room exists alongside the clinician's intention to impart something about theory as it applies to practice. Indeed, the case study is situated, in the words of Laurence Spurling (1997), "at the crossroads of theory and practice" (p. 65), and "it offers a format in which theory can be integrated with practice and turned into coherent communication" (p. 66). The interrelation between theory and the case study has become so interdependent that there is, Ian Parker (2018) remarks, "an expectation that a dense review of conceptual issues will at some point give way to a case example" (p. 9). Theory has been described in a number of ways: It is "a way of thinking" (Castle, 2013, p. 2), an object to think with (Turkle, 2007), "a frame for our listening and interpretative activities" (Zeavin, 2018, p. 70). Above all, theory is "an instrument" and "not an idol" (Canestri, 2012b, p. 161). It is formulated in the clinic, according to Jorge Canestri (2012a), as "intermediate theoretical segments" by the analyst with the patient, which Canestri explains are "hypotheses of conjunction between the observable and theory" (p. xxi). In this, theory constitutes the innovations of clinicians who commit their thinking about the efficacy of their practice to writing. Thus, theory provides guidance to clinicians for their work, in detailing principles of, and strategies for, treatment. Engaging with theory facilitates clinical wondering by expanding one's capacity and extending one's frame of reference. It triangulates the relationship between the analyst and her/his object, the patient. In functioning as a transitional object (Winnicott, 1953), theory opens up a space for thinking between the analyst and the patient and, in doing so, it assists the clinician by heightening their self-awareness and self-reflectivity about the transference and countertransference.

Theory forms part of the psychoanalytic frame, which facilitates the work between the analyst and the patient (Birksted-Breen, 2010–2011; Zeavin, 2018). It is an aspect of the psychoanalytic apparatus that is introjected and identified with by the analyst (Zysman, 2012, p. 152). Theory is, Samuel Zysman (2012) reminds us, akin to "any other object", in being "introjected", "projected", "attacked", debased", "idealised", "an identity sign" or "completely alien" (p 152). Theory functions for the analyst, to that end, as both an external and an internal object simultaneously. Theories are not taken in wholesale. Various traditions of psychoanalysis have developed from Freud's work – for example, Kleinian, Jungian, Lacanian, Independent, Contemporary Freudian, Relational – partly because clinicians have interpreted Freud's writings in different ways and also because their clinical experiences have challenged some of Freud's ideas. Psychoanalysis is a practice-led discipline, so theory, while being borne out of work in the clinic, is subject to being developed in tandem with clinical needs and insights. In this, there is a recognition that theory is indispensable while at the same time a product of the socio-cultural context prevalent at the time of its production. In general, theories, Werner Bohleber (2012) remarks, "can help the clinician to concretely conceptualise that which is inside the patient that he has not yet understood, but has sensed and perceived intuitively; they can thereby bring it out, capture it in words, and make it communicable" (p. 5). In this way, theory can function as a container to facilitate a deeper understanding of the patient's material.

The non-clinical case study and vignette

Rachel Blass (2018) writes about her experience of teaching theories of Kleinian psychoanalysis to students, concluding that "[t]eaching psychoanalysis is a difficult task" (p. 89). Part of the difficulty lies in how to present material in such a way "to allow the student to experience it, to feel it" (p. 77), rather than simply taking it in at an abstract, intellectual level (p. 76). "The mind", Blass (2018) remarks, "needs to be opened up to digesting [Melanie Klein's] ideas" (p. 74). This can be challenging when the ideas are "affectively disturbing" (p. 74). Blass differentiates between "content" and "meaning and truth" with reference to "psychoanalytic propositions" (p. 73). She believes that "experiential teaching" of, what she terms, "the Kleinian worldview" can be accomplished partly through "close reading" of Kleinian writings (p. 77). This approach is echoed by Thomas Ogden (2009a), who concentrates on analytic works "as a piece of writing and an experience in reading" (p. 54). For him, words "create experiences to be lived out by the reader" because "writing does not re-present what happened; it creates something that happens for the first time in the experience of writing and reading" (p. 63). To tap into the experiences pervading the written text, Ogden advocates reading texts aloud, in the process, "immersing ourselves intellectually and emotionally in the way the author thinks/writes" (p. 52). This is because reading is not a passive experience. While reading the text, the reader is "being read by the writing" (Ogden, 2012a, p. 2), or, as Ogden explains, the text offers the reader an opportunity to "read oneself" or engage in "self-reflection" (p. 2). Therefore, "reading creatively" results in a "personal set of meanings and ideas using the text as a starting point" (p. 1). Blass and Ogden are talking about ways of imparting psychoanalytic knowledge through the learning experience itself. While the text is important, it is the experience of engaging with the text that becomes central in the student's taking in of material. Blass (2018) foregrounds the act of reflecting in her seminars on Kleinian texts. She stresses how "important" it is that "these reflections come alive for the student" because "true learning and conviction is gained through immediate experience" (p. 89). This recognises the fact that material can be presented, but what the recipient does or is capable of doing with the material is a separate process, and one that also provides fertile ground for learning about oneself. As Ogden (2009a) puts it, in the process of reading aloud, seminar participants in his group get a sense of "who [the writer] is becoming, and, perhaps most important, who we are becoming as a consequence of the experience of reading the work together" (p. 52).

Judith Edwards has written about how and why she incorporates film (2010) and poetry (2015) into her teaching at the Tavistock Clinic in London. Describing film as "a powerful medium for projecting as well as containing emotional experience", Edwards believes that it can "convey something of the atmosphere which may be generated and experienced in a clinical session" (2010, p. 81). She adds that "[s]pecific films may also provide excellent illustrations of psychological processes" (p. 81) and therefore are useful for introducing students to clinical concepts, such as countertransference (p. 80). This is because, as Edwards comments elsewhere, "The power of images and music together may create an extra dimension not possible with words alone" (2014, p. 791). Her attendance is to the "experience engendered" (p. 80) by a film and especially to what is "evoked" in terms of associations (2014, p. 94). Writing about poetry, Edwards (2018) believes that "Analysts and therapists who read and listen to poetry being read are training themselves to resonate with dreams, with free association, and the primary process which reveals conflicting states involved with wishes and desires" (p. 282). This is because "unconscious phantasy can be tapped into" through writing, reading and listening to poetry, "even if these phantasies are not explicit in a poem, poet or reader" (p. 282). In her reading of the film, *Morvern Callar* (2002), Edwards (2010) reminds readers that hers "is not a definite view", arguing that she thinks "it is vital that we consider our specific views to be provisional, and open to question" (p. 97). This is important advice for anyone who works clinically, because a capacity for curiosity, wonder and surprise is vital for clinical work, alongside the recognition that every occurrence is provisional and context-specific. It can be difficult to hold onto an openness to experience in the face of the persecutory anxiety induced by states of not knowing and not understanding.

Candida Yates (2001) refers to "the possibilities of a more feeling-ful way" of "learning" in her discussion of teaching psychoanalysis to academic students on a psychosocial studies programme (p. 334). Incorporating some of the "culture" of "clinical work" into one's teaching of psychoanalysis, can, Yates argues, "encourage a more reflexive approach to both teaching and learning" (p. 334). Ogden's writings (2009a, 2009b, 2009c, 2012a, 2016, 2018) about how the analyst reflects on the experience of analytic work, as well as on the experience of transmitting psychoanalytic knowledge to others have been instructive for clinicians wishing to develop and expand their capacity for insight. In writing about his approach to teaching psychoanalysis, as mentioned earlier, Ogden (2009a) advocates reading clinical texts aloud to enable seminar participants to become aware of all the component parts of a text because they "contribute to the effects created and the ideas conveyed in the medium of language" (p. 52). He insists that reading "sentence by sentence, paragraph by paragraph" is "essential" (p. 52). He slows everything down to bring the process itself into focus. This close reading is attending to more than just the words on the page: the act of reading aloud and in the context of a group is evoking an experience; an experience that the seminar group can then reflect on together as individuals and as a group. Ogden is encouraging those who work with him in his seminar group to be present with the text and the experience that the encounter is evoking in each one of them. This is because Ogden appreciates that "an analytic experience – like all other experiences – does not come to us in words. An experience cannot be told or written; an experience is what it is" (Ogden, 2005, p. 16). Thomas Ogden's co-authored book with Benjamin Ogden (2013) brings literary criticism into dialogue with clinical psychoanalytic practice. In reflecting on the contribution that clinical analytic writers can offer to literary critics, they consider the "qualities" and "the experience of the practice of psychoanalysis" because "psychoanalytic concepts are only one part of psychoanalysis":

> its close attention to the effects of language and to other forms of human expression, its interest in the relationship between the use of language and the individual's attempts to express and understand himself, its therapeutic dimension, its way of understanding the unconscious as both an individual

and an intersubjective phenomenon, and its use of the qualities of aliveness and deadness of language as measures of the status of an analysis at any given juncture.

(p. 3)

I have found this to be true in my own teaching of psychoanalysis to students. Whether they are in clinical training or studying psychoanalytic ideas as part of an academic programme, students engage with the material in more depth if they are able to connect with it in an emotional way. This experience is most effective if it is made available to students in a live encounter, in the here and now of the class-room. This takes careful planning in advance of the class and mindful facilitation during the class itself. There is an important distinction between the needs of clinical and non-clinical students: while one group is preparing themselves for, or in the early stages of, clinical work with patients and so a capacity for self-reflectivity is vital, the second group is embarking on an academic course of study in which self-reflectivity is a significant feature. Whatever the career trajectory of students, the encounter with psychoanalysis offers them a meaningful experience to integrate into their life and work. In this chapter, I will concentrate on my work with trainees on clinical trainings and with clinicians attending further professional development training seminars or workshops. I will focus on my clinical teaching because the central argument that I will make here is for the usefulness of incorporating, what I call, non-clinical case studies and vignettes into clinical training programmes. I will outline an approach to clinical teaching, which I have been developing and which I refer to as the "Cultural Encounters Case Study Method" Method.

The Cultural Encounters Case Study Method

The Cultural Encounters Case Study Method brings together clinical, academic and artistic materials in the teaching of psychoanalytic theory to trainees and practitioners. I will refer to both as participants throughout, as the Method is an experiential and participatory approach to learning. I will also identify the lecturer or clinician who leads the training or further professional development group as a facilitator, as the Method departs from the imparting of theoretical knowledge through more intellectual means. The Method is grounded in theory, practice and experience, and is underpinned by an exploratory, interactive, collaborative, facilitative and creative approach to learning. I understand my role as being one in which participants are invited, as Thomas Ogden (2009c) expresses it, "not to be taught, but to discover" (p. 1). In this, my objective is to present participants with an experience, provide a frame for that experience and facilitate them in their encounter. Their response to the experience is influenced by their history, environmental context and personality, as well as their transferences to the material, to one another and to me. While I invite them to engage with the material and encourage them to reflect on the experience, how they engage and what they do with the encounter is specific to each individual and their capacity to take in, to use the object and, thus, to symbolise (Bott Spillius et al., 2011b). Writing about the engagement with theory, Deborah Britzman (2015) remarks, "what is felt in theory is anxiety" (p. 51). This relates to how the individual relates to the object, particularly to what is perceived as new (p. 51). This "emotional use of theory" (p. 52) can provoke persecutory anxiety and the employment of a range of psychical defences to protect against the experience of not knowing and not understanding. Experiences evoked in reaction to the learning situation include "danger of exposure", "defamiliarization", vulnerability that "something might happen to us", and anxiety that "a great deal will be lost should more be thought" (p. 52). This anxiety relating to learning might manifest as "resistance to theory, hostility to reading, hatred of language through worries over jargon, writing inhibitions, and fear of theory" (p. 52). Above all, Britzman is writing about, what she calls, the "psychoanalytic ethic", which involves "tolerat[ing] the opening of the mind" that demands "listening with a difference to the conflicts of meanings audible and inaudible just at the point that they reach defensive mechanisms of closure" (p. 52).

One of the characteristic features of the Cultural Encounters Case Study Method is the inclusion of non-clinical case studies and vignettes in the training or further professional development context. Non-clinical case studies are cultural objects produced in the fields of film, literature, music and the visual and performing arts. Michael Rustin (2019) refers to these objects as "artefacts of cultural production" (p. 269). They might include films, television programmes, plays, poems, novels, short stories, drawings, paintings, installations, sculptures, art performances, songs, sound pieces and pieces of music. This list is not exhaustive. Non-clinical case vignettes are excerpts, extracts or clips from the aforementioned. Non-clinical case studies and vignettes are the result of creative endeavours, and might be fictional, based on real life or an amalgam of both. They might be contemporary or historical productions. They might be structured using narrative as a device to contextualise their subject, or they might operate outside or against narrative conventions. They might be self-reflective about the environmental context from which they arise or document it unreflectively all the same. They might, though do not have to, depict aspects of the clinical encounter between analyst and patient. They do however demand an engagement from the individual. The engagement might be intellectual or emotional; usually both. The engagement will have, even if it is subtle, a somatic element to it. The experience engendered will be sensory in some respect. So, while cultural objects provide something, they also demand something from the subject in return, even if the subject is not aware of the demand or their reaction to it. Making use of cultural objects as non-clinical case studies and vignettes takes them out of their context, demands work of them in ways they were not intended, and reads them differently and sometimes against themselves. The naming of them as non-clinical case studies and vignettes recognises this re-routing and their specified purpose within the clinical training and discussion sphere. They remain cultural objects in their own sphere but are transformed into non-clinical case studies and vignettes when they enter the clinical conversation.

Vicky Lebeau (2001) refers to "the clinical situation" as psychoanalysis' "unique domain" (p. 5), and Stephen Frosh (2010) makes a distinction between psychoanalysis inside and outside the clinic: "Without analyst and patient both being there, locked into their transferential relationship, interpretation in the psychoanalytic sense cannot take place" (p. 3). It is this "live encounter" between the analyst and the patient that characterises psychoanalysis; "[a]nything else, therefore, is not psychoanalysis, however much appeal there is to the language or theoretical constructs of psychoanalysis" (pp. 3, 3–4). He refers to the employment of psychoanalytic concepts outside the clinic as "intellectual activities" (p. 4), and while reiterating that "none" of these activities "however carefully they employ psychoanalytic ideas, are in fact psychoanalysis" (p. 4), they can make a contribution to our experience and understanding of culture, society and politics. Frosh works hard to operationalise psychoanalysis "as opening out some questions and perceptions" rather than "possessing a 'truth'" (p. 39). This off-the-couch and outside-the-consulting-room approach to psychoanalysis is often referred to as "applied psychoanalysis", which Salman Akhtar and Stuart Twemlow (2018b) tell readers means "to denote the employment of basic psychoanalytic principles . . . for deepening understanding of cultural phenomena at large" and more broadly "sociocultural phenomena" (p. xxxi). They distinguish "applied psychoanalysis" from "clinical psychoanalysis", while tracing their origins back to Freud (p. xxxi). Their *Textbook of Applied Psychoanalysis* includes thirty-five chapters, each of which focuses on a different discipline or theme, including anthropology, philosophy, religion, medicine, prejudice, education, cyberpsychology, architecture, poetry, dance and music. Their book is situated within a rich tradition of psychoanalytic approaches to a diverse range of fields, for example, film (Gabbard, 2001a; Kuhn, 2013a; Sabbadini, 2014a; Piotrowska, 2015), literature (Phillips, 2002; Gabbard, 2007; Ogden and Ogden, 2013, Buechler, 2015), art (Goldstein, 2013; Hagman, 2017; Carey, 2018; Townsend, 2019) and music (Schwarz, 1997; Rose, 2004; Jaffee Nagel, 2013; Wilson, 2015). This also includes multidisciplinary areas of enquiry, such as psychosocial studies (Clarke and Hoggett, 2009; Frosh, 2010; Woodward, 2015; Thomas, 2018) and the psycho-cultural approach (Bainbridge and Yates, 2011; Yates, 2014; Bainbridge and Yates, 2014a; Richards, 2018). Work in psychosocial studies focuses on the inter-relation between the individual and the group, together with the psychical/unconscious and social and cultural aspects of experience. It is informed by psychoanalytic thinking (Frosh and Baraitser, 2008; Frost and McClean, 2014; Woodward, 2015). Like psychosocial studies, the psycho-cultural approach is underpinned by a psychoanalytic approach, particularly object relations, and an attendance to the internal and external worlds of subjects, particularly as they relate to our production of, engagement with and attachment to cultural objects (Yates and Bainbridge, 2014a; Yates, 2014, 2018). The triangular relationship dynamic enacted by psychosocial studies, the psycho-cultural approach and psychoanalysis was discussed in Chapter 1.

The Cultural Encounters Case Study Method shares an interest in exploring the unconscious dynamics underpinning cultural objects and socio-cultural contexts more broadly, in alignment with the commitment of people working in applied psychoanalysis, psychosocial studies and with the psycho-cultural approach. Having said that, the parameters of this Method are more precise, principally in the way in which the cultural object is used in clinical training and discussion contexts, and the purpose of its inclusion. Analytic work with non-clinical case studies and vignettes might at first appear to approach a text the way cultural studies critics or critical theorists do: as a thing in itself, the amalgam of a set of discourses produced within a cultural and societal context with material and ideological effects. And indeed, there is an aspect of this approach to cultural objects integrated into the Method from my background and training in textual analysis and critical theory. While the analytic readings resulting from an engagement with cultural objects might be of interest to those in cultural studies and critical theory, the primary target audience for non-clinical case studies and vignettes is trainees and clinicians. The naming of them as non-clinical case studies and vignettes makes this distinction explicit. It refers to their usage rather than their being, so the employment of them for a particular purpose in a particular context does not cancel out their qualities as a cultural object; one that exists in the world in its own right with a multitude of meanings and significances in different contexts. Writing with reference to psychoanalytic approaches to literature, Lucy Rollin and Mark West (1999) comment: "We must try to allow the literary work its 'life', its integrity as an artistic entity" (p. 11).

It is important to say something about wild analysis at this point. Freud (1910a) writes about the potential accuracy of statements made outside of the psychoanalytic clinical setting by people untrained in the method, which sometimes in spite of their clumsiness can even be "beneficial", but that this misuse of the technique ultimately damages the profession of psychoanalysis in increasing "prejudice" against it (pp. 8–9). Intellectual "knowledge" of the unconscious and the methods of psychoanalysis is of no use to the patient (p. 7). Such knowledge, Freud says, "would have about as much impact on neurotic symptoms as distributing menus would have on hunger during a famine" (p. 7). What is central to psychoanalysis is the emphasis on managing the relationship with the patient, namely transference, together with the patient's symptoms and resistances to treatment (p. 7). As mentioned earlier in this chapter, it is the experience itself that is central. Adrienne Harris and Jonathan Sklar (1998) warn against the "overly magisterial", "decontextualized" and "imperialistic" use of psychoanalysis for analysing other disciplines, specifically film, which is their focus (pp. 222, 223). This "uncritical" (p. 222), "ahistorical" (p. 225) and "authoritarian" (p. 235) use of psychoanalysis, unfettered from the clinic, is ignorant of the complexity of film as a cultural genre in and of itself with its own history, discourses and methods. Harris and Sklar are specific in their condemnation of particular types of psychoanalytic applications which include, for example, readings of "a film as personal pathology of a character, a director, or writer or treating a film as a species of individual psychobiography or a reading of cultural trends of consciousness" (p. 225). To avoid engaging in wild analysis, Rollin and West (1999) advise psychoanalytic readers to be "gentle and informed" in their approach and be mindful not to "distort the work" (p. 11). The wild analysis that Harris and Sklar previously refer to seeks to colonise the text by fixing its meaning in an omnipotent gesture towards certainty. There is a desire for omniscience evident in wild analysis, as it is written about by Harris and Sklar. This is antithetical to the Cultural Encounters Case Study Method, which advocates a tentative approach, namely an openness to the experience of engaging with a non-clinical case study or vignette and a receptiveness to reflecting on the experience of this encounter. The meanings of the non-clinical case study or vignette are understood as indefinite, provisional, illusive and ultimately unknowable. The point of engaging with a non-clinical case study or vignette is not to establish mastery or prowess but to offer an opportunity to test out one's developing knowledge, skills and capacities with the recognition that this tells one something about oneself rather than anything in particular about the object. This touches on ethics more generally, which is an important feature of the writing of case studies and vignettes when including material by patients. Writing about examples drawn from literature, Jeremy Holmes (2014) writes that they "provide case-illustrations without the attendant difficulties of confidentiality and non-generalisability" (p. ix).

Roleplays do not tend to be used in psychoanalytic trainings and further professional development trainings, although they are incorporated into trainings for psychoanalytically-informed treatments, such as Mentalization-Based Treatment (Bateman and Fonagy, 2016). Roleplays perform a useful function in other modalities of psychotherapy and counselling, in that they provide participants with an opportunity to test out skills and knowledge in controlled environments, where anxiety can be contained before participants bring what they have learned into the consulting room (Tolan and Lendrum, 1995). Roleplays are also used for the purpose of assessing trainees in particular. Infant observation takes the place of roleplays in psychoanalytic contexts. This is because in infant observation the observer has a more immediate, immersive and authentic experience to navigate and reflect upon, in order to develop capacities, skills and knowledge. The demands placed on the observer, alongside the observer's training and personal growth, contribute towards the development of "a psychoanalytic attitude" and "a developed sensitivity to emotion" (Rustin, 1989, p. 20). Infant observation gives the observer a chance to witness the development of an infant within her/his home environment first-hand. It also provides the observer with an opportunity to be with the experience of finding oneself in another's space, to sit with the feeling of not knowing, and to develop a capacity to wait without knowing what one is waiting for. The psychoanalytic encounter itself foregrounds a "waiting *with*" rather than a "waiting *for*" (Baraitser and Salisbury, 2020, p. 9). The aforementioned experiences facilitate the observer allowing the experience itself to unfold in all its complexity without deciding in advance what the experience might mean or attempting to theorise about it prematurely (Thomson-Salo, 2014, p. 3).

Janine Sternberg (2005) refers to this as "Living in the question" (p. 6), which is incredibly difficult to do because it requires a shift in oneself rather than simply learning and applying a concept or skill. The infant observation seminar is an integral part of the observation experience (Thomson-Salo, 2014, pp. 9–10). The seminar group comprises four to six observers, and each seminar is led by the same experienced clinician, usually with experience of working with children and adolescents. Every seminar focuses on the observation notes of a different observer. The observation notes are taken as soon as possible after the observer has left the infant's home and record everything the observer can remember of her/his experience. The seminar leader facilitates the exploration of observation material and contains the group as individual members develop their skills, capacity for self-awareness and insight, and confidence. The infant observation experience concludes with a lengthy seminar paper in which observers are tasked with integrating experience with theory. The Cultural Encounters Case Study Method is informed by infant observation in providing a space for the participant to observe and become more receptive to what is going on within and outside her/himself, in addition to representing her/his experience of observing. Thus, participants share aspects of the experience of the observer in being trained over time, as Sternberg (2005) writes, "to look, notice, feel, be aware of how what she sees impacts on her, reflect, remember, process, think, and then write about it all" (p. 6). The seminar group becomes an important site for testing out ideas and gradually learning more about *how* one processes and relates to experiences. This is made possible by the group operating as a thinking-mind that provides holding, as each individual develops their skills and capacities in relation to the material presented. This, in turn, is facilitated by the facilitator who contains the group through the framing of activities and discussions.

I will present a selection of non-clinical case studies and vignettes from art, literature, film and music to give a sense of how they can be employed within clinical trainings and further professional development seminars and workshops. This is a small sample of material that I have used myself, and I introduce it here to illustrate some of the workings of the Cultural Encounters Case Study Method. The Method has three principal characteristics. Firstly, it opens up a space for registering and reflecting on one's experience of engaging with non-clinical case studies and vignettes in a live encounter. This live encounter takes place within the context of an exploratory group, which is facilitated by an experienced psychoanalytic practitioner. Secondly, it provides space to explore one's theoretical understanding of clinical concepts, in a creative way that is designed to foster the development of a capacity for reverie, symbolisation, alpha-function and containment. Thirdly, it presents a practical opportunity to learn and hone clinical skills by applying them and reviewing their application within a controlled setting. The Method is not rooted in any particular cultural objects; rather it brings together clinical concepts and cultural objects as creative sites for playing with ideas through encounter and experience. In opening up spaces for thinking and feeling, the Method provides opportunities to work towards integrating theoretical knowledge with capacities and skills required for clinical practice. I have chosen a number of cultural objects that are readily and widely available, should readers wish to access them for a more direct experience with the material I write about here.

The non-clinical case studies and vignettes explored later can be introduced at any stage of clinical training and for groups including recently qualified clinicians and/or practitioners who have been working in practice for many years. The facilitator will need to adjust their approach, depending on the knowledge-base and clinical experience of the group. I will discuss two examples (art and music) that provide opportunities to develop capacities for self-awareness and self-reflectivity, particularly as they relate to engaging with and making use of the countertransference experience. I will write about a further two examples (literature and film) to show firstly how non-clinical case studies and vignettes can be used to illustrate the employment of clinical concepts for thinking about the patient within the contexts of the consulting room and her/his life. Secondly, I will explore how non-clinical case studies and vignettes provide opportunities to discuss the practicalities involved in the psychoanalytic consultation and assessment process (literary example), as well as why it is important for clinicians to understand the state of mind of the patient, based on how s/he is talking, acting and relating to the analyst in the clinic (film example). I will write about non-clinical case studies and vignettes under four sub-headings: "Art: Allowing ourselves to have an experience", "Literature: tuning in to experiences that come to us in words", "Film: Getting a sense of how the patient might be experiencing the world" and "Music: Attuning ourselves to experiences that come to us outside of words".

Art: allowing ourselves to have an experience

The first example is a series of non-clinical vignettes. These are photographs from Mark Gerald's (2003–) "In the shadow of Freud's couch: Portraits of psychoanalysts in their offices". This is an ongoing photographic project by Gerald, a psychoanalyst and photographer. It operates at the boundaries between the clinical and the artistic.

Gerald (2003) photographs analysts in their consulting rooms, commenting that he is interested in "seeing people . . . in their surface appearance and in the deeper sense of who they are". Subjects include Martin Bergmann (Figure 2.1), André Green, Anni Bergman (Figure 2.2), Joyce McDougall, Eyal Rozmarin (Figure 2.3), Susie Orbach and Andrew Samuels. Gerald (2011) visits analysts in their own environment, "houses for the unconscious" (p. 436), where they are surrounded by objects of their own choosing. The places in which we see patients are meaningful for us (p. 435). These environments operate – consciously and unconsciously – as sites of "self-expression" (p. 438). This is because "our offices remain repositories of our patients and our own inner worlds" (p. 437); they "live" in us (Gerald, 2016, p. 651). The environment in which we work reflects something of our inner world because, as Gerald (2011) says, "[i]nhabited space comes to inhabit us" (p. 437). They are conduits for the processes of projection and introjection. Those things about ourselves which are outside of our awareness

Figure 2.1 Martin Bergmann, New York, 2003

Source: © Mark Gerald

Figure 2.2 Anni Bergman, New York, 2003

Source: © Mark Gerald

Figure 2.3 Eyal Rozmarin, New York, 2004

Source: © Mark Gerald

can sometimes be reflected in ways that only another mind can help us to see. When working with clinical groups, I show participants a series of photographs from the project and ask for their impressions – words that come into their minds when they see the pictures – and usually a lively conversation ensues. There is an enjoyment in observing the other, in seeing things in others that they might not see in themselves, in observing without being observed. This is pleasurable partly because it gives a sense of omniscience and omnipotence. It also takes away the feeling of being evaluated or assessed, which can be intrusive and inhibiting, and allows participants to immerse themselves in the experience. It takes time to become aware of how one is reacting to a situation.

The function of these non-clinical vignettes is to open up a space for partici-pants to begin engaging with material in an authentic way, by saying what they actually think, rather than trying to find the correct answer (there is none). It also provides an opportunity to help participants to begin to reflect on their associa-tions to aspects of the photographs, as well as the associations of other members of the group. If they react to a photograph in a particular way, what is it about that photograph that leads them to make that determination? It could be anything from the framing of the shot, the lighting, an object in the room, a colour, an aspect of the analyst in the photograph. These are all part-objects that can be projected onto, and, as such, they result in a complex array of associations with attendant mean-ings. If participants say someone in the photograph looks serious or sad or angry, what is it about the person that suggests that is the case? This facilitates partici-pants honing their attention so that their observation skills become more precise, while they are given the chance to articulate what it is that is affecting them and in what ways. So, the act of observing others becomes a vehicle for self-observation and self-reflection.

Gerald (2011) commences his paper by stating that it is "a paper about looking at ourselves" (p. 436). These non-clinical vignettes provide an opportunity to look at ourselves while in the process of looking at someone else. What do participants' reactions, in effect their assumptions, tell them about themselves? Gerald's pho-tographs also lead to conversations about the clinical rooms in which participants practise or attend analysis and supervision, and the particularities of those spaces (Rendell, 2017, pp. 113–127). How do they and their patients navigate the clinical space, for example, the transitional spaces between the front door and the consult-ing room and between the door of the consulting room and the couch? What is that experience like for them, and how do they negotiate the experience? What transferences do they and their patients have to the objects in the room, the room itself, the building in which the analysis takes place and the geographical location of the building? How do their patients make use of the objects in the room? Do patients use tissues or cushions or blankets, for example, if they are provided? Can patients allow themselves to make use of the objects in the room? How might this help participants to reflect on how their patients make use of, or not, the ana-lyst and her/his interpretations? If there are pictures on the walls, what do they or their patients see in them?

What impact might any changes in the location of the analysis or in the objects in the consulting room have on the patient and on the treatment? Adrienne Harris and Isaac Tylim (2018) relay the experience of a colleague who had made some changes to her consulting room over the weekend and the formidable impact the changes had on her patient:

> Consider the case of a colleague of ours who had been having weekly sessions with a five-year-old boy who had been part of the foster care system. One Monday, she brings him to her office after a weekend during which the walls were painted and the furniture changed. The boy walks with her into the room, looks around and faints.
>
> (p. 3)

Harris and Tylim are writing about the impact not just of changes on the patient but of unanticipated changes – the effect of surprises, shocks. They insist that "attention to materiality" is fundamental to analytic work, and warn readers that "[s]hifts in the frame can, under certain contexts, have catastrophic consequences" (p. 3). The "materiality" of the analytic space can also impact on the clinician (Kahr, 2011b). How, for example do participants negotiate working in rooms that are shared and which might include objects that have been chosen by someone else? How might these things, at the edges of the session, be significant as vehicles for accessing the internal world of the patient? These non-clinical vignettes facilitate participants considering the links between the materiality of the consulting room and the analytic frame, particularly how every material change, however small, impacts on the patient and the analytic process at various levels of psychic functioning.

Conversations about the "materiality" of the consulting room lead on to discussions about the setting's function as part of the analytic frame or holding environment for the work. The frame includes the practical arrangements for the session, including the frequency of the sessions, the fees and the analyst's maintaining of a space free, as much as possible, from intrusions or interruptions, including in her/his own mind. As Dana Birksted-Breen (2010–2011) remarks, "The analyst's attitude is part of the setting" (p. 56), while Lynne Zeavin (2018) comments that the frame is "inextricable from the analytic relationship", namely "the transference relationship" (p. 59). The frame represents the reality principle, in incorporating the beginning and ending of sessions, the fees, the analysts breaks and so on. It is a reminder to the patient that s/he does not control the setting; it exists independently of the patient's wishes or demands. The frame, while sometimes perceived as persecutory by patients who find the boundary difficult, also provides holding and containment, because the consistency and regularity of the analytic environment, together with the attitude and behaviour of the analyst, all keep a space open for the unexpected to emerge in the analytic work itself. The organisation of analytic treatment leads patients to regress, and so it is important to facilitate that "safely, comfortably, and in a controlled way" (Eichler, 2010, p. 17). How does the treatment facilitate regression in the patient (and the analyst)? How is the analyst's management of the patient's regression linked to her/his holding of the analytic frame? How do participants manage the patient's regression and any challenges arising from this state? In what ways might the physical layout of the room and its contents, particularly the couch (Sabbadini, 2014c), be linked to the analytic frame and the regression of the patient? These non-clinical vignettes ease participants into the Cultural Encounters Case Study Method as a frame for exploration and reflection.

Literature: tuning in to experiences that come to us in words

The second example is a non-clinical case study which I use for two purposes: firstly, to introduce the Oedipus Complex as a clinical concept and to explore how Oedipal configurations might manifest in the words, actions and relationship patterns of children and adults; secondly, to facilitate thinking about the place of, and the practicalities involved in, the consultation process in psychoanalytic work, as well as the rationale for undertaking a clinical assessment. "My Oedipus Complex" is a short story by Frank O'Connor (1963). O'Connor's story describes the idealised existence of five-year-old Larry, who lives alone with his mother while his father is away during the First World War. During this time, Larry enjoys, what amounts to in his mind, unlimited access to his mother. He characterises his waking moments as "feeling myself rather like the sun ready to illumine and rejoice" (p. 12) or "feeling like a bottle of champagne" (p. 15). His father is presented as a distant and benign figure, whom Larry refers to as being like "Santa Claus" (p. 13). His father's comings and goings are represented in the "big figure in khaki peering down at [him]" and "the slamming of the front door and the clatter of nailed boots down the cobbles of the lane" (p. 12). His father's return from the War is deeply persecutory for Larry, puncturing his omnipotence and idealised relationship with his mother. Larry's father's presence is experienced by Larry as intrusive and castrating. These castrating gestures are enacted by his mother. His mother's remonstrations of "talking to Daddy" (p. 14), "Don't Wake Daddy!" (p. 16) and "Poor Daddy" (p. 17) prove to be confusing and distressing for the child, who goes from spending time in his mother's bed to being warned "don't interrupt again!" (p. 14). Larry perceives his father as an interloper stealing his mother's attention, "a total stranger" and an enemy, against whom he engages in "skirmishes" (p. 19). Over the course of the story, Larry begins to experience mixed feelings towards his parents, where before they had been all good (mother) or all bad (father). This is especially evident upon the birth of his younger brother Sonny. Larry externalises the war waging within himself as he increasingly begins to feel ambivalence towards both his father, whom he "couldn't help feeling sorry for" (p. 22), and his mother, who is "quite sickening about Sonny". Sonny becomes the repository for much of Larry's animosity projected previously onto his father. This facilitates Larry repairing the internal image he has of his father, which in turn enables him to acknowledge that while his father is not perfect, he is "better than nothing" (p. 22).

This non-clinical case study is useful for introducing and exploring the psychical processes forming part of the Oedipus Complex, conceived of by Freud to make sense of the child's developing relationships with her/himself and others. Freud uses the narrative sequences from a Greek myth to draw parallels between it and the psychical, sexual and emotional development of the child and her/his anatomy (Sophocles, 1984[1977]). The Oedipus Complex, as it was formulated by Freud (1905, p. 107, 1908, 1909[1908], 1909a, 1931, 1933[1932]), is a theory of desire and sexual difference. It seeks to give meaning to the phantasies attached to the child's earliest interactions with her/his caregivers, tracing her/his movement through desire and aggression, identification and separation. Estimating the Complex's beginning to three–five years, Freud argues that the child should have sufficiently worked through the process by the time s/he reaches the latency period (Laplanche and Pontalis, 1967, pp. 282–287). This non-clinical case study serves a didactic purpose, so it requires a lot of preparation on the part of the facilitator, who needs to identify scenes from the short story which illustrate the operations of Oedipal dynamics. While serving a didactic purpose for imparting the psychical features of the Oedipus Complex, this non-clinical case study is also useful for providing opportunities to reflect on experiences that come to us in words.

What is evoked in the reader when reading the words on the page? How does the narrator position himself within his own story? How does the patient narrate her/his story and, through her/his narration, frame her/his experiences? In verbally articulating what has transpired during a session in a supervisory context, for example, how does the analyst become a narrator of a new story? This non-clinical case study facilitates participants to observe the nuances within words and syntax, and how nuances can be missed, depending on how one verbally frames what has happened during a session. Writing in relation to the reporting of material from infant observation experiences, Esther Bick (1964) comments:

> In the seminars it comes out very clearly from the beginning how difficult it is to "observe", i.e. collect facts free from interpretation. As soon as these facts have to be described in language we find that every word is loaded with a penumbra of implications. Should the student say the nipple "dropped" from the baby's mouth, "fell", was "pushed", "released", "escaped", etc? In fact, he finds that he chooses a particular word because observing and thinking are almost inseparable. This is an important lesson, for it teaches caution and reliance on consecutive observations for confirmation.
>
> (p. 26)

Putting words on experience is difficult. This challenge is evident, particularly when it comes to the retrospective reporting of experience, because the relationship between observation and representation can become blurred through the lens of perception (Bick, 1964, p. 26).

"My Oedipus Complex" (O'Connor, 1963) is particularly useful when read together with a screening and discussion of another non-clinical case study, the film *Cyrus* (2010). *Cyrus* features two Oedipal triangles, each involving two men and one woman: Cyrus, Molly and John, and John, Jamie and Tim. The film represents two men – Cyrus and John – suffering Oedipal rivalrous rage because they believe the woman in their life is being taken away by another man: for Cyrus, it is his mother; for John, it is his ex-wife. The film also represents the fact that one can occupy different positions within an Oedipal dynamic, depending on the context. For example, while John occupies the interloper for Cyrus in the triangle with Molly, John perceives Tim as the interloper in another Oedipal triangle with Jamie. The film represents John's and Cyrus's movement from a two-person relationship towards a three-person relationship and from enmeshment and dependence through to separation, loss and a growing independence. Viewers are treated to the uncomfortable spectacle of two men coming to the painful realisation – to a greater or lesser extent – that their primary object is separate, different and possessing a subjectivity of her own and a desire that is not directed solely towards either of them. While "My Oedipus Complex" portrays the experiences of the young child through the retrospective reporting of an adult, *Cyrus* displays the continued presence of Oedipal dynamics in the life of the adult; one in a dramatic way (Cyrus) and another in a subtle yet equally painful fashion (John).

These non-clinical case studies lead to clinical discussions about how multiple Oedipal triangles arise in work with patients and also in one's own practice between, for example, the analyst, patient and clinical supervisor; the analyst, her/his own analyst and clinical supervisor; the analyst, patient and another person or people in the patient's life outside the consulting room. I also incorporate "My Oedipus Complex" (O'Connor, 1963) as a non-clinical case study to help participants to reflect on their approach to the consultation process, particularly as it relates to the practice of clinical assessment (Hobson, 2013; Cooper and Alfillé, 1998, 2011). The consultation process is, Judy Cooper and Helen Alfillé (2011) remind readers, "an introduction to a very different way of relating" (p. 2). It offers the patient an experience and more properly functions as "an invitation [to the patient] to consider the meaning" of her/his experience (Ogden, 2012b, p. 173). The consultation process also incorporates a clinical need to assess the patient's "suitability" (Mordecai and Waydenfeld, 1998, p. 87) for psychoanalytic treatment, or "whether the patient and analyst are able to work together" (Reith et al., 2012, p. 5). The clinician must exercise clinical judgement in determining whether psychoanalytic treatment is indicated or contra-indicated, and, if contra-indicated, whether a referral to another clinical practitioner, different psychotherapeutic modality or another form of treatment might be more appropriate. I ask participants to read the story and invite them to engage in hypothetical thinking: Larry is not a patient; however, engaging in thinking about him *as if* he were a patient offers participants an opportunity to reflect on their own professional practice, as well as to hear how other people might manage the consultation process, which prompts further reflection. This also encourages participants to play with ideas, which is important in analytic work because one needs to have a flexibility in one's thinking, which demands a capacity for creativity. We consider why Larry might present for treatment. There are a number of elements to consider here: what might Larry's presenting issue be, and what might be unconsciously underlying it (the symptom)? This is important for many reasons, one of which is the fact that the clinician must carefully manage the patient's demands (Eichler, 2010, pp. 11–14). This can be difficult when the patient is in pain and wants it to go away or to stop, especially when the patient believes that the process itself might increase the intensity of her/his pain.

Another point for discussion relates to the details that can be gleaned from "My Oedipus Complex" (O'Connor, 1963) about the patient's history and current situation. Which of these details are directly stated, and which are inferred by the text, or indeed assumed by the participants? This reminds participants of the importance of not pre-emptively moving to "fill in the gaps", to circumvent the process and attempt to evade the anxiety of not knowing. What difficulties might the patient have engaging in psychoanalytic treatment and why? This relates to the patient's motivation and readiness, so both desire and need are addressed here. This is also relevant to the patient's psychical defences and what can be perceived of their utilisation during the consultation process. This question relates, moreover, to the analyst's capacity for "clinical judgement" (Crick, 2013, p. 201), when assessing whether a psychoanalytic treatment would be appropriate for this particular patient at this moment in time. Participants are also invited to reflect upon the difficulties they think they might experience working with Larry and why. This prompts participants to reflect on their reactions to Larry and to what might be evoked in their countertransference, as well as any transferences they might develop based on their own prior experiences (Ogden, 2012b). They are, furthermore, asked to consider how such transferential and countertransferential elements might impact on the treatment, and how they might address this impact. Making use of "My Oedipus Complex" as a non-clinical case study provides participants with space to become aware, through engagement with other group members, of how they come to make clinical formulations and decisions. Consideration of this non-clinical case study also facilitates participants appraising their own transferences to the consultation process and how their framing of it has been influenced by their transferences to training analysts, clinical supervisors, other members of the clinical training team and the psychoanalytic writers they have read.

Film: getting a sense of how the patient might be experiencing the world

The third example is a non-clinical case study. I will show in more detail how I make use of non-clinical case studies to introduce clinical concepts, particularly with regards to the importance of getting a sense of how the patient might be experiencing the analyst and other people in the patient's life. It is necessary to gain a reliable impression of the patient's state of mind, with regards to how the patient might be interpreting her/his experiences. This is crucial when thinking about analytical technique, particularly in relation to the framing and timing of interpretations. This is because the offer of an interpretation will be perceived by the patient as an experience, which will be filtered through the same psychical organising principles framing other aspects of her/his experience. I will attend to aspects of the paranoid-schizoid position and how they might manifest in the con-sulting room, by scrutinising a number of scenes – non-clinical vignettes – from the film *Shame* (2011). Making use of a non-clinical case study in this way demands a lot of preparatory work from the facilitator. S/he needs to be clear about which concepts s/he is introducing to participants and how the chosen scenes from the film display the workings of the concepts in a precise yet detailed way. The facili-tator also needs to decide whether s/he is making use of a non-clinical vignette so that participants can observe something, or if s/he is showing a scene to provide participants with a chance to apply a concept to elucidate something. There also needs to be space left available, of course, for insights that might emerge in the live encounter of the group experience and so cannot be known in advance.

Films offer viewers an opportunity to become absorbed in an experience. Tania Zittoun (2013) refers to films as "transitional phenomena" (p 140) and "symbolic resources" (p. 144), which facilitate "a form of everyday creativity" (p. 144) and a "more complex understanding of real-life events" (p. 142). As spectators, we are seduced by films through image, dialogue, colour, sound and music, as well how the scenes are shot and the characters are positioned, including objects that appear at the edges of a shot (Aaron, 2007). Thus, viewers are presented with a fabricated set-up that elicits, nevertheless, an authentic experience to reflect upon. Glen Gab-bard (2001b) has written about films as sites for projections and containment, with particular reference to the cinema:

> audiences do not attend films merely to be entertained. They line up at the local multiplex to encounter long-forgotten but still powerful anxieties that stem from universal developmental experiences. They seek solutions to problems in the culture that defy simple answers or facile explanations. The screen in the darkened theatre serves as a container for the projection of their most private and often unconscious terrors and longings. As with all forms of art, when we study film we study ourselves.
>
> (pp. 13–14)

Films also offer an opportunity to explore the intricate mechanisms through which human beings communicate with one another, how verbal and non-verbal modes can often be at odds with each other, and the importance of a close attendance to these disjunctions in the consulting room. While film as a medium might present the interiority of characters, it is not an interior narrative as such. Film represents, in audio-visual terms, situations and behaviours – the externalised manifestation of psychic states – which can be thought about and reflected upon. I will discuss my use of the film *Shame* (2011) as a non-clinical case study. *Shame* is a feature film directed by the visual artist Steve McQueen, and features Brandon Sullivan, a 30-something-year-old man of Irish descent who lives and works in New York. The film's narrative arc revolves around a visit from his younger sister Sissy and the effect growing tensions have both on their relationship and on each of them as individuals. Whereas Brandon initially appears to be self-contained in his life and successful in his work as an executive of some kind, Sissy is represented as an emotional mess without a place to live of steady employment. Their relationship is an uneasy one, and viewers are given hints that something happened years earlier that continues to impact on them in the present day, although no details of any specific trauma are confirmed.

This historical event or series of events in the lives of Brandon and Sissy, alluded to without being named, is, it seems, unnameable. It is unthinkable too, to the extent that both siblings act out physically in increasingly erratic ways. This leaves viewers witnessing a series of self-destructive behaviours without a clear context, a visualisation of the compulsion to repeat (Freud, 1914) resulting in physical compulsivity and psychic fragmentation. The film presents a man incapable of experiencing psychic pain. He is in pain, but he is unable to suffer his pain. "Psychic pain", in the words of Robbert Wille (2011), "has an existential connotation, as when patients impress on us that they are suffering from life – that life itself is painful" (p. 24). Brandon concretises his pain, splits if off and projects it onto and into those around him. His bodily activities serve, unconsciously, as desperate attempts to stave off thinking and feeling through action. In other words, this non-clinical case study shows the use that can be made of the body to get rid of experiences rather than holding in mind thoughts and feelings too painful to bear (McDougall, 1989; Rosenfeld, 2014; Lemma, 2015a). In this, *Shame* illuminates, in resonant terms, the secondary effects of certain psychic mechanisms at work and why treatments that deal mainly with conscious, cognitive, symptomatic and/or behavioural aspects are unlikely to make a long-term intervention. This is because the personality, in these cases, is organised around such a rigidly structured psychic apparatus without the psychic space available to contain anxiety and so is designed to evacuate it whenever it arises.

I integrate *Shame* as a non-clinical case study as a way to illustrate the operation of paranoid-schizoid states of mind (Klein, 1946; Joseph, 2005; Elizabeth Bott Spillius et al., 2011a; Hinshelwood and Fortuna, 2018), particularly as they relate to the function of part-objects and part-object relating. Brandon identifies as a part-object and relates to part-objects. "Part-object" is a term used to refer to the subject's reducing another person to a body part, an aspect of her/his personality or a function the person performs. There is no recognition of the other person as a whole object – separate, different and with a subjectivity of her/his own. There is no capacity for ambivalence. The other person is perceived unconsciously as a narcissistic extension of the self and is related to as such. Splitting and projection predominate: If the split-off part is good, the projector craves to be around the part-object; if it is bad, the projector tries to avoid the part-object. This all happens outside of conscious awareness. People who relate to others as part-objects also tend to identify as part-objects and treat themselves as such. This non-clinical case study includes a number of non-clinical vignettes which provide specific examples of part-object relating in action, the way in which it operates both as a defence against overwhelming persecutory anxiety while also resulting from the psyche's inability to process experiences in a symbolic way.

We first hear Brandon's name in the film on an answering machine. A woman is calling a man's name: "Bran-don . . . Bran-don". What we see is not his face or his profile but his penis as he walks nakedly around his apartment and towards us. The female voice, another part-object, is his sister Sissy, but we do not know that yet. In fact, the first time we hear her name is when Brandon finds her naked in his shower, as he directs his gaze towards and away from and towards her vagina. The film presents viewers with many part-objects: the many women (and man in the nightclub) whom Brandon interacts with via his penis before moving quickly on. The woman in the bar whose vagina functions merely as a vehicle through which he can access the beating he provokes from her boyfriend after he aggressively shoves the fingers he has just inserted into vagina towards her boyfriend's nose. The many body parts – lips, nipples, eyes, vaginas, anuses – in the pornographic magazines he throws out onto the street in black plastic bags, together with sex toys, food from his fridge and his laptop. This scene of literal evacuation comes directly after he has an altercation on the sofa with Sissy when she walks in on him masturbating in the bathroom. A later scene follows a second altercation with Sissy on the sofa in which he tells her, "Try doing something. Actions count, not words". He goes on to literally enact this utterance. The sexual scene that follows Brandon's second altercation with Sissy features him engaging in a threesome with two women, the camera's focus moving quickly over parts of all three participants' bodies as they move frenetically on the bed. The visual image is accompanied by a telephone message with Sissy's tearful voice, "Brandon I need you. We're not bad people. We just come from a bad place", which is entangled with a classical score while Brandon moves energetically on the bed with the two women. The two aforementioned scenes suggest more than part-object relating. They infer severe splitting to the point of fragmentation (Bott Spillius et al., 2011a, p. 345), which occurs when the subject is unable to differentiate between the good and the bad, to keep them separate. This results in a confusional state, well represented by the dizzying array of body parts the audience witnesses in both scenes, the camera moving so fast we are unable to take in what we are being presented with. This prompts discussions about how one might hold one's position in the consulting room when flooded by the patient's projections – in other words, when the transferential-countertransferential relationship is characterised by the analyst's functioning as a "toilet-breast" (Meltzer, 1967, p. 20; Lemma, 2015b, pp. 150–159) for the patient's evacuation of unbearable aspects of her/himself.

It is important for the analyst to have a felt sense of the patient's state of mind as that will impact on how the patient relates to the analyst and to the analytic process more broadly. This will also give the analyst an indication of how the patient might receive interpretations, or indeed whether the patient has the capacity to take in something from outside her/himself. This is unlikely in the case of Brandon, who endeavours to empty himself of unbearable thoughts and feelings. He does this through various bodily activities, including jogging, fidgeting, masturbating, engaging in sexual encounters with others and watching Internet pornography. The eye and the penis become the organs through which he rids himself of that which is unbearable and too difficult to feel. They might appear to facilitate him taking in experiences, but it becomes evident over the course of the film that they function as muscular organs that evacuate in action, what is too much for his mind. An exploration of part-objects in this non-clinical case study leads on to clinical considerations of patients who do not have a capacity to contain themselves. If this is the case, the patient's self-awareness and self-reflection are limited to the extent that experiences cannot be articulated verbally but are, as mentioned earlier, acted out, repeatedly, and sometimes in alarming ways. This can be anxiety-provoking for the clinical practitioner who needs to sit with the experience and contain the patient's projections, emptied out and into the clinician as a toilet-breast. This can be precarious work with patients who engage in excessive splitting and so can put pressure on the psychoanalytic practitioner to collude or enact split off parts of the patient.

This non-clinical case study impresses on participants the integral part played by containment in the analytic process, and what a strain it can be to contain massive amounts of projective identification, when the analyst is being utilised as a toilet-breast. Containment is an unconscious, intersubjective process whereby the patient splits off and projects what is too much to bear into the analyst (Caper, 1999; Cartwright, 2010). If the analyst is receptive to the projection, rather than enacting it and attempting to push it back into the patient, s/he can bring meaning to the patient's experience and over time might be able to offer it back to her/him in a more manageable form. In the analytic situation, this would be in words via an interpretation. Therefore, if the analyst who has been projected into recognises the projection as a communication rather than simply being an attack on the mind (which it could also be), the analyst can transform what is unbearable and unthinkable for another into something that is potentially meaningful. If this process is repeated time and again, the patient who relies on projective identification as a mode of communication and defence might be able to gradually develop a capacity to think her/his own thoughts. Analytically, this is a delicate task that takes great psychic resourcefulness on the part of the analyst and painful perseverance in the case of the patient. As Antonino Ferro (2013) describes it: "The patient cannot immediately have the space necessary for parts that are difficult to integrate – otherwise, why would they have split them off? – and more time and work is necessary to develop this potential in the patient" (p. 3). It is also dependent on the patient's capacity to be able to accept something from the object rather than enviously destroying that which s/he needs from another (Caper, 1999, p. 144), as well as finding an object in the first place who is receptive to her/his projections. This facilitates an exploration of how participants formulate, pitch, deliver and time interpretations, and the relationship between that and the holding of the analytic frame and the intrapsychic and interpsychic aspects of containment (Riesenberg-Malcolm, 1985). This use of a non-clinical case study requires participants to be familiar with the concepts, as well as have experience working with patients who have a tendency to act out and in rather than think.

Music: attuning ourselves to experiences that come to us outside of words

The fourth example is a selection of non-clinical vignettes. These non-clinical vignettes are excerpts from pieces of music. I select them to help participants to reflect on the feeling in the room and to hone their capacity for reflecting on transference and countertransference. I usually choose pieces without lyrics or in which the lyrics are distorted or in languages which might be unfamiliar to participants. I play a series of excerpts of equal length, usually two and a half minutes each (I do not share this information with participants). I incorporate pieces from different genres of music. Some pieces I have used in the past include "Bass society" (Perri O'Neill, 2006), "Sanvean" (Dead Can Dance, 2007), "The Hunt" (Sepultura, 1993), "At the beach" (David Wingo, 2011), "Close encounters of the second mind" (Vincent de Moor, 2007), "4'33''" (John Cage, 2010), "White Kross (Live)" (Sonic Youth, 1991) and "End Credits Suite" (Nicholas Britell, 2016). I use a mobile speaker to play the pieces, which I move after each piece, placing the speaker in different locations around the room: in front, behind and beside participants, including on the floor. I play each piece without providing any details about them.

I use music and sound pieces as non-clinical case vignettes in a number of ways, two of which I will briefly outline here. Firstly, I invite participants to listen to each piece and write down words to describe thoughts, feelings or bodily sensations they experience as they listen to the music. I tell them to write whatever comes to mind, even if it does not make sense or seem to be connected to anything. Secondly, I invite participants to listen to the pieces and imagine that the patient is telling them her/his story. I ask them to write words that describe the patient's affective state as s/he tells her/his story, as well as words that express the impact that the patient telling her/his story has on them. In both of the aforementioned, I encourage participants to close their eyes if it helps them to focus on their thoughts, feelings and bodily sensations in reaction to the music, after which we discuss what they have written as a group and how it might relate to their experiences in the consulting room. Part of the discussion involves participants associating to the words they have written on the page. Participants are invited to sit with the word and articulate what related words, experiences, people, situations and so on come to mind as they stay with the word, often surprising themselves with the links that emerge between words that they heretofore thought were random and meaningless. As Wilfred Bion (1963) writes, "the name is an invention to make it possible to think and talk about something before it is known what that something is" (pp. 87–88).

These non-clinical vignettes also help participants to listen to more than just the words spoken and tune into the tone, pitch, speed and rhythm of the music and the voice, if one is present. "Meaning and unconscious phantasies may be expressed", according to Alessandra Lemma (2016[2003]):

> through the way the patient speaks rather than in what he says: a harsh tone, a soft, barely audible voice or a fast-paced delivery can convey far more about the patient's psychic position at the time the words are spoken than the words themselves.
>
> (p. 174)

Music assists participants to become unstuck from the words, the narrative, the manifest content and allow their minds to wander; to exercise "evenly-suspended attention", as Freud (1912a) has referred to it. Freud advises against "deliberate attention" (p. 112). This leads to the listener prematurely selecting and disregarding material and thus "following his expectations and inclinations" (p. 112) rather than what the patient is communicating. It is necessary for the analyst to develop a capacity to get a sense of the atmosphere or feeling in a room, what Paula Heimann (1949/50) refers to as "a freely roused sensibility" (p. 75). As an early advocate of the importance of the countertransference as "an instrument of research into the patient's unconscious", Heimann (1949/50) stresses the integral part played by the "analyst's emotional response" (p. 74) to the patient. Much work has been done on the countertransference in psychoanalytic practice, particularly how analysts bring awareness to and manage their countertransference, as well as the place of the countertransference in the formulation and delivery of interpretations (Racker, 1968; Brenman Pick, 1985a; Mitrani, 2001; Oelsner, 2013; Waska, 2015). It is crucial that clinical practitioners develop an awareness of the operation of countertransference and a capacity to reflect on its potential source and impact because, as Heimann (1949/50) points out, interpretations made "without consulting [one's] feelings" are "poor" (p. 74). Countertransference, as a term used to describe the analyst's reaction to the patient, might be registered at the level of thoughts, feelings or bodily sensations.

Countertransference is, Heimann (1949/50) contends, "the most dynamic way in which [the] patient's voice reaches [the analyst]" (p. 75). In this, it refers to what is evoked in the analyst in response to being with a particular patient. The use of excerpts from music as non-clinical vignettes provides participants with a chance to be with the impact of a stimulus (in this case, music; in the clinical situation, a patient) and allow her/himself to be with the experience and register what is going on within her/himself. While listening to what the patient is saying, as well as the sounds and silences in the room, what does it mean for the analyst to listen to what is going on within her/himself? This includes the analyst becoming aware of what is being evoked by the other in her/himself as well as her/his own transference to the other. As part of the experience of working with these non-clinical case vignettes, projections are revealed through group discussion, when participants express radically different impressions of the pieces and the listening experience itself. Projections become all the more visible because participants relate to the task in a variety of different ways, so their assumptions and fantasies become part of the conversation. They gradually become aware of the particular aspects of the music they associate to and even how the position of the mobile speaker impacts on how they interact with the material. These non-clinical vignettes, moreover, help participants to tap into the ebb and flow of the session, the moment-to-moment shifts in the transference-countertransference dynamic. Betty Joseph (2015) spent decades honing an extraordinary clinical aptitude for carefully tracking the nuances of transference and countertransference in the session. Joseph's attendance to the "movement" and "constant change" (p. 2) in the room calls to mind the mutability, flexibility and sometimes repetitions of the musical score (Sabbadini, 2014b, p. 119).

As participants reflect together as a group, they become attentive to the evocative nature of the music, and this leads to clinical considerations of the evocative nature of sound and silence within the analytic setting (Jaffee Nagel, 2013). Donald Meltzer (1976a) refers to "the emotional music of the voice" (p. 27) and Harriet Kimble Wrye (1997) to "listening . . . with our whole bodies" (p. 362–363). Christopher Bollas (1987) makes reference to his work with a patient who "wanted . . . to hear my voice", which Bollas came to realise was the patient's "need for a good sound" (p. 21). This is a reminder to the analyst that "at certain times in the analytic sound chamber, content doesn't matter at all; it is the rhythms, tones, staccatos, and mellifluous sounds of the analyst's voice that matters" (Kimble Wrye, 1997, p. 360). Patients regress in the clinic (Eichler, 2010, pp. 17–28). The melody of the voice conjures up the emotional resonances of the patient's earliest experiences. Sound, Amal Treacher Kabesh (2013) comments, forms part of the facilitating environment, with sound "enabling a capacity to inhabit one's body" (p. 68). Thus, the analyst's voice comes to represent, as part of the regressive quality of an analysis, "the powerful reverberations and timbres" (Kimble Wrye, 1997, p. 360) of the sounds made by the mother's voice in early life. This is stored by us in the very fibres of our being and provides texture to our experience of the "soundspaces" (Treacher Kabesh, 2013, p. 67) we inhabit. The use of non-clinical vignettes in languages participants might be unfamiliar with facilitates them tuning into the voice as sound rather than as the deliverer of content. To focus, furthermore, on listening as an activity solely performed by the ear for the receipt of content reduces oneself and the patient to a part-object and misses the potential impact the analyst's voice as sound might be enacting on the patient and vice versa. This invoking of listening with more than the ear gestures towards how the voice (and any sound, as well as silence) can be absorbed into the self and encourages the practice of attuning oneself to its reverberations by sitting long enough to allow something to happen within oneself.

Chapter 2 has introduced the Cultural Encounters Case Study Method within the context of the central position occupied by clinical case studies and vignettes within the history of psychoanalysis. The Method brings non-clinical case studies and vignettes into clinical training and further professional development contexts for three reasons. Firstly, they are objects that produce meanings so they provide opportunities to interpret. Secondly, an engagement with them facilitates encounters that evoke experiences so they become occasions to reflect. Thirdly, in integrating these different facets of experience, they encourage meaning-making and, in the process, the development of an aptitude for clinical insight. In this way, non-clinical case studies and vignettes operate as creative sites for playing with theoretical concepts as well as pedagogical tools to open up a space for thinking and feeling for participants. In doing so, they provide moments to work towards integrating theoretical knowledge with capacities and skills needed for clinical practice. These include key clinical concepts (knowledge); self-awareness, self-reflectivity and self-reflexivity (capacities); and observation, analytical and interpretative skills.

Chapter 3

The culture-breast

The breast occupies a central position in psychoanalysis. It is the female breast that takes centre stage, as one of the biological markers of sexual difference, and in its literal and metaphorical functioning as a feeding apparatus that also provides emotional succour to the dependent infant. The word designates the feeding experience and so covers both the bodily organ and baby bottle. The breast points to the paramount importance of the mother in the developing infant's life. It is, moreover, a discursive representative for her and the person of the caregiver more generally. The term "the breast" is fundamental in psychoanalytic discourse as a metaphor for the environmental context and provision, an external stimulus, and a space for the psychical operation of introjections and projections. The breast stands in for the infant's relation to the mother as a part-object and the reduction of her in perception to a body part and a function she performs. In this, the breast is, for the infant, all about her/him. It is with and against the breast that fierce battles get played out between that which is considered to be good and that which is thought to be bad. It is hugely persecutory for the infant that the breast cannot be controlled, and so the breast also serves as a painful reminder of the reality of dependence and need. This experience is not limited to the infant. We continue to experience dependence and need, and so our earliest interactions with the breast have an enduring influence on every encounter we engage in with others and the world around us for the rest of our lives. The experiential residues affect how we relate to ourselves. The psychoanalytic literature is replete with references to breasts: good breast (Klein, 1946, p. 2), bad breast (Klein, 1946, p. 2), no-breast (Bion, 1965, p. 82), feeding-breast (Meltzer, 1973, p. ix), toilet-breast (Meltzer, (1990, pp. 38–40), penis-breast (Joseph, 1960, p. 529), breast claustrum (Bick, 2001, p. 13), psychosomatic breast (Magnenat, 2016), couch-breast (Meltzer et al., 1986, p. 60), Earth-breast (Schinaia, 2019), breast universe (McDougall, 1989, pp. 33–34), genius breast (Brenman Pick, 2008, p. 189), apple-breast (Watson, 1990, p. 133), toffee-apple breast (Brenman Pick, 1985b, p. 166), hope breast (Wittenberg, 1975, p. 64), head-breast (Meltzer, 1976b), container-breast (Anzieu, 1979, p. 23; referencing Bion), patched breast (Green, 1986, p. 152), phallic breast (Bergler, 1937, p. 197), breast-complex (Bergler, 1937, p. 197). To this terminology I add the culture-breast, which is the focus of Chapter 3.

Chapter 3 will commence by providing an overview of the psychoanalytic discourses of the breast, as they appear in the work of Sigmund Freud, Melanie
Klein, Wilfred Bion, Donald Winnicott, André Green and Donald Meltzer, among
others. Following this, I will outline the conceptual parameters of the term "the
culture-breast", after which I will examine the applicability of the culture-breast
to clinical considerations of case material within the context of my work as a psychoanalytic psychotherapist and lecturer with experience of teaching academic
courses and on clinical training programmes. I will introduce and discuss the
extensive use of cultural objects for psychical ends. I will focus specifically on
the unconscious use made of cultural objects (film, art, literature, music) as screen
memories, psychic retreats and containers. By introducing "the culture-breast" as
a new clinical concept, I will foreground both the importance of cultural objects in
the psychical lives of patients and, by extension, appeal to clinicians to not underestimate their regular appearance in the free associations of particular patients.
While I have encountered this phenomenon many times in my clinical work and
academic and clinical teaching, I will choose examples from my own personal
experience to illustrate the culture-breast's psychical operations. In this, I will
present a "psychosocial case study" in this chapter, one wrought from my own
personal experience but employed in the service of reflecting on a phenomenon
that has emerged in my clinical work with patients.

Psychoanalytic discourses of the breast

There are over 10,000 references to the word "breast" in the Psychoanalytic
Electronic Publishing (PEP) database (1998–), an online subscription-based
archive of books, journal articles and videos relating to psychoanalysis. The term
appears to describe the bodily organ with reference to feeding, weaning, sexuality,
gender and physical illness (Rinder, 1958; Sarlin, 1981; Lebovici and Kestemberg,
1993; Lubbe, 1996; McDougall, 2004; Coll-Planas, Cruells and Alfama, 2017).
Authors also focus on affects, such as greed, envy, contempt, rage and ambivalence, as they relate to an engagement with the breast, whether in infant observation settings or in the consulting room (Boris, 1986; Miller, 1987; Herzig, 2001;
Stone, 2015). The word can be found in the titles of articles about the long-term
impact of the infant's relation to the breast on the formation of psychopathological
symptomology in the adult, as well as the development of emotional difficulties
more generally and patients' attempts to manage them through behavioural repetitions (Eisenbud, 1965; Greenspan, 1979; Nurka, 2015; Magnenat, 2016). The
breast also shows up as a discursive concept (Berke and Schneider, 1994), a representational symbol (Fine, 2010), an illusory product forming part of a market-
ing strategy (Covington, 2018, p. 252), a site for psychical evacuations (Meltzer,
1967), an emblem for the Earth and the challenges of climate change (Schinaia,
2019), and a metaphor for the mind of the analyst (Astor, 1989), to name but a
few instances. Some authors attend to the psychical functions of the nipple in
relation to fetishism and castration anxiety (Grossman, 1995), or as the mother's

unconscious way of managing distance and closeness between her and her infant (Hering, 1986). The breast is fundamental to the advancement of psychoanalytic theories of the unconscious, the enduring influence of early-life experiences in the psychical life of the adult, the operations of psychopathological symptomology, and transference-countertransference dynamics in the analytic relationship. The relationship with the breast as a material, discursive and internal object, and the attendant feelings, phantasies, defences and behaviours this provokes constitute the cornerstone of psychoanalytic understandings of the psyche.

In a discussion about reality-testing, Sigmund Freud (1925) cites its "first and immediate aim" as "not to *find* an object in real perception which corresponds to the one presented, but to *refind* such an object, to convince oneself that it is still there" (pp. 237–238). Freud is referencing and extending his earlier consideration (1905) of the abiding importance of the infant's relation to the breast, which is "the child's first and most vital activity" (p. 181) and "the prototype of every relation of love". And so, "The finding of an object is in fact a refinding of it" (p. 222). Freud makes this comment with reference to the "first beginnings of sexual satisfaction", which he claims are linked to "the taking of nourishment" (p. 222). This link later becomes dislocated when the sexual instinct becomes "auto-erotic", after a period of which the "original relation" is "restored" (p. 222), when the latency period is over. Thus, this "refinding" requires and is prefigured by a "los[ing]" of "the object", the breast, which Freud speculates happens "just at the time, perhaps, when the child is able to form a total idea of the person to whom the organ that is giving him satisfaction belongs" (p. 222). The process of weaning is linked in passing by Freud (1926) to castration (pp. 129–130) and elsewhere (1931) to penis envy and the female child's raging against her mother for not giving her a "proper penis" or "enough milk" (p. 234). Elsewhere Freud (1933[1932]) traces this rage back to the child's "avidity" for nourishment and the insatiability of the instinct (p. 122). So, the rage is ultimately associated with loss. The child, Freud suggests, "never gets over the pain of losing its mother's breast" (p. 122). The child takes refuge in her/his own body, which "can provide sensations at any moment" (Freud, 1930[1929], p. 67). This is an attempt to retain the illusion of omnipotence because the fact that "other sources evade . . . from time to time" is deeply persecutory for the child (p. 67). In fact, it is the loss of the breast, among other losses experienced through and as separations from the body, that gives rise to the psychical state of narcissistic injury (Freud, 1923b, p. 144, n. 2).

In dealing with the breast's fundamental place in terms of the development of the sexual instinct, Freud writes that the sexual instinct itself is "aroused" by the mother's caregiving activities, in which she "strokes", "kisses", "rocks" the baby, as she "teach[es] the child to love" (p. 223). She is, as Freud (1917[1916–1917] b) puts it, "the first *love*-object" (p. 329). A "mnemic image" or "memory trace" is laid down, Freud writes (1900–1901, p. 565), associating "the excitation of the need" with "a psychical impulse" to "re-evoke" and "re-establish . . . the original satisfaction" (pp. 565–566). Freud (1917[1916–1917]a) differentiates between sucking that aims at the "intake of nourishment" and "sensual sucking" for "pleasure", and makes an analogy between the infant's "expression of blissful satisfaction" at the breast and what transpires "after the experience after sexual orgasm" in later life (p. 313). It is also, Freud explains (1931), at the breast that the infant's early experiences of passivity and activity play out against the backdrop of her/his negotiation of the "satisfactions" of being "suckled, fed, cleaned, and dressed" (p. 236). This "being suckled" and, more generally, the experience of *being done to* brings with it enjoyment and satisfaction but also evokes a "striv[ing]" for the activity of *doing* and "active sucking" (p. 236). The breast occupies a pivotal place in the mind, with the child speculating that birth takes place out of the breast (Freud, 1905, p. 196) or between the breasts (Freud, 1917[1916–1917]c, p. 319). This early attachment to the breast continues to be significant unconsciously and can become a point of fixation as a result of trauma when patients might regress back to that early time psychically (Freud, 1917[1916–1917]d, p. 274). There are some, Freud (1923[1922]) remarks, who remain "eternal sucklings". These "cannot tear themselves away from the blissful situation at the mother's breast", instead "persist[ing] in a demand to be nourished by someone else" (p. 104). The pain of the loss of the breast is, in these cases, too much to bear.

Melanie Klein (1932a, p. x) extends and adapts Freud's ideas about the breast, particularly as they relate to its originary status in psychic life and enduring influence in the unconscious of the adult. The breast figures as an essential actor in Klein's paranoid-schizoid (1975b) and depressive positions (1975a), which she developed over the course of her career. It is the relationship with the breast that forms the basis for all subsequent relationships (Klein, 1952a, p. 99) and to which Klein (1957) "attribute[s] fundamental importance" (p. 157). The psychical and physical relationship with the breast as "the first object" (Klein, 1946, p. 2) and "primal object" (Klein, 1957, p. 178) dominates object relations, which Klein asserts "exist from the beginning of life" (1946, p. 2). As a part-object, the breast represents and stands in for the mother, and, as such, it becomes the locus of introjections and the depository for projections. This process of taking in and emptying out, as it plays out in relation to the breast, sets the foundations of the ego and plots the course of its future development (Klein, 1946, pp. 5–6, 1957, p. 178). This is not without its challenges. The relationship with the breast also underpins the evolution of nascent feelings, such as envy, greed and jealousy (Klein, 1975b), as well as love, guilt and the desire to make reparation (Klein, 1975a). The breast is, at times, loved and hated, coveted and feared, idealised and denigrated. As Klein (1952a) puts it, "the fundamental experiences of happiness and love, of frustration and hatred, are inextricably linked with the mother's breast" (p. 99).

In the paranoid-schizoid position, the infant's mind splits the breast into a "good (gratifying)" and a "bad (frustrating)" breast (Klein, 1946, p. 2), entirely separate and unrelated to each other: "The good breast – external and internal – becomes the prototype of all helpful and gratifying objects, the bad breast the prototype of all external and internal persecutory objects" (Klein, 1952c, p. 63).

In the depressive position, the child slowly begins to experience the mother as a whole person rather than simply as a part-object or series of part-objects to gratify her/his needs (Klein, 1952b, p. 76, 1960, p. 272). The child now has to come to terms with the fact that it is the same mother who both provides for and frustrates her/him, towards whom s/he feels love and hate, or ambivalence. The breast is both good and bad, at different times, and sometimes at the same time. The child's "libidinal fixation to the breast develops", according to Klein (1935), "into feelings towards her as a person. Thus, feelings both of a destructive and of a loving nature are experienced towards one and the same object and this gives rise to deep and disturbing conflicts in the child's mind" (p. 285). Thus, the ongoing relation to the breast arouses significant anxiety (Klein, 1948) – of a persecutory (Bott Spillius et al., 2011c) or depressive nature (Bott Spillius et al., 2011d). This intense relation with the breast in early life is internalised and, as an internal object, forms "part of the underlying meanings of the later adult's evaluations of life, and his or her activities" (Hinshelwood, 1994, p. 66).

Wilfred Bion develops Melanie Klein's work on the breast, especially as it deals with the emotional experience of feeding (Bion, 1962a, p. 34). It is at the breast that the infant will find physical, emotional and mental nourishment. He refers to the "mental alimentary system" (Bion, 1962a, p. 102, n.12.6.1), and makes a link between the taking in of milk and love. Love, he writes, is "comparable with milk for the mental welfare of the child" (p. 33). The breast signifies the mother as well as her capacity for thinking and containment (Bion, 1962b, p. 116). The breast is, Bion (1965) writes, "the source of emotional experiences" for the infant (p. 81). This encounter has a profound effect on the infant, particularly when the breast is sought and it is not there. Bion (1965) refers to the absence of the breast with terms like "no-breast" or "no-thing" (p. 82). The persecutory gap opened up by the absent breast outside is internalised as a bad breast inside. So, the painful experience of an absence becomes incorporated as a painful presence. Instead of recognising a need for a good breast to satisfy, the experience is one of persecution and a need to get rid of a bad breast. This confusing experience is deeply distressing, and the infant's mind does everything to rid itself of the sensation, as it is too much for the mind to bear. In Bion's words (1962a): "the need for the breast is a feeling and that feeling itself is a bad breast; the infant does not feel it wants a good breast but it does feel it wants to evacuate a bad one" (p. 34). He is particularly interested in the processes by which this emotional experience plays out and its link with the development of a capacity for thinking alongside the development of disorders of thought.

Bion (1962b) emphasises the frustration experienced by the infant when s/he encounters the no-breast. The infant can react to this situation in one of two ways: if s/he modifies the frustration, it will become a thought; if s/he evades it, it will be split off and evacuated via projective identification:

> The model I propose is that of an infant whose expectation of a breast is mated with a realization of no breast available for satisfaction. This mating is

experienced as a no-breast, or "absent" breast inside. The next step depends on the infant's capacity for frustration: in particular it depends on whether the decision is to evade frustration or to modify it.

(pp. 111–112)

Projective identification, described by Bion (1962a) as an omnipotent mechanism, comes into play when frustration becomes "intolerable". It is an "early form of that which later is called the capacity for thinking" (p. 37), and is "employed to fulfil the duties of thought until thought takes over" (Bion, 1970b, p. 28). Bion (1962a) considers the communicative function of projective identification, in which the infant arouses feelings in the mother that s/he is unable to tolerate or those that s/he "wants the mother to have" (p. 31). So, projective identification is used here in an attempt to get rid of something (the bad breast) while also making an effort to give it to another and, in doing so, make the other experience what the subject cannot.

Bion (1962a) uses the term alpha-function (pp. 28–30) to denote the mother's processing of projections as thinking. This requires the mother to accept projections as a communication rather than an attack, because an attack would lead to her defending against the projection. The mother intuits and receives the infant's projections, or beta-elements, via reverie, which is "the receptor organ for the infant's harvest of self-sensation gained by its conscious" (Bion, 1962a, p. 116), "a state of mind . . . open to the receipt of any 'objects' from the loved object" (Bion, 1962b, p. 36). The mother's alpha-function transforms beta-elements (projections) into alpha-elements. In the process, experiences that were intolerable and meaningless for the infant have been returned as manageable and meaningful experiences. When re-introjected by the infant, they are potentially comforting rather than intrusions that need to be split off and evacuated via projective identification. Bion refers to this process as containment, which will be discussed in more detail later in this chapter. The breast is also, for Bion, in an abstract sense, "a link between two objects" (Bion, 1994, p. 251), as well as the "conjunction" itself, an alpha-element (p. 250).

Donald Winnicott (1968a), a psychoanalyst and paediatrician with vast experience with infants and their mothers and a supervisee of Melanie Klein for a period, remarks that "a 'good breast' is a jargon word, and it means satisfactory mothering and parentage in a general way" (p. 25). He concentrates on the literal and metaphorical aspects of the breast in his examination of the infant's earliest weeks and months of life and their formative effect on the development of her/his personality: "the word *breast* and the idea of breast-feeding is an expression that carries with it the whole technique of being a mother to a baby" (p. 26). Bringing together the infant's inherited potential and the facilitating environment provided by the mother, Winnicott writes of the "richness" of the breast-feeding experience for the infant, which is a "sensuous" experience (p. 30), involving "the total personality" (p. 29). So much is communicated and played out between the infant and her/his mother in this feeding experience, whether it is the "ruthlessness" displayed by the infant in using "unprotected objects" or her/his efforts to "protect the breast" (p. 31). As Winnicott observes, "even when babies have teeth they but seldom bite to do damage" (p. 31). The survival of the breast, and by extension the mother, is of paramount importance to the psychic development of the infant (p. 32): The mother

> has one job when the baby bites and scratches and pulls her hair and kicks, and that is to survive. The baby will do the rest. If she survives, then the baby will find a new meaning to the word love.
>
> (p. 31)

The mother's capacity for holding – both the infant's aggression and her own – is an element of her "good-enough care" of the infant (Winnicott, 1960a, p. 49). Holding forms part of "environmental provision" or "the maternal function", which also includes handling and object-presenting (1960b, pp. 26–27). These three aspects of physical and emotional care facilitate the infant developing a sense of her/himself as a person with an inside and an outside, an integrated being with a mind and a body, and an individual who can relate to objects outside of her/himself. Adaptation to the infant's needs is "almost exact" (Winnicott, 1988, p. 101) in the earliest period of life, gradually becoming less so as the growing infant begins to adapt to external reality, "the world not created by the infant" (p. 101). Thus, the infant's "illusion of having created external objects" (p. 101) and "illusion of magical creative power . . . and omnipotence" (p. 106) gives way to the reality of living in "the world that was there before the infant" (p. 111). This happens in parallel with the growing child's movement from absolute dependence through to relative dependence. This negotiation of need and, in time, desire (p. 102) is worked through in relation to the breast and, over time, a series of transitional objects that represent the mother and help to mediate between feelings of loss and omnipotence.

Where the breast occupies the place of the "first object", the transitional object is the "first possession" (Winnicott, 1953, p. 4). The transitional object is positioned in the transitional space between "the subjective and that which is objectively perceived" (p. 4). As a "not-me" or "other-than-me" object, the transitional object has symbolic value as a stand-in for the mother, as well as functioning as something that facilitates the developmental and ongoing task of moving between internal and external reality. As Winnicott puts it, "The transitional object is never under magical control like the internal object, nor is it outside control as the real mother is" (p. 13). While the relation between the child and her/his transitional object revisits the ebb and flow of her/his attachment to the breast, it is, according to Winnicott, an object in its own right, which means that it goes further and so makes something new possible: It is

> symbolic of some part-object, such as the breast. Nevertheless, the point of it is not its symbolic value so much as its actuality. Its not being the breast

(or the mother), although real, is as important as the fact that it stands for the breast (or mother).

(p. 8)

Many psychoanalytic clinicians have both challenged and developed the earlier or sometimes contemporaneous work of Freud, Klein, Bion and Winnicott to formulate their own theories of the infant's relation to the breast, the breast's actual and symbolic function, as well as its long-standing impact on psychical development throughout the life cycle. The "first representation of the external world", Joyce McDougall (1989) reminds readers, is the "mother's body", what she terms "the breast universe" (p. 33). At the beginning, the mother is, according to McDougall, "a total environment" and "something much vaster than simply another human being" (p. 32). She discusses this all-encompassing sense of the mother alongside related terms, "mother universe" and "magical breast universe" (p. 34), in the context of the infant's navigation of states of enmeshment and separateness, as they relate to the mind and the body. In her exploration of the early "psychosomatic matrix" (p. 33), McDougall traces the disentanglement of the psychological from the somatic in the infant's mind, what she refers to as the " 'desomatization' of the psyche" (p. 34). This move towards symbolic functioning takes place alongside the infant's push towards being "completely merged with the mother universe" (p. 34). This to- and fro-ing towards "somatic and psychic autonomy" (p. 34) can be disrupted along the way and lead to a split developing between the mind and the body and the experiencing of psychosomatic symptomology as a consequence, when "conflict and psychic pain" are suffered and communicated through "somatic discharge" (p. 48). McDougall states that she found instances of adult patients presenting with psychosomatic symptoms who were psychically reacting to situations like infants. Infants, she remarks, "cannot use words with which to think, they respond to emotional pain only psychosomatically" (p. 9). The patient becomes firmly attached to her/his psychosomatic symptom(s) in a way that mirrors the infant's earlier attachment to "the breast universe".

Andrea Celenza (2014) discusses maternal erotic transferences within the context of Margarete Hilferdig's focus on the "erogenous breast" (p. 25), Jean Laplanche's enigmatic signifier and his theory of general seduction (p. 26), and the "sensual and erotic nature of mother/infant interaction in and of itself" (p. 25). The "underlying erotic elements constituting (preoedipal) maternal longings" (p. 27) persist throughout development and then manifest in the transference with adult patients, emerging in "nonverbal and/or subsymbolic form" (p. 25) as "longings" (p. 34). Psychoanalysts have written extensively about the psychical processes underlying acts of feeding and their impact of other aspects of the individual's life. "Eating, more than any other bodily function, is drawn into the circle of the child's emotional life", writes Anna Freud (1946, p. 125). Feeding is thus an intense experience that is registered in the feelings of both parties. Drawing on the writings of Bion and Winnicott, Alessandra Lemma (2012) puts forward the view that the mother "provides psychic nourishment" in giving the infant her mind at the same time that she presents her breast: "it is a breast with a mind" (p. 308). Lemma argues that the mother facilitates the infant developing a capacity to feel gratitude through communicating a sense of her enjoyment of the feeding experience to the infant. If the infant perceives that the mother does not in fact enjoy "feeding", s/he assumes that the mother is "withholding" her mind (p. 308). This enacts a split between the bodily experience of being fed and the emotional experience of being taken in by the other. This provokes feelings of resentment and envy. If this experience becomes internalised as a formative object relation, the adult patient can become caught in a damaging repetition compulsion in which s/he enacts relational scenarios that lead to cycles of deprivation and envy.

Having said that, the mother's enjoyment of what she has to give can also provoke envy, as Klein (1957) puts it: "Envy is the angry feeling that another person possesses and enjoys something desirable – the envious impulse being to take it away or to spoil it" (p. 181). John Steiner (2008) explores the link between the repetition compulsion, the death instinct and envy in patients who feel humiliated by what they perceive as their lack. In doing so, they sidestep their need by attempting to "possess the goodness" being offered through a process of identifying with the object, thus occupying the position of someone who has something to give rather than someone open to receiving (p. 139). Identification with the one who has something to give is also considered by Irma Brenman Pick (2008), who uses the term "genius breast" (p. 189) to describe a patient's envious attack on her via projective identification. As a result, the patient attempts to evacuate any envious feelings she might be experiencing by splitting them off and projecting them into the analyst. The analyst becomes the quality, in this case "genius", which the patient both "worships" and "envies" (p. 188). This move enacts a conflict between envy and greed: an attempt to greedily gobble everything up that the other has so that the other retains nothing, tempered by an envious resentment that the other has anything at all (Klein, 1957, p. 181). This is played out via a series of introjections and projections with the analyst as desired and envied object.

Anna Freud and Donald Winnicott have commented on what they consider to be the differences between breast-feeding and bottle-feeding and their psychical consequences. In a piece on losing and being lost, Anna Freud (1967) traces the "double identification" experienced by "chronic losers" of material objects as one of identifying with parents perceived to be "neglectful, indifferent, and unconcerned toward them" on the one hand while playing out that relationship with the multiple objects they consistently lose on the other (p. 16). The original loss of "the mother's breast, the bottle, the child's own fingers" (p. 11) is "displaced" (p. 15) instead of being mourned. The melancholic attachment is then repeated again and again with things in the external environment. This is because, Anna Freud explains, "the infant directs value cathexis to any object from which satisfaction can be obtained, irrespective of the object being animate or inanimate, part of the internal or of the external world" (p. 10).

This is in contrast to Anna Freud's (1946) remarks in another article about infantile neurotic feeding disturbances in which she makes the point:

> Where infants are breast-fed, and the milk and breast are in fact part of the mother and not merely, as with bottle-fed babies, symbolic of her, the transition from narcissism to object love is easier and smoother. The image of food and the mother-image remain merged into one until the child is weaned from the breast.
>
> (p. 125)

The appearance of the term "merely" signifies Anna Freud's privileging of the mother's breast above the bottle. There is an intimation that the infant can identify a difference between the experience of drinking milk from the breast of the mother and drinking milk from a bottle and that this differentiation has an impact on psychical development. In his paper on "Breast-feeding as communication", Winnicott (1968a) believes that the survival of the object is of paramount importance in the face of the infant's attacks. He distinguishes between the "survival" of the breast and the bottle, with the observation that the dropping and breaking of the bottle is an "extremely traumatic experience" for the infant (p. 32).

André Green (1986) uses the term "patched breast" within the context of his theory of the "dead mother complex" (p. 152). He introduces his paper, "The dead mother", by referring to the Kleinian employment of the word "breast" to "designate the mother" and remarks that the term includes within it the recognition that the act of sucking includes taking in more than the breast: "her smell, her skin, her look and the thousand other components that 'make up' the mother" (p. 148). The breast as "metonymical object" has, Green tells readers, "become metaphor to the object" (p. 148). He makes it clear that the dead mother complex does not refer to the actual death of the mother or "a real separation from the object" (p. 149). "The essential characteristic", according to Green, is her physical "presence" and the fact that while present she is "absorbed by a bereavement" (p. 149). The dead mother complex includes "a premature disillusionment" and both the loss of "love" and "meaning" (p. 150). This takes place at a time when the infant believes that s/he is "at the centre of the maternal universe" and thus s/he is responsible for the mother's affect. In fact, the infant is left, Green says, with the burdensome sense that the mother's affect is a "consequence of his drives towards the object" (p. 150). The patient's dead mother complex reveals itself in the transference (p. 149) and is "the repetition of an infantile depression" (p. 149). The child will be confronted by her/his impotence when her/his efforts to repair the mother fail (p. 150). The patched breast, among other strategies, will emerge as a defence against the infant's overwhelming anxiety (p. 150). Green describes it thus: "a piece of cognitive fabric which is destined to mask the hole left by the decathexis, while secondary hatred and erotic excitation teem on the edge of an abyss of emptiness" (p. 152).

The ego is left with a "hole", with the consequence that its "compromised unity" depends on either "fantasy" or "knowledge", which results in "artistic creation" or "highly productive intellectualization" (p. 153). These "precocious idealized sublimations", however impressive they might appear in their outward expression, represent valiant attempts to deal with a trauma and merely paper over the loss that forms an integral part of the patient's ego. The patched breast is related to another concept, "the mind object", described by Edward G. Corrigan and Pearl-Ellen Gordon (1995a) as "an object that originates as a substitute for maternal care" which "organizes the self, providing an aura of omnipotence", a "precocious, schizoid solution" to loss (p. xiv). The mind object is, according to Corrigan and Gordon (1995b), "a psychic structure that replaces the relationship to a real object" (p. 9). As such, the mind itself becomes the breast that nourishes the psyche so that the subject begins to feed off her/himself. To return to Green's idea of the patched breast: the long-term impact on the person with a dead mother complex is a disruption in matters relating to loving another person; s/he can "create" but is unable to "love" (Kohon, in Green dialogues with Kohon, 1999, p. 53). As Geraldine Crehan (2004) puts it in a clinical application of Green's concept in her paper on the emotional effects of the death of a sibling in childhood: "Love then, is not truly possible, for the subject's love is mortgaged to the dead mother. Identification with the dead mother leaves a core that is frozen and therefore not really free to love another" (p. 216).

Donald Meltzer (1990, pp. 38–40) introduces the term "toilet-breast" to describe a part-object relation to the breast as something that absorbs and contains persecutory projections. He refers to the toilet-breast as one of the "maternal functions as the modulator of mental pain" (Meltzer et al., 1986, p. 68). A container is sought in the external environment for the "psychic pain" (1967, p. 20) that is unbearable for the subject. Meltzer describes the toilet-breast as "a receptacle in order to unburden oneself" (Meltzer in Meltzer and Harris, 1974, p. 140) and a container into which "the self that is in a state of chaos and desperation" is projected (1974, p. 140). As a part-object, the toilet-breast is "valued and needed, but not loved", so "depressive anxieties" are not present (1967, p. 20). The toilet-breast constitutes a paranoid-schizoid relation to the world, where persecutory anxiety dominates the psyche and the need is to evacuate the too-muchness of experience via splitting, projection, projective identification and evacuation. Meltzer (Meltzer et al., 1986) makes a distinction between, what he terms, the "toilet-breast" and the "feeding-breast". They are two types of container, distinguished by their function (Meltzer et al., 1986, p. 59). This severe and rigid splitting results in "geographical confusions" (1967, p. 20) between the "inside and outside of the object", between "external reality and psychic reality" and between the upper and lower regions of the mother's body (1967, p. 21). This "horizontal splitting", as Meltzer refers to it, separates the lower parts of the body from the upper parts and aligns them with different functions.

The "toilet functions" are aligned with the buttocks, while the "breasts, nipples, eyes and mouth . . . and . . . mind" are aligned with the "feeding function" (1967,

p. 21). Thus, the feeding-breast is connected with introjective processes while the toilet-breast is connected with projective processes. When this split is enacted in the consulting room, the analyst might be treated like the toilet-breast, so that s/he becomes a repository for the bad parts of the self, while any goodness can only be taken in from people outside the room (1967, p. 20). This rigid policing of the boundaries between the feeding-breast and toilet-breast operate out of an anxiety about "soiling, polluting and poisoning" the feeding-breast (1967, p. 20). So, there is an attempt on the part of the patient to protect the goodness of the feeding-breast from contamination by the badness that has been projected into the toilet-breast. The analyst's role in this situation is to contain the "massive" projective identification (1967, p. 22) that is persistent until such time that the patient can begin to integrate these different aspects of her/his experience.

Meltzer's ideas about the toilet-breast have been applied to reflect on, for example, early development (Negri, 1994) and the behaviour of adult patients in and around the consulting room (Lemma, 2015b). Romana Negri (1994) reports on her observation of the infant Giacomo in a hospital setting and his reaction to his mother's breast during and after the experience of defecating:

> the gestures of turning his head backwards and still holding his mouth in front of the nipple suggest that he is associating the bothering dirty feeling with the breast, and we can see some possible confusion between the dirty nappy and the breast, as though the fact of being bothered by his dirty bottom is caused by the breast, which is disturbing him, becoming the "toilet breast".
>
> (p. 123)

Negri is writing here of the confusional state experienced by the infant when confronted by the toilet-breast. An unpleasant sensation or feeling is experienced; an attempt is made to identify where it is coming from, but it is unclear where it is coming from, so an effort is made to attach the sensation or feeling to something tangible, at which point it is possible to move away from it. The subject unwittingly endeavours to enact something in a physical way that cannot be thought through psychically.

Alessandra Lemma (2015b) takes Meltzer's concept to explore how patients make psychical use of the consulting room toilet which often becomes, in the patient's mind, "the analyst's toilet" (p. 143). She explores two case studies, one of which centres on a female patient, Ms. H, and the operations of the toilet-breast in the patient's transference to the building in which the consulting room was housed, the consulting room toilet, and the analyst within the consulting room (pp. 150–159). Lemma shows how the physical space of the toilet can be used literally and concretely by patients trying to evacuate the bad aspects of themselves to keep the consulting room and the analyst within it good. Ms. H gradually went from using a toilet across the road from the building in which the consulting room was located to making use of the consulting room toilet as "the first prototype of a safe container for felt-to-be dangerous or unacceptable feelings and parts of the self" (p. 157). Over time, Lemma was able to facilitate the material being brought into the room by means of her making an interpretation. After which, the patient began to move from acting out her "messy, angry part" (p. 153) unconsciously in the consulting room toilet to relating to the analyst as a toilet-breast. Eventually Lemma believes that this balancing of the good and bad projections in the transference can be worked through towards a more depressive state of mind.

Two applications of psychoanalysis work directly with the breast and observe the infant's relation to the breast and what s/he does with it: infant observation (Sternberg, 2005; Thomson-Salo, 2014) and parent-infant psychotherapy (Baradon, 2005, 2015). I previously discussed infant observation within the context of its forming part of the clinical training of psychoanalysts and psychoanalytic psychotherapists in Chapter 2. Esther Bick (1964) developed and incorporated infant observation into the clinical training programme in child psychotherapy at the Tavistock Clinic in 1948. The approach is now widely utilised in psychoanalytic training programmes (Boyle Spelman, 2013), as well as in specialist and further professional development courses attended by professionals in other fields, such as teachers, nurses and social workers (Diem-Wille, Steinhardt and Reiter, 2006; Shulman, 2019), whose work requires a high degree of self-reflectivity and an insight into early development and its impact on behavioural and relationship patterns (Thomson-Salo, 2014, p. 3). Infant observation presents trainees with an experience of directly observing an infant as s/he develops within her/his own environmental context during the first two years of life. It also offers observers an opportunity to witness pre-verbal, non-verbal and unverbalisable aspects of experience, as well as how anxieties and psychical defences get played out against the backdrop of the breast. The term "infant", *infans*, "implies", Winnicott (1960a) writes, "not talking" (p. 40), so the observation of this phase of life becomes "a place where verbalization has no meaning" (Winnicott, 1968b, p. 91). The method requires a precise attention to detail coupled with a reflective approach to presenting what one has observed about the infant, the environment and oneself.

Psychoanalytic parent-infant psychotherapy developed from the work of Selma Fraiberg (1982; Shapiro, Fraiberg and Adelson, 1976) in the United States of America and Françoise Dolto (1995) in France among others and is underpinned by psychoanalysis, attachment theory, theories of human development and neuroscience. Clinicians work with a baby and her/his primary caregiver when, in the words of Tessa Baradon (2002), "there has been a dis/ruption or distortion in the normal course of bonding" (p. 25). In focusing on the "relationship" (p. 25) between the two, parent-infant psychotherapists attend to the "behavioural and affective interactions" (p. 27) between them, as well as how they relate to the psychotherapist as a third figure. So, the psychotherapist works with them as a couple but also as individuals (Masur, 2009, p. 469). The psychotherapist offers the dyad a clinical intervention (Baradon, 2015, p. 50) by working with the unconscious dynamics underpinning the relation between the two, as well as exploring what and how the baby and caregiver might be trying to communicate to each other. The psychotherapist occupies a number of roles according to Baradon: a clinical observer, an analytic therapist, a transference figure and a new object (p. 50). The clinician assesses, among other things, the mother's capacity for reflectivity, attunement and containment, the impact of intergenerational trauma on the pair, as well as any developmental difficulties evident in the child (Masur, 2009, pp. 467–468). The psychotherapist facilitates the caregiver becoming more curious and reflective about their baby, as well as developing a heightened awareness of how they, as an adult, are relating to their baby and the impact of their behaviour on the baby. The caregiver is also offered an opportunity to develop interpretive skills to help them to recognise more accurately what their baby is trying to communicate to them and how they might respond to the baby in a way that is reassuring and containing (Hogg, 2019, p. 29).

What is "the culture-breast", and how might it work within the context of the previous discussion of psychoanalytic discourses of the breast? This neologism, which is familiar yet strange, is embedded within psychoanalytic understandings of the breast as both an internal and external object. I introduce the culture-breast as a new clinical concept for the consideration of psychical material that appears in the consulting room via the patient's free associations, behavioural repetitions and transference to the analyst, as well as in the analyst's countertransference. The term also refers to the unconscious use made of cultural objects more broadly outside the clinic.

The culture-breast

How might culture be understood as a breast? What does it mean to say we are fed by culture? Why are some of us subject to being fed by the breast of culture to greater or lesser extents? What does the term "culture" signify here, and why have I used a hyphen for the concept "culture-breast"? The "culture-breast" brings together two words and a hyphen to form a hybrid: combined yet separate, together yet apart, enmeshed yet differentiated. The appearance of the hyphen draws attention to the fact that the concept conjoins two words to form a new word, a third word. The hyphen occupies an in-between space, part of each word yet an entity in its own right. Not a word itself in this instance, the hyphen is situated between a dash and a minus sign. Its appearance *does* something, enacts a change. It impacts on meaning. In this, the inclusion of a hyphen gestures towards a transitional space, a space for thinking and reflection, a space for playing. The hyphen, moreover, draws attention to the constructedness that underpins all concepts.

Culture is, in the words of Raymond Williams (1985), "one of the two or three most complicated words in the English language" (p. 87). This is how Williams begins his entry on "Culture" in *Keywords: A Vocabulary of Culture and Society*, before tracing the etymology of the term in different contexts (pp. 87–93). The entry on "Culture" in Giorgio Nardone and Alessandro Salvini's *International Dictionary of Psychotherapy* (2019) defines it as "[a] broad concept used by different disciplines with different meanings", continuing that "the therapist must know how to 'build' their interventions considering the cultural aspects of the person in front of them" (p. 172). The word is positioned "most fundamentally", according to Julian Wolfreys (2004), in opposition to "nature" (p. 37). Cláudio Laks Eizirik (1997) points to the fact that, in German, "*Kultur*" was used, during the eighteenth century, synonymously with "civilisation" (p. 789). Sigmund Freud was interested in culture and wrote many papers on different aspects of culture, including literature, art and religion (Frosh, 2010, pp. 40–68). Since then, culture has emerged in different ways within psychoanalytic writings; for example, Allan Frosch (2006) and Jeffrey Rubin (1997) have explored discursive "cultures" operating within the field of psychoanalysis; Thomas Kohut (2003) has examined psychoanalysis within the wider "cultural" context; while Warren Poland's (2002) introduction to a special journal issue and the contributors in Salman Akhtar and Stuart Twemlow's book (2018a) have used psychoanalysis as an analytical tool to look closely at different "cultural" forms. In their introduction, Akhtar and Twemlow (2018b) describe their endeavour as "applied psychoanalysis", which they use to "denote the employment of basic psychoanalytic principles. . . [f]or deepening the understanding of cultural phenomena at large" (p. xxxi). Among its potential meanings, Wolfreys (2004) remarks that the word "culture" "signifies an acquaintance with the humanities, fine arts, and other intellectual or scientific pursuits" (p. 37). Eizirik (1997) includes "works and practices of intellectual and especially artistic activity" (p. 790) among contemporary uses of the term, when he cites "music, literature, painting, sculpture, theatre and film, sometimes with the addition of philosophy, scholarship, history" (p. 790) among culture's objects.

I use the word "culture" very specifically in this chapter to denote cultural objects, resulting from creative endeavours and arising from the fields of film, art, literature and music. These cultural objects originate and are consumed within particular social and historical contexts. They might be one-off creations or mass produced, and access to them might be exclusive to one or two galleries, for example, or shared by millions of people at different times, in a variety of ways and in a range of locations around the world. The term "object" as it appears in "cultural object" has a number of meanings. Firstly, the use of the word "object" points to the thingness of culture (Connor, 2011; Turkle, 2007), for example, a sculpture, painting, novel, DVD or CD. Secondly, cultural phenomena facilitate experiences and encounters (Kuhn, 2013a; Gabbard, 2001a), like the experience of listening to a piece of music, visiting an exhibition, watching a film or reading a poem. Thirdly, as external objects, cultural objects also function, like *people*, as internal objects in the psyche (Bott Spillius et al., 2011e; Scharff, 2020), providing a number of creative and defensive functions. In psychoanalysis, the term "object" also features in concepts, such as "part-object" (Bott Spillius et al., 2011f), "transitional object" (Winnicott, 1953), "transformational object" (Bollas, 1987) and "mind object" (Corrigan and Gordon, 1995a), all of which will be discussed in due course.

The culture-breast refers to the psychical use made of cultural objects. We all make use of cultural objects of one form or another unconsciously. These cultural experiences are necessary. They enrich our lives, a fact that is becoming increasingly recognised in creative arts therapies (Irish Association for Creative Arts Therapies, 1992–; Northern Ireland Group for Art as Therapy, 1976–), arts and health initiatives (Arts & Health, 2011–; National Alliance for Arts, Health & Wellbeing, 2012–), as well as in the practice of social prescribing (Walker et al., 2019; Redmond et al., 2019). To depend on cultural objects for psychical survival is a phenomenon that is the reserve of particular individuals, however, and is the focus of this chapter. The individual does not present as psychotic (Bion, 1962a, pp. 24–27), autistic (Rhode, 2018) or perverse (Wood, 2014) in their relation to cultural objects, and so cannot be subsumed into the aforementioned psychopathological categories. They do not present as being addicted to particular cultural objects or experiences (Sweet, 2013). The culture-breast describes a process; a process of relating to and through cultural objects. It is a phenomenon that I have witnessed many times in clinical and educational contexts, and it is also a phenomenon that is of relevance to me as a person, a clinician and an educator. It is a phenomenon, in other words, that I know about from my work but also from my personal experience. In cases where the culture-breast is in operation, cultural objects become the domain through which the individual experiences the world. The person appears most alive when engaging in or talking about cultural experiences. It is not that the person is affectless when they are relaying other experiences; rather there is an intensity of feeling evident when their free associations touch on cultural objects. It is, furthermore, not that they turn away from the world, so much as that their approach to the world is mediated through their relation to and identification with cultural objects.

Cultural objects also operate as a protective filter through which difficult experiences can be managed and held at bay, thus providing a defensive function to enact a screen between the individual and that which is unbearable. At certain times, the individual will engage in an accelerated use of cultural objects, and with a fervour that amounts to an almost manic intensity. This tends to be during particularly difficult periods in the person's life. This unconscious co-option of cultural objects generally begins in early childhood and persists into adulthood. The individual is unaware of the extent to which s/he relies on cultural objects. This might go unnoticed by others as well, because the individual may be seen as "cultured", something that is acceptable, even lauded, within certain societal spheres, for example, in academia and the arts. This use of cultural objects is usually made necessary because of environmental deprivation, to the extent that cultural objects take on a care-taking function performed, in less adverse circumstances, by the adults in the child's life. The culture-breast operates as a part-object in the psyche. The external cultural object is utilised as a site for introjections and projections. This psychical over-investment in cultural objects leaves the individual feeling drained and as if something is missing. While being surrounded by loved ones, friends and work colleagues, the individual often experiences a painful isolation that feels like they are "cut off from life". It can take some time for this material to emerge in the transference and in discursive repetitions. It is important that the psychoanalytic practitioner does not dismiss or minimise the appearance of such

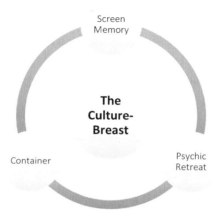

Figure 3.1 The culture-breast

material as evidence of displacement or avoidance. It is essential that the clinician does not bring the patient's attention to, what might appear to be, her/his behaviour too soon, by challenging the patient's use of cultural objects. It is crucial that the practitioner recognises that the patient is enmeshed with her/his cultural objects; it is how s/he relates and is essentially not just a doing but a being.

I will trace the contours of the psychical operation of the culture-breast through an attendance to three themes: the provision of framing as a screen memory, the provision of safety as a psychic retreat, and the provision of meaning as a container (Figure 3.1). Following this, I will discuss the working-through process, in which the patient needs to be weaned off her/his dependence on cultural objects and onto the psychoanalytic psychotherapist, which requires a gradual shift in the patient's relation to her/his cultural objects from identifying with them to being able to make use of them (Winnicott, 1971a). This demands a movement from the paranoid-schizoid position to the depressive position, which makes possible an increased capacity to relate to one's objects more generally as whole objects rather than part-objects. This, in turn, facilitates the development of a satisfactory rather than a gratifying attachment to one's cultural objects, together with an amplified ability to feel psychic pain and the immediacy of experience more broadly. I will do this from the perspective of my work as a clinician, and include examples from my own personal experience to illustrate the clinical points I make. In this, I will include a psychosocial case study for the purpose of psychoanalytic reflection. Psychosocial studies was explored at length in Chapter 1. I am using the term "psychosocial case study" here to refer to the inter-relation between the psychical and the social, the personal and the environmental in the formulation of psychoanalytic concepts and clinical technique and knowledge (Spurling, 2019; Frosh, 2019a). In writing about work in psychosocial studies, Liz Frost and Helen Lucey

(2010) remark, "psychological issues cannot be validly abstracted from social, cultural and historical contexts" (p. 3).

Clinical insight does not arise solely from one's experience of working with patients in the clinic. It does not simply materialise from what one does with the patient's story and experience. Clinical insight emerges from the experience of being both inside and outside the clinic, from how one approaches one's life as much as from how one approaches one's work. Our clinical training, supervision, personal analysis, clinical work, reading and further professional development all contribute towards the continuing evolution of our clinical expertise for working with patients. Our skills, knowledge and clinical experience all make it possible for us to work with patients. But none of us are merely clinicians. We can only be who we are, however much experience or knowledge or skills-based training we acquire. The writing of any clinical case study includes the observations and reflections of the clinician on the patient's material, in order to develop a new clinical theory, hone a skill or make a contribution to psychoanalytic knowledge. The clinician's subjectivity is central to these tasks. While clinicians might write eloquently of their countertransference, they rarely include more detailed information about the personal experiences that lie behind their capacity to make meaning of the dynamics that play out in the consulting room (Ogden, 1999, pp. 157–197). The psychoanalytic case study rests squarely on the patient in terms of detail, with the clinician framing everything from off stage. The psychosocial case study, as I am presenting it here, brings the clinician's subjectivity and environmental context into view, in the service of making transparent the psychical, social, cultural and indeed historical processes through which individual clinicians develop particular aptitudes for noticing certain things.

In the early stages of my clinical work as a trainee psychoanalytic psychotherapist, I began to notice that images would come to my mind as I walked towards the front door and greeted a patient for the first time. These images might relate to aspects of people whom I knew or had met, colours, shapes, objects, places. The images might be clearly defined or fuzzy. They might be singular or have multiple parts to them. They might appear slowly or in quick succession. They might be associated with experiences I had had, or scenarios I had heard or read about. They might relate to "real" life or appear fantastical. Sometimes the images would be accompanied by words or have stories attached to them; sometimes not. These images could be described as thoughts or memories or fantasies. What is important about them is that they emerged in visual form. I did not know what the images meant, or how they might be connected to one another or to my patient, but I realised, over time, that they were significant. I held them lightly. I did not try to figure them out. I did not try to push them from my mind. At first, I thought they told me something about my reactions to, and perceptions of, my patient, and thus gave me an insight into myself. And indeed they did. In time, however, I came to appreciate that the images also told me something about my patient and the work ahead of us.

At the same time, I observed that I might listen to a certain piece of music or a song at different times during a patient's treatment. I noticed that I would listen to the same track repeatedly and that thoughts about a particular patient would become present while listening. These thoughts were mixed in with other thoughts about a whole manner of other things, so I was not aware of any connection at first, and the associations to specific patients took some time to emerge. I would allow the thoughts to settle in my mind, and to proliferate. It might be the title, lyrics, the melody, the rhythm, the artist or band that prompted a reaction in me. It might be a moment in the track, discernible in my affect and how a particular response would be repeated time and again at that specific point in the song. I am not unique in this regard. Lots of psychoanalytic psychotherapists become aware of connections to patients in their thoughts and feelings. This is a feature of countertransference. Countertransference is not limited to the feelings and thoughts the practitioner experiences when the patient is present. The treatment continues between sessions. Faye Carey (2018) has written, for example, of the "visual countertransference", which includes "the images that arise spontaneously in the therapist's mind" and how the therapist makes "sense" of such imagery (p. 4). Elsewhere Alexander Stein (2007) has explored how "Music is a sophisticated language of semantic, harmonic, intervallic, rhythmic, and scalar relationships" (p. 82), which can hold affects and memories outside of awareness. Cultural objects and experiences more generally can come to mind in the free-floating attention of the clinician as well as in the free associations of the patient while together in the consulting room.

I believe I am particularly attuned to registering, identifying and reflecting on some of the unconscious resonances of these stray thoughts relating to cultural objects and experiences because of my personal experience. I could sidestep this uncomfortable reality by focusing on my academic training and experience with cultural objects, textual analysis and theoretical practices of reading. I could choose examples from my clinical work with patients to illustrate how the culture-breast operates. While both the aforementioned would be relevant, they would not be entirely accurate, because my formulation of the culture-breast has been made possible, in a significant way, by my own personal experience which required me to reflect on it, which in turn facilitated me being able to reflect on what might be going on for patients in this regard. In her book *Psychoanalysts Talk*, Virginia Hunter (1994a) invited eleven prominent psychoanalysts to discuss one of her cases, prefacing each case discussion with an interview with the analyst. The interviews she conducted included details about each analyst's personal history, professional and theoretical investments, as well as the social and cultural environment in which they were located (Hunter, 1994b, p. 2; Grinberg, 1994, p. xi). "The analyst's choice of theory or even creation of theory may be affected by the analyst's personality and history", according to Hunter (1994c, p. 11). By bringing each analyst's case discussion and interview together, Hunter enables readers to appraise how the particularity of each analyst's subjectivity has influenced her/his approach to the same case material. "Subjectivity", Hunter writes,

Figure 3.2 Psychical operations of the culture-breast

"will influence technique, interpretation, focus, activity, gratification, responsive-ness, empathy, the way the defenses are analysed, and countertransference". It is "subjectivity", she continues, "that causes each psychoanalytic dialogue to be unique" and "is also the major reason for the differences among psychoanalyses" (p. 7). Gail Lewis (2009) and Sasha Roseneil (2019a) have both integrated aspects of their personal experience with their clinical acumen and theoretical knowledge to explore, in a more explicitly psychosocial way, the psychodynamics of race and racism (Lewis) and sexuality and heteronormativity (Roseneil), as well as their material effects.

I will provide some brief remarks about my personal history to frame the dis-cussion of the culture-breast as it relates to the screen memory, psychic retreat and container (Figure 3.2).

Context

I am the eldest of three children. My father worked outside the home in skilled manual work. My mother worked in the home and also briefly, while I was a teenager, part-time outside the home in skilled manual work. Money was very tight, and its scarcity formed the basis of daily arguments between my parents. I was the first person in my extended family to complete secondary school and go to college. I wonder now if my interest in education set me apart from my parents and if this was a source of aggravation to them. My enduring memory of growing up was my father was always angry. He would fly into rages almost the moment he walked in the door, and the rows would last for most of the evening. His mood dominated the house. The atmosphere was tense, turbulent, unpredictable. Living there felt like a permanent state of walking on eggshells. He could also be playful and taught us many games, but his mood was erratic to the extent that any playfulness usually ended as a row. The one place I felt safe was the local library, because it was quiet there. I was born shortly after my mother's own mother died. She was anxious and sad. My abiding sense of her growing up was she wanted to be out of the house, shopping, walking, visiting. She was preoccupied and turned in on herself; absent in her presence. She developed some serious medical condi-tions at different points, which were a source of added worry for her.

I dropped the eggs on the kitchen floor: cultural objects as screen memories

A memory comes to my mind, unbidden, over and over again: I am in the kitchen. I am young, four, maybe five years old. I am at the fridge and I open the door. The fridge light comes on. I enjoyed drinking the gripe water, meant for my younger sibling. I opened the door, there were eggs in an open com-partment, they dropped and smashed on the floor. My mother arrived into the room just as they landed and punished me. I associated gripe water with grapes and further with Grace Poole, a character in the novel, Jane Eyre *(1847), who was the caretaker of Bertha Mason, the first wife of the lead male protagonist, Mr Edward Rochester, and otherwise known as "the mad woman in the attic".*

This memory is a screen memory, the significance of which has only become apparent to me as I write this chapter. In the context earlier, I wrote that grow-ing up in my family home felt like "a permanent state of walking on eggshells". Sometimes, I was responsible or held responsible for breaking those eggshells. It is impossible to walk on an eggshell without breaking it. The pleasure in drinking the gripe water was partly because it was meant for someone else, my younger sibling, whom I resented and towards whom I felt a fierce ambivalence. This memory is also about the excitement of doing something by myself and for myself, away from and outside the awareness of my mother. And it starkly represents the "gripe" I harboured towards my younger sibling at the time.

"Not only *some* but *all* of what is essential from childhood has been retained in these memories", Sigmund Freud (1914) writes with reference to screen memories (p. 148). These screen memories, while "well-preserved", "do not necessarily cor-respond to the important experiences of childhood years" (Freud, 1916–1917[1915–1917]), p. 200). They are characterised by their "unusual sharpness", according to Jean Laplanche and Jean-Bertrand Pontalis (1967, p. 410). What distinguishes them is the fact that they seem "so commonplace and insignificant" (p. 200). While appearing on the surface to be "indifferent childhood memories" (Freud, 1899, p. 309), once submitted to analysis, they can often be found to "illustrate the most momentous turning-points" of life (p. 316). Freud goes further to say that "with a thorough analysis all that has been forgotten can be extracted from them" (Freud, 1916–1917[1915–1917], p. 201). He links screen memories to dreams because they emerge in visual form (Freud, 1899, p. 309; see also Freud, 1916[1915–1916]): "They represent the forgotten years of childhood as adequately as the manifest con-tent of a dream represents dream-thoughts" (Freud, 1914, p. 148). Like dreams, these "scenes" (Freud, 1899, p. 309) or "mnemic images" (pp. 306–307) are a prod-uct of "condensation", "displacement" (Freud, 1916–1917[1915–1917], p. 200) and "repression" (Freud, 1901a, p. 45). They are "substitutes" for "other and more important impressions" (Freud, 1901a, p. 47), so that "essential elements of an experience are represented in memory by inessential elements of the same expe-rience" (Freud, 1899, p. 307). They "screen" (Freud, 1916–1917[1915–1917]) or "conceal" (Freud, 1899, p. 309) aspects of the experience that have been "suppressed" (p. 306). This is because screen memories are a "compromise" between representing an experience and protecting the mind of the subject from becoming overwhelmed by distress. So, screen memories contain elements that are "latent" or "inaccessible" to the conscious mind (Freud, 1916–1917[1915–1917], p. 201), "*omitted* rather than forgotten" (Freud, 1899, p. 306). They are an amalgam of "phantasies" (Freud, 1899, p. 315), including "residues of memories relating to later life" (p. 320), woven into a childhood memory. They are constructions, which are "formed" rather than "emerge", displaying to us "our earliest years not as they were but as they appeared at the later periods when the memories were aroused" (p. 322).

Screen memories are an aspect of the culture-breast (Figure 3.3). They provide a frame for experiences. They give a sense of the atmosphere of childhood, rather than a factual account of a particular situation (LaFarge, 2012). They are imbued with an affective retrospection because they emerge from conscious memory as well as being entangled with unconscious phantasies. An analysis of them provides an impression of "indelible childhood experiences" and "unconscious phantasies" (Laplanche and Pontalis, 1967, p. 411). Cultural objects and experiences become interwoven with the aforementioned to form screen memories that hold affective resonances that would be too overwhelming to experience directly. So, there is, as it were, a double screening process that takes place. I will briefly outline three screen memories for the purpose of discussion and illustration:

> *I was hospitalised with a chest infection for a brief period when I was five years old. I told the nurses I was going to get married to the Hulk. I loved watching* The Incredible Hulk *(1977–1982). When my father came to collect me to bring me home, he lifted me up on his shoulders. I felt so tall.*
>
> *When I was ten years old I had a painting on my wall, above my bed, with a magician standing on a concrete plinth with his arm raised towards a dragon. There was light coming out of his hand. Magic. The magician was tiny and the dragon was huge. The light emanating from the hand on his outstretched arm was the only thing keeping the dragon from engulfing him.*
>
> *I read C.S. Lewis's (1950) novel,* The Lion, the Witch and the Wardrobe, *when I was eight years old. One of my favourite scenes is when Lucy pushes through the fur coats in the wardrobe to find herself out in the magical, snow-covered landscape of Narnia. There is a street lamp in the clearing, where she meets the faun Mr Tumnus, half-man and half-goat, carrying an armful of Christmas presents.*

All three screen memories above relate to my relationship with my father: desired yet feared. Anticipation and hope underpin each scene. But it is precarious. Charming Bruce Banner can turn, without a moment's notice, into the rage-filled Hulk with teeth clenched, wreaking havoc and violently destroying everything around him. He is mighty and he is out of control and uncontrollable. The excitement at seeing a magical creature like a faun, Mr Tumnus, is tempered by the fact

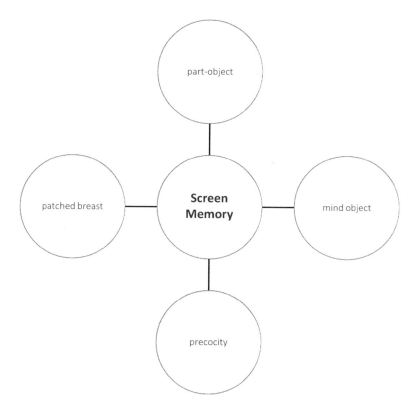

Figure 3.3 Cultural objects as screen memories

that he is half-man, half-goat. The mythological figure Baphomet is represented as a man with goat's hooves, who in turn is associated with the Devil, whose domain is Hell, a place of unrelenting punishment and agony. All three screen memories revolve around the dynamics of power and powerlessness. Phantasies of omnipotence are projected onto each cultural object, most concretely illustrated in the tiny magician's magical control over the huge dragon bearing down on him. The outstretched hand also represents the stark reality of a small child holding up a hand, in a desperate plea to an adult to stand back or stop what they are about to do. Each memory incorporates cultural objects – a television programme, a painting, a novel – to hold these feelings, allowing them to surface and be held for experiencing in a manageable way, while protecting against the latent thoughts that underpin them. I watched *The Incredible Hulk* routinely, went to sleep with the painting above my bed every night, and the passage from *The Lion, the Witch and the Wardrobe* continues to be one of the scenes I most prize in literature. So, these cultural objects were accessible to me on a regular basis. Each of them was held in high regard by me, not just for their artistic merit but because they held such emotive intensity.

Screen memories, as they relate to the culture-breast, are constructed from part-objects. These part-objects are stray thoughts, feelings, phantasies. They are not connected and might be in conflict with one another. They are a feature of the paranoid-schizoid position, holding projections. They are glued together with reminiscences of cultural objects and experiences. These part-objects are beta-elements collected together to form something that makes sense intellectually. While they appear to have a coherence, they have not been worked through via a process of symbolisation. Their coherence is dependent on the operations of intellectualisation and rationalisation. Cultural objects provide narrative holding for the projection of unbearable experiences that are too much for the mind to bear consciously. The unbearable element that underpins the screen memory has been split off and projected out into a cultural object that provides holding at a safe distance, so that the feelings can be managed without becoming overwhelming. These cultural objects are kept close – whether materially (like the poster of the magician and the dragon) or conceptually (like the scene from *The Lion, the Witch and the Wardrobe*). They persist over many years. The cultural object provides a concrete reference point for the screen memory. Patients presenting with screen memories showing aspects of these features tend to describe childhoods marked by precocity and often display a grandiosity linked to intellectual development and achievement. This intellectual precocity develops in reaction to impingements emanating from the child's environmental context. In writing about premature intellectual development, Donald Winnicott (1949a) remarks that it results from a situation when "an infant has to cope with an environment which insists on being important" (p. 185). The child is forced into *doing* rather than *being*, because the environment demands attention. The mind is harnessed by the infant, partly to meet the environment's demands and partly to mediate between her/him and the experience of persecution in reaction to the impingements enacted by the environment. This situation might result in the child developing, what he terms, "a false integration", which features "some kind of abstract thinking which is unnatural" (p. 185).

In environments that are not "good-enough", to use Winnicott's phrase, or "tantalizing" (Winnicott, 1949b, p. 246), the development of the infant's "mental functioning" can go into overdrive so that it becomes "*a thing in itself,* practically replacing the good mother and making her unnecessary" (p. 246). The key word here is "practically". The mother is still physically present, but the infant's mind has taken over some of her emotional and psychological functions to the extent that the infant has developed a "mind-psyche, which is pathological" (p. 247). With the mind object, the child becomes "compliant" with the environment (Stewart, 1995, p. 45), while ruthlessly demanding from her/his own mind, thus repeating the experience of being demanded upon by the environment and also establishing an exhausting mental cycle of draining and replenishing. This results in a feeling of "emptiness", which Harold Stewart (1995) says often brings the adult patient to therapy. It is more precisely, as Stewart puts it, "the emptiness of their lives" (p. 41) that patients report, externalising the internal feeling of emptiness they experience back into the environment. This is because the mind does not give selflessly. The mind's pre-eminence enacts a split between the omnipotent mind and the vulnerable body – the body becoming largely disregarded – so that the mind becomes "localised in the head" (p. 252). Peter Shabad and Stanley Selinger (1995) describe the development of the mind object as "a counterphobic movement" and a mental compensation for an inability to physically meet the demands of the impinging environment (p. 216). It is a matter of psychical survival for the infant (p. 217), who henceforth exists psychically in a "mental self-embrace" (p. 218). This mind object provides the psychological and emotional succour that the dead mother is unable to give, because she is taken up with her own emotional demands. The mind object feeds off intellectual pursuits, so that cultural objects become a melange of part-objects that function as a patched breast, covering over the developmental loss experienced by the adult patient, which remains present but split off, denied and projected into cultural objects and experiences.

I like my nature filtered through culture: cultural objects as psychic retreats

> I had recently relocated from an urban location to a rural location. The move was difficult for me. I felt I had to give up too much and the loss was overwhelming. People kept asking me how I was finding it. I felt under pressure to say something positive, all the while feeling resentful and despondent. I regularly reproduced the line that the scenery was beautiful and that I had never experienced weather quite like this. I also continuously complained that there was no culture. I meant art galleries, plays, arthouse films. This was untrue but it is how it appeared to me at the time. Everywhere I looked there was nature in all its wildness. I felt like I was living at the end of the earth. One day I responded to someone's question in a way that took me by surprise: "I like my nature filtered through culture".

I had known for some time that I co-opted cultural objects to mediate the rawness of experience, but had not represented this fact to myself before with such clarity. The aforementioned utterance, "I like my nature filtered through culture", is an example of insight, arrived at through many years of experience. Its verbalisation is accompanied, in the moment, by a feeling of surprise, not because the knowledge is new but because of the precision with which it is synthesised and communicated. It is akin to a psychoanalytic interpretation that has been heard and taken in. It *does* something. Something changes in that moment. A psychic link is made. Something is gained at the same time that something is lost. I no longer use cultural objects in the way that I once did – as part of a psychic retreat.

There was a time when I gave myself over to cultural objects for the purpose of becoming absorbed in the experience, which, in itself, functioned as a protective filter between me and the immediacy of an external environment that I found too persecutory.

Psychic retreats are, according to John Steiner (1993), "states of mind which [provide] protection from anxiety and pain . . . states which [are] often experienced spatially as if they [are] places in which the patient [can] hide" (p. xi). He lists a variety of terms to describe these psychical states of withdrawal: "psychic retreats, refuges, shelters, sanctuaries or havens" (p. xi). Steiner employs a series of visual images to refer to a system of defences which keeps the patient safely tucked away from unbearable contact with the analyst: "protective armour . . . hiding place . . . like a snail coming out of its shell . . . a house . . . a cave . . . a fortress . . . a desert island" (pp. 1, 2). A psychic retreat can also be composed of "groups of people" (Steiner, 2011, p. 3). Analysis itself can become operationalised by the patient as a psychic retreat (Steiner, 1993, p. 3). The workings of this system of defences, which Steiner refers to as, "pathological organizations of the personality" (p. 2), serve to leave the patient psychically "stuck, cut off, and out of reach" (p. 2). Steiner uses words like "isolation" (p. 2), "avoidance" (p. 3), "dependence" (p. 3) and "trapped" (p. 9) when writing about the impact of the psychic retreat on the patient. A psychic retreat is more precisely "a grouping of object relations, defences and phantasies" (p. 2); a melange of "objects or part-objects" (p. 2). Its function is to provide security, safety, protection. This comes at a cost. The enactment of a psychic retreat has the effect of stalling the treatment, so while the psychic retreat is constructed, in Steiner's estimation, spatially, it also has temporal elements and effects. Time seems to stand still there. Nothing moves. So, while the psychic retreat endeavours to maintain an "equilibrium" (p. 3), it also contains and enacts destructiveness (p. 4) that can harm the patient's relation to her/himself, to the analyst and to others outside the consulting room.

Todd Haynes directed a film entitled [Safe] (1995), in which the word "safe" is encapsulated within square brackets. This stylistic gesture performs, in its very figuration, the tension between safety and entrapment underpinning the operation of a psychic retreat. The film features "Carol", a self-described "homemaker", who lives in suburbia with her husband and "his" son, as she gradually begins to develop physical symptoms that are inexplicable and resist interpretation by others yet give her life meaning. She becomes, as it were, allergic to her life, in the process catapulting herself out of one situation and exchanging it for another, equally stifling one. The external situation changes – she moves from her suburban home to a communal retreat in the desert – yet the internal situation remains the same. The film ends with her looking at herself in a mirror within an igloo-like structure within the communal retreat within the desert. This psychic retreat has layers. While the psychic retreat might offer the patient some relief from what is perceived to be the unbearable, intolerable, overwhelming pain of reality, the air is stale there. It produces somewhat of a psychic entombment, as it sucks the life out of experience. The experience becomes muted, dulled, drained of its aliveness.

Steiner locates the psychic retreat between the paranoid-schizoid and depressive positions (p. 11). In addition to mapping out the intricate web of defences clustering around the patient, Steiner is interested in tracing how the patient might be brought out of the retreat slowly, gently, steadily. This entails the careful monitoring of the patient's anxiety and the moment-to-moment atmosphere of the session: "if the minute movements are attended to, a transient and briefly bearable 'taste' of the anxiety which is experienced on emergence from the retreat can be registered by the patient and interpreted by the analyst as it becomes observable" (p. 10). In addition to evoking anxiety and suffering, emergence from a psychic retreat can provoke feelings of embarrassment, shame and humiliation (Steiner, 2011, p. 3), as the patient feels "seen" and judged by a hostile other.

Psychic retreats are a feature of the culture-breast (Figure 3.4). They offer a sense of psychic safety from experiences which are overwhelming. The original experience that is being protected against is filtered through a second experience with a cultural object, which keeps the original experience at a distance, while at the same time enabling some of the affect to be felt. Through "splitting and

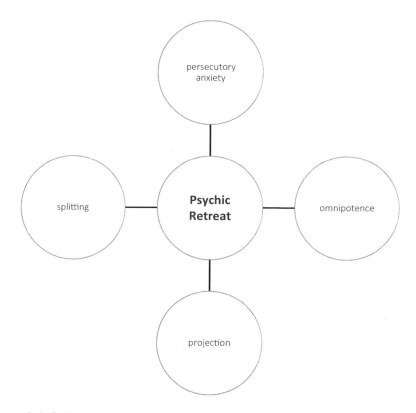

Figure 3.4 Cultural objects as psychic retreats

projective and introjective processes" (Steiner, 2011, p. 2), common defences forming part of psychic retreats, the two experiences become intermingled to the extent that the cultural object becomes central in the patient's relation to the original experience that is being defended against. The cultural object becomes a conduit as it were. I will introduce and discuss three brief vignettes to illustrate the inclusion of cultural objects in the construction of psychic retreats:

> *I read and read and read. On the bus or train, at the bus stop or train station, while eating lunch, while watching television. I always had a book to hand. When meeting someone, I would read right up to the moment they were beside me.*
>
> *I listened to music for hours, the same song over and over. Sometimes I wore headphones; other times not. When I was twelve years old, a neighbour from next door arrived at the front door with an armful of her records. She offered them to me.*
>
> *I watched as many films as I could. It did not matter what review they received – one star or five stars – I was there. I loved going to the cinema. I laughed aloud at the beginning of each film, as the sound boomed out from the speakers on the wall.*

The previous three examples give a sense of my relentless pursuit of cultural experiences. There is a manic quality to each endeavour: "I read and read and read", "I listened to music for hours, the same song over and over", "I watched as many films as I could". This manic quality is evident in the laugh I uttered at the beginning of each film in the cinema. This involuntary laugh was also an expulsion of anxiety, because my father did not like the television loud. He would punish us for putting the sound up "too high". So, there is also desperation. Each example represents an attempt to fill up every moment with an experience of my own choosing. This display of omnipotence exposes the impotence of the situation I found myself in while I was growing up. While I could decide which book I would read, song I would listen to or film I would see, I could do nothing about the ongoing turbulence of my external environment. This external turbulence, soaked up by me as a young child, was internalised so that it also churned around inside. Thus, the feeling of too-muchness was not just a result of the external situation but also something that emanated from within myself. While my actions might point to the presence of greed – wanting more and more, as if nothing could ever be enough – it also illustrates a process of emptying out. The example in which I describe myself listening to the same song "over and over" suggests that I am draining the object of all aliveness; however, this belies the fact that the object is being used in this instance for the purpose of evacuation. Being in an experience with the object, in other words, facilitated the emptying out of unbearable feelings. These unbearable feelings were also emptied out into other people, for example, the next-door neighbour who offered me her records, possibly because she found my constant playing of the same song unbearable to listen to. Reading, listening to music and watching films allowed me to be some-where while being somewhere else. The repetitive nature of the behaviour also illustrates how dependent I was on the use of cultural objects to interrupt feelings of anxiety and provide a buffer between me and the environmental intrusions around me.

Cultural objects sometimes function as the glue that holds a psychic retreat together. This is an example of the psychopathological functioning of the culture-breast, in which cultural objects and experiences become part of the patient's psychical defence system. While patients might make use of cultural objects and partake in cultural experiences for a variety of conscious reasons, the way in which the aforementioned have become a constituent element of the psychic retreat remains unconscious. John Steiner (1993) remarks that "[t]he patient's view of the retreat is reflected in the descriptions which he gives and also in unconscious phantasy as it is revealed in dreams, memories, and reports from everyday life" (p. 2). I would add that the patient's description of her/his rela-tion to cultural objects and experiences, as well as her/his associations to cultural objects and experiences, tell us something about the structure and function of a particular psychic retreat. It also gives us an indication of what the retreat is defending against. Thus, the cultural objects are, in this instance, not simply the means by which a patient communicates unconscious aspects of a psychic retreat; they are fundamental to the workings of the retreat itself. Steiner (1993) writes of his experience of seeing the presence of psychic retreats across a spectrum of patients, from those exhibiting neurotic to psychotic characteristics (pp. 5, 11). In addition, he remarks on the "range and pervasiveness" (p. 3) of the retreats he has witnessed, from those that appear to be intractable, in which the patient seems to be imprisoned within her/his own defensive system, to those that show some signs of being part of the patient's psychical structure without dominating it completely.

"All gradations of dependence on the retreat are found clinically", Steiner (1993) informs readers, "from the completely stuck patient at one extreme to those who use the retreat in a transient and discretionary way at the other" (p. 3). Not all engagements with cultural objects suggest the presence of a psychic retreat or the psychopathological co-option of cultural objects as part of a retreat's dynam-ics. It is the way in which the cultural object is used, as well as the choice of object itself, that is significant. The part-object functioning of cultural objects as integral to a psychic retreat will become evident to the clinician from the way in which the patient speaks about her/his relation to a particular cultural object or selection of objects, as well as from the frequency with which s/he speaks about the object(s) and the affect attendant to her/his speech acts. The impact of the patient's speaking about particular cultural objects will also register in the clinical practitioner's countertransference. Psychic retreats are, as Steiner (2011) reminds readers, defensive structures to protect the patient from feeling anxiety or pain (p. 1). This might be persecutory anxiety emanating from paranoid-schizoid states of mind or depressive anxiety arising from depressive states of mind. Whatever the source of the anxiety or the psychical positioning of the patient, the patient seeks to sidestep the feelings arising within her/him (p. 11). The cultural object assists her/him in this regard.

Steiner (1993) observes that the psychic retreat serves to assist the patient in avoiding "contact" with the analyst as well as with "reality" (p. 3). He reports that this happens in the case of "perverse, psychotic, and borderline patients" (p. 3). I would counter that all patients seek, in large or small part, "the avoidance of contact with reality" (p. 3). This is because psychic and/or external reality can be crushing. This is something that Steiner (2020) has recently argued in acknowledging that "[j]ust as we need defences, we need illusions", with the proviso that "we also need to be able to emerge from the illusion and face reality" (p. 1). Reality is both denied and acknowledged at the same time, via a process of experiencing what is unbearable through an engagement with a cultural object. The retreat facilitates the patient avoiding while also acknowledging reality by means of an omnipotent attempt to frame and control what counts as reality in that particular moment. This is through a process of absorption in the experiencing of the cultural object via splitting off aspects of experience and projecting them into an array of cultural objects, as well as individuals in the vicinity (such as the next-door neighbour in the example from my own experience). What is pertinent from the perspective of the culture-breast is that the various psychic dynamics get played out in and around cultural objects. Steiner (1993) draws readers' attention to the fact that "what appears as a relatively straightforward split between good and bad is in fact the result of a splitting of the personality into several elements" (p. 7). These split-off parts of the self become lodged in particular cultural objects, some of which are exchangeable while others endure in their importance.

I borrowed books from the teacher's glass case: cultural objects as containers

When I was ten years old I had a teacher who made an indelible impression on me. She lent me books. Classics. "Coming-of-age stories" by novelists mainly from the nineteenth century. She kept these books in a glass case in the classroom beside her desk. Over the course of one school year she lent me a number of books: I can't remember all their titles, but I do remember reading authors like Jane Austen, Charles Dickens, Herman Melville, Charlotte Brontë and Walter Scott. I loved borrowing these books, her books. It made me feel special, like I was visiting my own private library. I read and read, and as I returned each book, she would open the glass case and invite me to take another. I don't remember whether my classmates were lent books from the glass case, but in my mind it was only me. The chosen one. Her favourite.

As I write this chapter, I have come to realise that each of these "classics" was a *Bildungsroman* – novels that chart the personal and professional development of their characters, and which usually feature a protagonist who has to overcome great environmental adversity to reach her/his potential. The experience outlined above became instrumental in my own development as a locus for multiple identifications. I identified both with the teacher and the books. I professed throughout my schooling and university education that I wanted to be either a writer or a teacher. In some ways, I have become both: I teach and I write, with some modifications. I wanted to teach at second level, a direct identification with the teacher, while I have ended up teaching at third level. I desired to write fiction, to carry on the "good" feeling I got from the novels I read, yet I have found myself writing non-fiction. I also identified with the classroom and the library, having manoeuvred myself, via my career, to spend much of my life in both. Perhaps, most starkly, I identified with the glass case itself within which the precious books were housed. The glass case was a safe space, full of knowledge and opportunity and hope. In some ways, it is with the glass case that this book began.

Containment is a clinical concept introduced into psychoanalysis by Wilfred Bion (1962a). A "dyadic, intersubjective process", according to Howard Levine (2011), containment takes place between two people. It

> requires the participation of an object, whose role is to help the individual, be it infant, child or analytic patient, to deal with the "too muchness" of their particular experience by intuiting aspects of the experience that the subject cannot stand to know, making sense of them and responding to that sense in a facilitating manner. When the object's participation in this process is successful, then the object absorbs, makes sense of in some way and then "re-presents" to the individual that which was absorbed, although in a newly transformed and now bearable way.
>
> (p. 190)

Central to containment is the psychical process of projective identification as an unconscious form of communication between two minds: one, for whom a particular experience is too much, and another into whom projections are lodged and held (Cartwright, 2010, p. 1). Melanie Klein (1955) links projective identification to the first three to four months of life when persecutory anxiety is intense and the infant uses splitting to manage it. She lists it among a number of what she terms "primitive" defences, including idealisation, denial and omnipotence. "Identification by projection," she remarks, "implies a combination of splitting off parts of the self and projecting them on to (or rather into) another person. These processes have many ramifications and fundamentally influence object relations" (p. 143). Betty Joseph (1989), commenting on the experience of the patient's employment of projective identification in the consulting room, writes, "Projective identification is a phantasy and yet it can have a powerful effect on the recipient" (p. 169).

Projective identification is utilised for a variety of reasons, including the need to get rid of intolerable thoughts or feelings; in an attempt to control, harm, or destroy the object; and in an effort to deny separation between the subject and the object. Projective identification takes place, among other things, at the breast. The infant's feeding at the breast is, according to Wilfred Bion, an emotional experience as well as a physical one. The process of containment integrates these two experiences, and perhaps this is why he uses metaphors of food, feeding, digestion and excretion to explore projective and introjective processes, psychical development and the formation of a thinking apparatus in the infant. The infant's first relationship is with a part-object, her/his mother's breast. This is where s/he will find mental, emotional and physical sustenance. Using phrases such as "mental alimentary system" (Bion, 1962a, p. 102, n. 12.6.1), Bion makes a correlation between the receipt of milk and love, the latter being "comparable with milk for the mental welfare of the child" (p. 33). The mother's love for her infant is expressed, in part, through her capacity for containment. In other words, the infant who finds herself/himself experiencing intolerable states splits off, evacuates and projects what Bion terms beta-elements into the mother. If the mother can receive these projections as a communication rather than simply an attack that needs to be defended against, she can bring her ability to think to bear on the situation in order to make sense of what feels to be, to the infant, overwhelming experiences.

Bion labels the mother's openness to receiving whatever the infant sends her way "reverie": It is

> that state of mind which is open to the reception of any "objects" from the loved object and is therefore capable of reception of the infant's projective identifications whether they are felt by the infant to be good or bad. In short, reverie is a factor in the mother's alpha-function.
>
> (p. 36)

As a result of her capacity for alpha-function, the mother transforms the beta-elements she receives from the infant into alpha-elements; what were otherwise meaningless, intolerable experiences now become both meaningful and manageable. They can now be re-introjected in a modified form by the infant. The infant is therefore contained ($\male$) by the mother as container ($\female$). Bion (1962a) uses the term "nameless dread" (p. 96) to refer to instances in which the infant projects intolerable states into the mother but instead of containing them, they are rejected and thus projected back into the infant without any modification or meaning having been made of them. This may be because the mother lacks the capacity to contain the projections (Bott Spillius, 1992, pp. 61–62) or because the infant is unable to tolerate or accept the mother's containing function (Caper, 1999, p. 144). If repeated time and again, this leads to an unbearable situation for the infant in which the experience of containment itself becomes something to be feared.

Culture-breast containers give meaning to experiences which would otherwise be meaningless (Figure 3.5). They both hold and transform the too-muchness of experience, offering it back to the patient in a more manageable and meaningful form. This is particularly in the case of traumatic experiences. This is achieved via processes of projective and introjective identification when the patient splits off aspects of her/his experience which are too much to manage and projects them into the cultural object. Repeated contact with the specific object is required for it

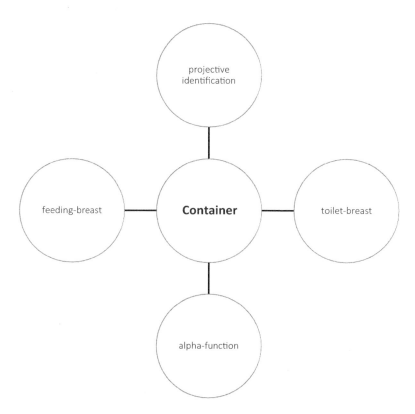

Figure 3.5 Cultural objects as containers

to provide meaning. This meaning is not simply intellectual; attachment to the cultural object will be conscious, but the psychical role it performs will be unknown to the person. I will explore and highlight the workings of the culture-breast as a container through a consideration of two brief vignettes:

> *I read and re-read William Golding's* The Lord of the Flies *(1954). It was my favourite novel, so prized that I would not read any of Golding's other novels.*
> *I visited Francis Danby's painting, "The Opening of the Sixth Seal" (1828), in the National Gallery of Ireland many times. My visits felt like a pilgrimage. I would gaze at it and attempt to take it in.*

The two vignettes reveal aspects of the emotional atmosphere of my childhood home: the chaos, the menace, the too-muchness. It is all here. William Golding's (1954) novel *The Lord of the Flies* tells the story of a group of boys, stranded on an island, and the gradual disintegration of order, empathy and civility among them. They become like beasts, completely identified with the id as the superego and ego fall away (Freud, 1923a). There is one scene, the last scene, which is deeply meaningful for me. It is when an adult naval officer "rescues" them from the island. As they emerge from the burning undergrowth, with three of their number deceased, they begin to cry. The officer "turned away to give them time to pull themselves together; and waited, allowing his eyes to rest on the trim cruiser in the distance" (p. 223). Francis Danby's (1828) painting "The Opening of the Sixth Seal" depicts the beginning of the apocalypse, as it is described in the biblical *Book of Revelation* (Figure 3.6). It is a large painting, and its detail is impossible to take in via the gaze. One ("The Opening of the Sixth Seal") details the moment at which things fall apart, while the other (*The Lord of the Flies*) represents the aftermath when nothing will ever be the same again. They are dramatic scenes, evocative yet difficult to describe in words. They demand to be felt, even if they cannot be understood. Both scenes are concerned with trauma – a small word that stands in for the enormity of an overwhelming experience too painful for the mind to comprehend. Trauma is a spectacle, one that is inarticulate to those in its midst. "The Opening of the Sixth Seal" (1828) happens because humankind deserves to be punished, which might also be said about the "shak[ing] and sob[bing]" boys (Golding, 1954, p. 223) at the end of *The Lord of the Flies*. Some of those same boys have also spent sections of the novel relentlessly bullying and punishing those most vulnerable among them. Growing up felt a bit like being on that island in Golding's novel, with all of us running around the house like lost children, some just bigger than others. I held both of these cultural objects close, literally and unconsciously. I bought copies of the novel and painting and displayed them in my bedroom.

The culture-breast is, above all else, a container. We all feed at the culture-breast; some of us more than others. Cultural objects can become containers for experiences, feelings and/or thoughts that are too difficult to manage. These unbearable experiences are held by the object at a safe distance – the patient sees what is within her/himself as if it forms part of the cultural object. The cultural object operates as a toilet-breast (Meltzer, 1967b, p. 20) on these occasions, to expel the too-muchness of experience. Cultural objects can also contain experiences that patients consider to be good, yet vulnerable to spoiling, so the experiences are split off and projected into the object for safe-keeping. The cultural object then becomes associated with these good experiences as a feeding-breast (Meltzer, 1973, p. ix), offering psychical nourishment. The culture-breast can function as a toilet-breast and a feeding-breast simultaneously, and oftentimes does. This is because patients who make use of cultural objects as containers have generally had access to a limited number of adults who could perform this role. The adults have oftentimes been professionals of one sort or another (teachers, social workers, general medical practitioners), so access to them has been structured and outside the child's control. In writing about psychic retreats, John

Figure 3.6 Francis Danby (1793–1861), "The Opening of the Sixth Seal", 1828, oil on canvas, 185 × 255 cm, NGI.162, National Gallery of Ireland Collection

Source: © National Gallery of Ireland

Steiner (1993) makes reference to "the containing function" in the context of the operation of a retreat:

> what appears as a relatively straightforward split between good and bad is in fact the result of a splitting of the personality into several elements, each projected into objects and reassembled in a manner which stimulates the containing function of the object.
>
> (p. 7)

The functioning of a psychic retreat and a container differs with regards to the culture-breast, in the way in which the patient employs the object.

In the case of a psychic retreat, contact with the object, often transferable, needs to be continuously maintained in order to cultivate the protective properties of the object. What I mean by "transferable" is that one cultural object – such as a particular film – can be exchanged for another object – a different film or song or novel, for example – without the experience produced being necessarily disrupted. There is a noticeable level of activity evident – this might be identifiable in the content or delivery of the patient's speech while talking about the cultural object(s) or experience(s), or in a sustained countertransference reaction that might be instantaneous or become more palpable over time. There is a repetitiveness to the engagement with the cultural object, and there is also often a manic aspect to this engagement, particularly in times of stress or distress. The use of the object is akin to the movement of a castle's drawbridge. The drawbridge is almost up, but it keeps lowering – the purpose of the cultural object is to attempt to close the gap and secure the defensive system. The use of a cultural object for the purpose of containment departs from this, though it might at first appear to replicate the work of a psychic retreat. In the case of a container, the cultural object is projected into via a process of projective identification. The object itself becomes significant to the patient. The experience engendered in the patient as a result of making contact with the object also takes on an importance in the patient's psychic life. The affect is often compelling and present from the first time the patient comes into contact with the object.

While a psychic retreat requires concrete contact with a cultural object (playing a song, reading a poem), containment by a cultural object is different in one significant respect: when the patient projects into the cultural object, the object holds and metabolises the too-muchness of experience, offering it back to the patient in a modified form, which can then be re-introjected by the patient in a more manageable and meaningful way. The patient is contained by the cultural object as a container (Bion, 1963, p. 6). This describes the process that happens between two minds in definitions of containment. For example, Elizabeth Bott Spillius and her colleagues (2011g) make reference to containment as a process in which "one person in some sense contains a part of another" (p. 280). Elsewhere, Duncan Cartwright (2010) introduces containment as developing from Bion's belief that "projective identifications, split-off parts of the self that are located in other objects, required containment in another mind if they were to be modified in some way" (p. 1). So, containment by a cultural object departs from containment by another person with a mind that is open to receiving the patient's projections. Containment by a cultural object is containment by the patient's own mind, performing two functions at once: projector and container. Containment is therefore limited, though this does not lessen its importance or effectiveness to patients who need it. Containment by the culture-breast transforms the patient's projective identifications into thoughts. As a result, the patient does not need to be in the vicinity of the cultural object or crave active engagement with it in the concrete way a psychic retreat demands. The relation to the cultural object is a symbolic one. It is meaningful, though the full extent of the meaning, what continues to be split off, eludes the patient. The full meaning of the patient's psychical attachment to cultural objects can only become possibly known, though not always, through a psychoanalytic process, with a practitioner who is attuned to the place of cultural objects in the psychical lives of us all.

Feeding and weaning

Donald Winnicott (1953) describes weaning as signifying a psychological process rather than simply something that occurs at the level of the physiological: "The mere termination of breast-feeding is not a weaning" (p. 17). Winnicott (1936) considers weaning "one of several critical times of early childhood" (p. 43), while René Allendy (quoted in Anna Freud, 1929, p. 494) refers to it as one of the "great complexes" alongside the Oedipus and castration complexes. It is central to early development and encompasses a great deal of emotional turmoil for the baby and her/his mother (Lubbe, 1996; Daws, 1997). Its beginning is, according to Melanie Klein (1952a), "a major crisis in the infant's life" (p. 118, n. 2). The term "weaning" routinely appears in clinical writings about the analytic process (Meltzer, 1978), particularly in relation to the experience of patients in reaction to the analyst's breaks (Joseph, 1966, p. 186; Segal, 1988, p. 171) or the termination phase of analysis (Segal, 1958, p. 180; Glover, 1927, p. 319).

In a discussion about the formation of symptoms, Sigmund Freud (1917[1916–1917e) gives an example of the feeling of disgust often experienced in reaction to instances when a "skin forms on milk" (p. 366). This is in contrast to the "satisfaction" once experienced while feeding at the breast (p. 367). Weaning, he says, is situated between these two states. Its "traumatic effects" have been repressed, and in its place the individual experiences disgust. Elsewhere, when considering castration, Freud (1926) likens it to "losing the mother's breast at weaning" (pp. 129–130). So, weaning is underpinned by loss. It is not just characterised by loss. Weaning provokes a state of ambivalence, which George Klein (1973) comments "involves the irreconcilability of the desire to be at the breast with a desire to be free of it" (p. 13). Winnicott (1963) makes a link between cases in which infants "wean themselves" and the infant's growing capacity for concern, which prompts the infant to become "inhibited", out of an effort to protect her/his mother from the expression of her/his oral sadism (p. 76).

Loss, ambivalence and concern are all constituent elements of the depressive position, which Melanie Klein (1952a, 106, n. 2) links with weaning and the loss of the breast: "The loss of the first loved object is felt to confirm all the infant's anxieties of a persecutory and depressive nature" (p. 107). The way in which weaning is managed has a long-lasting effect on the infant, so much so that Klein recommends "a careful and slow weaning" because "an abrupt weaning, by suddenly reinforcing [the infant's anxiety], may impair his emotional development" (p. 118). It is in the depressive position that the child slowly begins to experience the mother as a whole person rather than simply as a part-object or series of part-objects to gratify her/his needs (Klein, 1952b, p. 76, Klein, 1960, p. 272). This process is not without its difficulties. The child now has to come to terms with the fact that it is the same mother who both provides for and frustrates her/him; towards whom s/he feels love and hate, or ambivalence. A similar weaning process needs to be undergone by the patient suckled by the culture-breast and relying on cultural objects and experiences to manage her/his relation with her/himself and the world around her/him. It is important that the psychoanalytic psychotherapist treating the patient does not underestimate the fact that the patient's psychical survival depends on these same objects; to be deprived of them before s/he has the psychical resources to manage the loss would be like being divested of oxygen.

Patients are weaned off their dependence on the culture-breast through the transference relationship (Figure 3.7). This is gradual and cannot be rushed. A significant amount of regression is required for the patient to latch onto the analyst and let go of the culture-breast. This is particularly difficult for patients who engage in intellectualisation and rationalisation. The loss of control can feel overwhelming, with the result that s/he can retreat back into a reliance on cultural objects to fend off the analyst and empty out any intensification of feelings brought on through engagement in the analytic process. The weaning process will provoke both frustration and pain. The analyst will notice a significant acceleration in the number of complaints uttered by the patient, about all aspects of life, while at the same time appearing to almost starve her/himself of cultural experiences that had hitherto appeared to bring the patient great pleasure. The frustration is a defence against pain and the loss of the dependence on the cultural object, which eventually, if it can be borne, will lead to the experiencing of intense loss at the original situation that led to her/him becoming dependent on the culture-breast in the first place. If this psychic pain can be experienced and worked through, the patient will come to a less gratifying and more satisfactory relation to cultural objects, and to her/his objects more broadly. Lisa Baraitser (2017) refers to working through as "the slow and arduous process of not just learning something mildly interesting about yourself, but becoming yourself" (p. 186). The patient's symbolisation of her/his relationship with the culture-breast leads to a recognition of cultural objects as a one-time, though no longer,

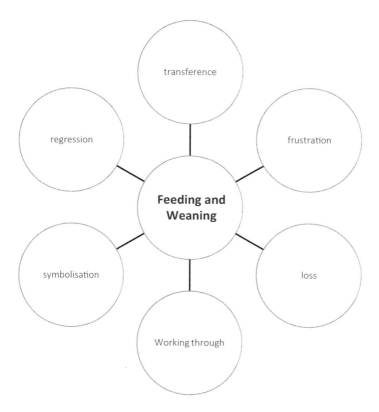

Figure 3.7 Feeding and weaning

necessity; a substitute for living life. This insight will free the patient up psychically to engage more fully in the world.

Chapter 3 has introduced "the culture-breast", a new clinical concept to address the therapeutic challenges encountered by patients whose environmental deprivation prompts their psychical reliance on cultural objects for functions optimally performed by human caregivers. While often showing an impressive resilience for psychical survival in the face of considerable environmental adversity, patients who depend on cultural objects in this way tend to develop rigid psychical defences which impact on their capacity to relate to themselves and others, while draining experience of aliveness. Part of the analytic work with patients who use cultural objects in this way involves weaning them off the culture-breast through the transference relationship, towards a more satisfactory relationship with her/ his objects, cultural and otherwise. This is painful work for patients and can take several years. I explored the operation of the culture-breast as a screen memory, a psychic retreat and a container through an analysis of brief vignettes from my own life. In doing so, I incorporated a psychosocial case study, and thus invite other psychoanalytic practitioners to reflect more on the evolution of their own clinical and theoretical innovations. We are more than our clinical work, and to put everything on our patients misses an opportunity to take a risk and learn something about ourselves, which, in turn, can facilitate us working in more depth with our patients.

Experience and the no-breast

In the documentary, *Max Richter's Sleep* (2020), Richter, who is a composer, musician and the subject of the film, says that "making creative things is . . . a kind of self-medicating in a way . . . you write the piece that you wish someone had written so you can listen to it". The documentary focuses on Richter's (2015) sumptuous and affecting work, *Sleep*, which has been performed live over an eight-hour period in a variety of locations, including London, Los Angeles, Sydney and Paris. Audience members are invited to listen to Richter, other musicians and a vocalist performing his "lullaby" (Ellis-Peterson, 2015) in concert; to fall asleep together. Music appears to function as a culture-breast for Richter (2020), who remarks that it "is my sort of vehicle for travelling through the world, you know, and for sort of, getting through life. It's like I write music to do that". It is a container. Richter and his creative partner Yulia Mahr carefully choreograph each concert to offer attendees an object while not foreclosing their experience of that object, or what they might do with their experience. The performance of *Sleep* (Richter, 2015) provides a facilitating environment for people to have an experience that is unique to each individual while also creating something that is shared with a group – some of whom are asleep and some of whom are awake. *Sleep* operationalises the evocative (Bollas, 1987), transitional (Winnicott, 1953) and transformational (Bollas, 1992b) aspects of music as a cultural object. It is a resonant reminder of music's affective pull. Richter (2020) makes an observation during the documentary which is relevant to the subject matter of this book, and particularly to my approach:

> I think of making a piece of writing and sort of creative work as sort of . . . It's like now moving from a space which we know into a space we don't know. And that's . . . that's the kind of interesting part. And actually it hardly matters what's there. It's that little process of just stepping into somewhere you don't know. At a certain point, it's almost like the piece starts dreaming.

The Culture-Breast in Psychoanalysis invites readers to move into a space of not knowing, and see what happens.

The experiencing of this space of not knowing can feel like a no-breast. Wilfred Bion uses the term "no-breast" to refer to a situation in which the infant moves towards the breast, with the expectation that it will be there, but instead finds that it is not. In this situation, there is "an infant whose expectation of a breast is mated with a realization of no breast available for satisfaction" (Bion, 1962b, p. 111). This experience is persecutory for the infant with the result that the absence outside is internalised and registered as an absence inside; a no-breast. This is not recognised by the infant as an absence, but rather as a presence; the presence being a bad breast or no-breast: "objectively there is an absence, but for the infant there is no such thing as an absence, merely the presence of something causing the pain" (Hinshelwood, 1991, p. 74). Inside and outside become indistinguishable. Bion refers to the "no-breast" as "the absent breast" (1965, p. 54), "a non-existent breast" (1965, p. 76), "a 'need-of-a-breast' bad breast" (1962a, p. 58), "a very bad breast inside" (1962a, p. 57). The no-breast "gives [the infant] painful feelings" (Bion, 1962a, p. 57), which are difficult to manage. These are an amalgam of "painful lumps of faeces, guilt, fears of impending death, chunks of greed, meanness and urine" (Bion, 1963, p. 31). The feelings become mixed up with bodily excretions; they become one and the same in the distressed infant's mind, a mess. Bion (1962a) writes of "two situations":

> one of which is an actual breast, indistinguishable from an emotional experience which in turn is thing-in-itself and thought, but in an undifferentiated state, and the other the bad "need-of-a-breast" bad breast which is equally an object compounded of emotional experience and thing-in-itself the two being as yet undifferentiated, it is clear that we have arrived at an object very closely resembling a beta-element.
>
> (p. 58)

These difficult feelings are referred to, by Bion (1962b), as "frustration" (p. 112). How the infant manages frustration will determine whether the experience becomes a thought. I use the word "whether" because it is presented as an either/ or by Bion; a split: "it depends on whether the decision is to evade frustration or to modify it. If the capacity for toleration of frustration is sufficient the 'no-breast' inside becomes a thought and an apparatus for 'thinking' it develops" (p. 112). The psychical process of evasion, evacuation, projection and gratification differs from modification and thought in a notable respect: "evacuation of a bad breast is synonymous with obtaining sustenance from a good breast" (p. 112). The development of thought requires "capacity", according to Bion (p. 111), specifically the capacity to tolerate frustration (p. 112).

These psychical processes, outlined by Bion with reference to the infant, persist into adulthood. They describe a number of mental states that are separate yet inter-related, and, sometimes, enmeshed: need, anticipation, expectation, realisation, surprise, frustration, reaction. Thus, they relate to how we encounter objects, react to situations and process experiences. They are bound up, as this book is, with how we take in experiences and what we do with those same experiences, particularly when they are not what we would anticipate or expect. This is especially true in situations when a demand is placed on us to think in ways that might be new or unfamiliar. I will return to something Bion (1962b) wrote, which I cited earlier: "evacuation of a bad breast is synonymous with obtaining sustenance from a good breast" (p. 112). Evacuation is aligned here with finding one external object to replace another external object; a good breast that is present to replace a bad breast that is absent. An object is sought in the external environment to get rid of an object in the internal environment. The two experiences – "evacuation" and "obtaining sustenance" – are not just related; they are "synonymous". Taking in and getting rid of are reduced to one and the same. I will include another quotation from Bion's work also cited earlier: "If the capacity for toleration of frustration is sufficient the 'no-breast' inside becomes a thought and an apparatus for 'thinking' it develops" (p. 112). Thought, therefore, displays a capacity not just to tolerate frustration over time ("becomes" and "develops" suggest it is not immediate) but to represent one's experience to oneself. To produce something from no-thing, and in the process to give to oneself rather than to get rid of; to make meaning. What was a no-breast becomes a thought. This process is akin to what it means to learn from experience (Bion, 1962a), to use an object (Winnicott, 1971a), to symbolise (Bott Spillius et al., 2011b).

Returning to this book as a reader, I have come to realise that *The Culture-Breast in Psychoanalysis* is, like all books, both a breast and a no-breast. The reader receives something, though that something might not be what the reader expects. This is because while the reader receives something from the book, this is not all the reader receives. The reader also receives whatever is evoked in her/him as a consequence of encountering the book, though that might not be evident at first. The reader thus receives something from her/himself, though s/he might not initially recognise it as such. This experience, which is unique to each reader, is related to, though also separate from, the book as an object. Bion has referred to experience as "O" when writing about the clinical situation (Giffney, 2013a, pp. 219–222). O emerges in the here and now. It is unknowable and can only be experienced (Bion, 1970b, p. 26, 1970d, p. 52). "The only point of importance in any session", Bion (1967b) remarks, "is the unknown. Nothing must be allowed to distract from intuiting that" (p. 381). This is one of the reasons I thought Jennifer Rubell's sculpture "Us" (2015a) was such a good fit for the cover image of this book. A book is never an "I"; it is always an "Us". It only makes sense within the context of an encounter with a reader. To return to a quotation from an interview with Rubell (2018), which I included in the preface, "The piece *is* the interaction between the person and the object", adding that "the object is the only part of the interaction that I have any control over. I can only offer a prompt to that interaction" (p. 34). I offer *The Culture-Breast in Psychoanalysis* to the reader as "a prompt" for her/his "interaction", and invite the reader to reflect on whatever emerges in the process.

References

Books and journal articles

Aaron, Michele (2007). *Spectatorship: The Power of Looking On*. London and New York, NY: Wallflower Press.

Abse, Susanna (2007). Review of Prophecy Coles (Ed.), *Sibling Relationships* (London: Karnac, 2006). *Journal of Analytical Psychology* 52.4: 509–511.

Ackerman, Sarah (2018). (How) can we write about our patients? *Journal of the American Psychoanalytical Association* 66.1: 59–81.

Akhtar, Salman (2012). Editor's introduction: The "new" applied psychoanalysis. *International Journal of Applied Psychoanalytic Studies* 9.4: 364–365.

——— and Stuart Twemlow (Eds.) (2018a). *Textbook of Applied Psychoanalysis*. London and New York, NY: Routledge.

——— (2018b). Introduction. In *Textbook of Applied Psychoanalysis* (pp. xxxi–xxxii). London and New York, NY: Routledge.

Anderson, Daniel (2019). Sexual polyphony and the necessary failure of group analysis. *Studies in Gender & Sexuality* 20.4: 238–241.

——— and Jackie Stacey (2018). (Conveners). Queer theory and psychoanalysis. Sexuality Summer School, University of Manchester, Manchester, UK.

Anzieu, Didier (1979). The sound image of the self. *International Review of Psycho-Analysis* 6: 23–36.

Arts & Health (2011–). URL www.artsandhealth.ie. Accessed 28 November 2019.

Association for Psychosocial Studies (2013–). URL www.psychosocial-studies-association.org. Accessed 5 March 2020.

Astor, James (1989). The breast as part of the whole: Theoretical considerations concerning whole and part objects. *Journal of Analytical Psychology* 34.2: 117–128.

Auestad, Lene (Ed.) (2012). *Psychoanalysis and Politics: Exclusion and the Politics of Representation*. London: Karnac.

——— and Amal Treacher Kabesh (Eds.) (2017). *Traces of Violence and Freedom of Thought*. Basingstoke and New York, NY: Palgrave Macmillan.

Bainbridge, Caroline (2011). From "the Freud squad" to "the good Freud guide": A genealogy of media images of psychoanalysis and reflections on their role in the public imagination. *Free Associations* 12.2: 31–59.

——— (2014). Psychotherapy on the couch: Exploring the fantasies of *in treatment*. In Caroline Bainbridge, Ivan Ward and Candida Yates (Eds.), *Television and Psychoanalysis: Psycho-cultural Perspectives* (pp. 47–65). London: Karnac.

———— (2019a). On the experience of a melancholic gaze. *British Journal of Psychother-apy* 35.1: 142–155.

———— (2019b). Box-set mind-set: Psycho-cultural approaches to binge watching, gender, and digital experience. *Free Associations: Psychoanalysis and Culture, Media, Groups, Politics* 75: 65–83.

———— (2020). Who will fix it for us? Toxic celebrity and the therapeutic dynamics of media. *Celebrity Studies* 11.1: 75–88.

————, Susannah Radstone, Michael Rustin and Candida Yates (Eds.) (2007). *Culture and the Unconscious*. Basingstoke and New York, NY: Palgrave Macmillan.

————, Ivan Ward and Candida Yates (Eds.) (2014a). *Television and Psychoanalysis: Psycho-Cultural Perspectives*. London: Karnac.

———— (2014b). Preface. In Caroline Bainbridge, Ivan Ward and Candida Yates (Eds.), *Television and Psychoanalysis: Psycho-Cultural Perspectives* (pp. xv–xvii). London: Karnac.

———— and Candida Yates (2011). Therapy culture/culture as therapy: Psycho-cultural studies of media and the inner world. *Free Associations: Psychoanalysis and Culture, Media, Groups, Politics* 62: i–v.

———— (2012). Introduction to special issue on media and the inner world: New perspec-tives on psychoanalysis and popular culture. *Psychoanalysis, Culture & Society* 17.2: 113–119.

———— (Eds.) (2014a). *Media and the Inner World: Psycho-cultural Approaches to Emo-tion, Media and Popular Culture*. Basingstoke and New York, NY: Palgrave Macmillan.

———— (2014b). Introduction: Psycho-cultural approaches to emotion, media and popular culture. In Caroline Bainbridge and Candida Yates (Eds.), *Media and the Inner World: Psycho-cultural Approaches to Emotion, Media and Popular Culture* (pp. 1–16). Bas-ingstoke and New York, NY: Palgrave Macmillan.

Baradon, Tessa (2002). Psychotherapeutic work with parents and infants – Psychoanalytic and attachment perspectives. *Attachment and Human Development* 4.1: 25–38.

———— (2005). "What is genuine maternal love?" Clinical considerations and technique in psychoanalytic parent-infant psychotherapy. *Psychoanalytic Study of the Child* 60.1: 47–73.

———— (2015). Preface. In Tessa Baradon, Michela Biseo, Carol Broughton, Jessica James and Angela Joyce (Eds.), *The Practice of Parent-Infant Psychotherapy: Claiming the Baby*, 2nd ed. (pp. xi–xiv). London and New York, NY: Routledge, 2005.

Baraitser, Lisa (2008). *Maternal Encounters: The Ethics of Interruption*. London and New York, NY: Routledge.

———— (2015). Temporal drag: Transdisciplinarity and the "case" of psychosocial studies. *Theory, Culture & Society* 32.5–6: 207–231.

———— (2016). Postmaternal, postwork and the maternal death drive. *Australian Feminist Studies* 31.90: 393–409.

———— (2017). *Enduring Time*. London and New York, NY: Bloomsbury Academic.

———— (2019). Introduction. *Studies in Gender & Sexuality* 20.4: 209–213.

———— and Laura Salisbury (2020). Containment, delay, mitigation: Waiting and care in the time of a pandemic. Waiting and care in pandemic times collection, 12 pp. URL https://wellcomeopenresearch.org/articles/5-129. Accessed 16 July 2020.

———— and Sigal Spigel (2009). Editorial. *Studies in the maternal* 1.1, no page numbers. URL www.mamsie.bbk.ac.uk/articles/10.16995/sim.170/. Accessed 29 June 2020.

Bartlett, Vanessa (2019). Psychosocial curating: A theory and practice of exhibition-making at the intersection between health and aesthetics. *Medical Humanities*. doi:10.1136/ medhum-2019-011694.

Bateman, Anthony and Peter Fonagy (2016). *Mentalization-Based Treatment for Personality Disorders*. Oxford: Oxford University Press.

Baudry, Francis (1984). An essay on method in applied psychoanalysis. *Psychoanalytic Quarterly* 53.4: 551–581.

——— (1992). Faulkner's *as I lay dying*: Issues of method in applied analysis. *Psychoanalytic Quarterly* 61.1: 65–83.

Bell, David (Ed.) (1999). *Psychoanalysis and Culture: A Kleinian Perspective*. London and New York, NY: Routledge.

Bennett, Jill, Lynn Froggett and Lizzie Muller (2019). Psychosocial aesthetics and the art of lived experience. *Journal of Psychosocial Studies* 12.1–2: 185–201.

Bergler, Edmund (1937). Further observations on the clinical picture of "psychogenic oral aspermia". *International Journal of Psychoanalysis* 18: 196–234.

Berke, Joseph H. and Stanley Schneider (1994). Antithetical meanings of "the breast". *International Journal of Psychoanalysis* 75.3: 491–498.

Bick, Esther (1964). Infant observation in psycho-analytic training. In Frances Thomson Salo (Ed.), *Infant Observation: Creating Transformative Relationships* (pp. 17–28). London: Karnac, 2014.

——— (2001). Anxieties underlying phobia of sexual intercourse in a woman. *British Journal of Psychotherapy* 18.1: 7–21.

Bion, Wilfred R. (1959). Attacks on linking. In *Second Thoughts* (pp. 93–109). London: Karnac, 1984.

——— (1962a). *Learning from Experience*. London: Karnac, 1984.

——— (1962b). A theory of thinking. In *Second Thoughts* (pp. 110–119). London: Karnac, 1984[1967].

——— (1963). *Elements of Psychoanalysis*. London: Karnac, 1984.

——— (1965). *Transformations*. London: Karnac, 1984.

——— (1967a). Commentary. In *Second Thoughts* (pp. 120–166). London: Karnac, 1984.

——— (1967b). Notes on memory and desire. In *Cogitations*, new extended ed. (pp. 380–385). London: Karnac, 1994.

——— (1970a). Introduction. In *Attention and Interpretation* (pp. 1–5). London: Karnac, 1984.

——— (1970b). Reality sensuous and psychic. In *Attention and Interpretation* (pp. 26–40). London: Karnac, 1984.

——— (1970c). Container and contained. In *Attention and Interpretation* (pp. 72–82). London: Karnac, 1984.

——— (1970d). Opacity of memory and desire. In *Attention and Interpretation* (pp. 41–54). London: Karnac, 1984.

——— (1970e). Medicine as a model. In *Attention and Interpretation* (pp. 6–25). London: Karnac, 1984.

——— (1977). *The Italian Seminars*, trans. Philip Slotkin. London and New York, NY: Routledge, 2018.

——— (1994). *Cogitations*, new extended ed. London: Karnac.

——— (1997). *Taming Wild Thoughts*. London: Karnac.

Birksted-Breen, Dana (2010–2011). The psychoanalytic setting. In Caterina Albano, Liz Allison and Nicola Abel-Hirsch (Eds.), *Psychoanalysis: The Unconscious in Everyday Life* (pp. 53–58). London: Science Museum, Institute of Psychoanalysis and Artakt.

Blass, Rachel B. (2010). How does psychoanalytic practice differ from psychotherapy? The implications of the difference for the development of psychoanalytic training and practice. *International Journal of Psychoanalysis* 91.1: 15–21.

――― (2013). Introduction: What does the presentation of case material tell us about what actually happened in an analysis and how does it do this? *International Journal of Psychoanalysis* 94.6: 1129–1134.

――― (2018). The teaching of Klein: Some guidelines for opening students to the heart of Kleinian thinking and practice. In Penelope Garvey and Kay Long (Eds.), *The Klein Tradition* (pp. 73–90). London and New York, NY: Routledge.

Boesky, Dale (2013). What does the presentation of case material tell us about what actually happened in an analysis and how does it do this? *International Journal of Psychoanalysis* 94.6: 1135–1143.

Bohleber, Werner (2012). The use of public and of private implicit theories in the clinical situation. In Jorge Canestri (Ed.), *Putting Theory to Work: How Are Theories Actually Used in Practice?* (pp. 1–22). London: Karnac.

Bollas, Christopher (1987). The transformational object. In *The Shadow of the Object: Psychoanalysis of the Unthought Known* (pp. 13–29). London: Free Association Books.

――― (1992a). Aspects of self experiencing. In *Being a Character: Psychoanalysis and Self Experience* (pp. 14–30). London and New York, NY: Routledge, 1993.

――― (1992b). The evocative object. In *Being a Character: Psychoanalysis and Self Experience* (pp. 32–42). London and New York, NY: Routledge, 1993.

――― (2009). The evocative object world. In *The Evocative Object World* (pp. 79–94). London and New York, NY: Routledge.

Boris, Harold N. (1986). The "other" breast – Greed, envy, spite and revenge. *Contemporary Psychoanalysis* 22.1: 45–59.

Bott Spillius, Elizabeth (1992). Clinical experiences of projective identification. In Robin Anderson (Ed.), *Clinical Lectures on Klein and Bion* (pp. 59–73). London and New York, NY: Routledge.

――― (2012). Developments by British Kleinian analysts. In Elizabeth Spillius and Edna O'Shaughnessy (Eds.), *Projective Identification: The Fate of a Concept* (pp. 50–60). London and New York, NY: Routledge.

―――, Jane Milton, Penelope Garvey, Cyril Couve and Deborah Steiner (2011a). Paranoid-schizoid position. In *The New Dictionary of Kleinian Thought* (pp. 63–83). London and New York, NY: Routledge.

――― (2011b). Symbol formation. In *The New Dictionary of Kleinian Thought* (pp. 184–193). London and New York, NY: Routledge.

――― (2011c). Persecution. In *The New Dictionary of Kleinian Thought* (pp. 438–440). London and New York, NY: Routledge.

――― (2011d). Depressive anxiety. In *The New Dictionary of Kleinian Thought* (pp. 310–315). London and New York, NY: Routledge.

――― (2011e). Internal objects. In *The New Dictionary of Kleinian Thought* (pp. 40–62). London and New York, NY: Routledge.

――― (2011f). Part-objects. In *The New Dictionary of Kleinian Thought* (pp. 434–436). London and New York, NY: Routledge.

――― (2011g). Container/contained. In *The New Dictionary of Kleinian Thought* (pp. 279–285). London and New York, NY: Routledge.

――― (2011h). Countertransference. In *The New Dictionary of Kleinian Thought* (pp. 288–294). London and New York, NY: Routledge.

Bowlby, John (1979). Psychoanalysis as art and science. *International Review of Psycho-Analysis* 6: 3–14.

Boyle Spelman, Margaret (2013). *Winnicott's Babies and Winnicott's Patients: Psychoanalysis as Transitional Space*. London: Karnac.

Brafman, A.H. (2018). *Life in the Consulting Room: Portraits*. London and New York, NY: Routledge.

Brenman Pick, Irma (1985a). Working through in the counter-transference. In Elizabeth Bott Spillius (Ed.), *Melanie Klein Today: Developments in Theory and Practice, Vol. 2: Mainly Practice* (pp. 34–47). London and New York, NY: Routledge.

———— (1985b). Male sexuality: A clinical study of forces that impede development. In Irma Brenman Pick, M. Fakhry Davids and Naomi Shavit (Eds.), *Authenticity in the Psychoanalytic Encounter* (pp. 159–171). London and New York, NY: Routledge, 2018.

———— (2008). Reflections on *envy and gratitude*. In Priscilla Roth and Alessandra Lemma (Eds.), *Envy and Gratitude*, revisited ed. (pp. 186–200). London: Karnac.

———— (2018). Working through in the countertransference revisited: Experiences of supervision. In M. Fakhry Davids and Naomi Shavit (Eds.), *Authenticity in the Psychoanalytic Encounter: The Work of Irma Brenman Pick* (pp. 48–62). London and New York, NY: Routledge, 2018.

Breuer, Joseph (1895). Fräulein Anna O. In Sigmund Freud and Joseph Breuer (Eds.), *Studies in Hysteria*, trans. Nicola Luckhurst (pp. 25–50). London: Penguin.

British Psychoanalytic Council (2017). (Convener). Contemporary developments in sexuality and gender and their impact on the consulting room. Psychoanalytic Psychotherapy Now Conference: The Inner World and the State We're In, Imperial College, London, UK.

Britzman, Deborah P. (2015). *A Psychoanalyst in the Classroom: On the Human Condition in Education*. Albany and New York, NY: State University of New York Press.

Brontë (1847). *Jane Eyre*. London: Penguin, 2006.

Budd, Susan (1997). Ask me no questions and I'll tell you no lies: The social organization of secrets. In Ivan Ward (Ed.), *The Presentation of Case Material in Clinical Discourse* (pp. 29–44). London: Freud Museum.

Buechler, Sandra (2015). *Understanding and Treating Patients in Psychoanalysis: Lessons from Literature*. London and New York, NY: Routledge.

Bullard, Ashley R. (2017). Review of Kath Woodward's *Psychosocial Studies: An Introduction. Journal for Psycho-Social Studies* 10.1: 84–87.

Burman, Erica (2008). Resisting the deradicalization of psychosocial analyses. *Psychoanalysis, Culture & Society* 13.4: 374–378.

Canestri, Jorge (2012a). Introduction. In Jorge Canestri (Ed.), *Putting Theory to Work: How Are Theories Actually Used in Practice?* (pp. xix–xxx). London: Karnac.

———— (2012b). Conclusions. In Jorge Canestri (Ed.), *Putting Theory to Work: How Are Theories Actually Used in Practice?* (pp. 157–183). London: Karnac.

Caper, Robert (1999). *A Mind of One's Own: A Psychoanalytic View of Self and Object*. London and New York, NY: Routledge.

Carey, Faye (2018). *The Place of the Visual in Psychoanalytic Practice: Image in the Countertransference*. London and New York, NY: Routledge.

Cartwright, Duncan (2010). *Containing States of Mind: Exploring Bion's "Container" Model in Psychoanalytic Psychotherapy*. London and New York, NY: Routledge.

Castle, Gregory (2013). *The Literary Theory Handbook*. Oxford: Wiley-Blackwell.

Cavanagh, Sheila L. (2019). Queer theory, psychoanalysis, and the symptom: A Lacanian reading. *Studies in Gender & Sexuality* 20.4: 226–230.

Cavarero, Adriana (2009). *Horrorism: Naming Contemporary Violence*, trans. William McCuaig. New York, NY: Columbia University Press.

Celenza, Andrea (2014). *Erotic Revelations: Clinical Applications and Perverse Scenarios*. London and New York, NY: Routledge.

Chabert, Catherine (2013). Response: What does the presentation of case material tell us about what actually happened in an analysis and how does it do this? *International Journal of Psychoanalysis* 94.6: 1153–1162.

Civitarese, Giuseppe (2013). *The Violence of Emotions: Bion and Post-Bionian Psychoanalysis*. London and New York, NY: Routledge.

Clarke, Carrie (2017). Re-imagining dementia using the visual matrix. *Journal of Social Work Practice* 31.2: 173–188.

Clarke, Simon and Paul Hoggett (2009). Researching beneath the surface: A psycho-social approach to research and method. In Simon Clarke and Paul Hoggett (Eds.), *Researching Beneath the Surface: Psycho-Social Research Methods in Practice* (pp. 1–26). London and New York, NY: Routledge.

Cohen, Jonathan (2007). Interdisciplinary psychoanalysis and the education of children. *Psychoanalytic Study of the Child* 62.1: 180–207.

Coles, Prophecy (Ed.) (2006). *Sibling Relationships*. London: Karnac.

Coll-Planas, Gerard, Marta Cruells and Eva Alfama (2017). Breast surgery as a gender technology: Analyzing plastic surgeons' discourses. *Studies in Gender & Sexuality* 18.3: 178–189.

Connor, Steven (2011). Introduction: Speaking of objects. In *Paraphernalia: The Curious Lives of Magical Things* (pp. 1–13). London: Profile Books.

Cooper, Judy and Helen Alfillé (Eds.) (1998). *Assessment in Psychotherapy*. London: Karnac.

——— (2011). *A Guide to Assessment for Psychoanalytic Psychotherapists*. London: Karnac.

Cooper, Steven (2013). The analyst's self-reflective participation and the transference-countertransference matrix. In Robert Oelsner (Ed.), *Transference and Countertransference Today* (pp. 269–288). London and New York, NY: Routledge.

Corrigan, Edward G. and Pearl-Ellen Gordon (1995a). Introduction. In Edward G. Corrigan and Pearl-Ellen Gordon (Eds.), *The Mind Object: Precocity and Pathology of Self-Sufficiency* (pp. xiii–xvii). Northvale, NJ and London: Jason Aronson Inc.

——— (1995b). The mind as an object. In Edward G. Corrigan and Pearl-Ellen Gordon (Eds.), *The Mind Object: Precocity and Pathology of Self-Sufficiency* (pp. 1–22). Northvale, NJ and London: Jason Aronson Inc.

Covington, Coline (2018). Populism and the danger of illusion. *Contemporary Psychoanalysis* 54.2: 250–265.

Crehan, Geraldine (2004). The surviving sibling: The effects of sibling death in childhood. *Psychoanalytic Psychotherapy* 18.2: 202–219.

Crick, Penelope (2013). Thinking about judgement in psychoanalytic assessment and consultation. *Psychoanalytic Psychotherapy* 27.3: 199–214.

Crociani-Windland, Lita (2018). The researcher's subjectivity as a research instrument from intuition to surrender. In Anne-Marie Cummins and Nigel Williams (Eds.), *Further Researching beneath the Surface, Volume 2: Psycho-Social Research Methods in Practice* (pp. 27–47). London and New York, NY: Routledge.

Cullington, Denise (2019). *The Rough Beast: Psychoanalysis in Everyday Life*. London and New York, NY: Routledge.

Cummins, Anne-Marie and Nigel Williams (2018). Introduction: Researching beneath the surface – A continuing journey. In Anne-Marie Cummins and Nigel Williams (Eds.),

Further Researching beneath the Surface, Volume 2: Psycho-Social Research Methods in Practice (pp. xiii–xxvii). London and New York, NY: Routledge.

Curtis, Hannah (2015). *Everyday Life and the Unconscious Mind: An Introduction to Psychoanalytic Concepts*. London: Karnac.

Dalzell, Thomas (2011). *Freud's Schreber between Psychiatry and Psychoanalysis: On Subjective Disposition to Psychosis*. London: Karnac.

Davids, M. Fakhry (2011). *Internal Racism: A Psychoanalytic Approach to Race and Difference*. Basingstoke and New York, NY: Palgrave Macmillan.

Daws, Dilys (1997). The perils of intimacy: Closeness and distance in feeding and weaning. *Journal of Child Psychotherapy* 23.2: 179–199.

Dethiville, Laura (2019). The squiggle. In Susan Ganley Lévy (Trans.), *The Clinic of Donald W. Winnicott* (pp. 13–24). London and New York, NY: Routledge, first pub. 2013 in French.

Diem-Wille, Gertraud, Korneilia Steinhardt and Helga Reiter (2006). Joys and sorrows of teaching infant observation at university level – Implementing psychoanalytic observation in teachers' further education programmes. *Infant Observation: International Journal of Infant Observation and Its Applications* 9.3: 233–248.

Dimen, Muriel (Ed.) (2011). *With Culture in Mind: Psychoanalytic Stories*. New York, NY and London: Routledge.

Dolto, Françoise (1995). Seminars on child psychoanalysis, trans. Olga Cox Cameron. In Carol Owens and Stephanie Farrelly Quinn (Eds.), *Lacanian Psychoanalysis with Babies, Children, and Adolescents: Further Notes on the Child* (pp. 33–47). London: Karnac, 2017.

Dwairy, Marwan (2015). *From Psycho-Analysis to Culture-Analysis: A Within-Culture Psychotherapy*. Basingstoke and New York, NY: Palgrave Macmillan.

Edwards, Judith (2010). Teaching and learning about psychoanalysis: Film as a teaching tool, with reference to a particular film, *Morvern Callar*. *British Journal of Psychotherapy* 26.1: 80–99.

——— (2014). Sifting through the sands of time: Mourning and melancholia revisited via the documentary *Nostalgia for the Light* (2011). *International Journal of Psychoanalysis* 95.1: 791–799.

——— (2015). Teaching, learning and Bion's model of digestion. *British Journal of Psychotherapy* 31.3: 376–389.

——— (2018). "This is not for tears: Thinking" – Poetry and psychoanalysis in orbit. *British Journal of Psychotherapy* 34.2: 270–284.

Eichler, Seth (2010). *Beginnings in Psychotherapy: A Guidebook for New Therapists*. London: Karnac.

Eisenbud, Jule (1965). The hand and the breast with special reference to obsessional neurosis. *Psychoanalytic Quarterly* 34.2: 219–247.

Eizirik, Cláudio Laks (1997). Psychoanalysis and culture: Some contemporary challenges. *International Journal of Psychoanalysis* 78.4: 789–800.

Elfer, Peter (2018). The contribution of psychoanalytically informed observation methodologies in nursery organisations. In Kalina Stamenova and Robert D. Hinshelwood (Eds.), *Methods of Research into the Unconscious: Applying Psychoanalytic Ideas to Social Science* (pp. 126–142). London and New York, NY: Routledge.

Ellis-Peterson, Hannah (2015). Sleep – The eight-hour live-broadcast lullaby for a frenetic world. *The Guardian*, 28 September. URL www.theguardian.com/culture/2015/sep/27/sleep-the-the-lullaby-for-our-frenetic-world. Accessed 31 July 2020.

Erreich, Anne (2018). Psychoanalysis and the academy: Working across boundaries with linguistics, cognitive/developmental psychology, and philosophy of mind. *Journal of the American Psychoanalytic Association* 66.6: 1065–1088.

Esman, Aaron H. (1998). What is "applied" in "applied" psychoanalysis? *International Journal of Psychoanalysis* 79: 741–756.

Ferro, Antonino (2013). *Supervision in Psychoanalysis: The San Paolo Seminars*, trans. Ian Harvey. London and New York, NY: Routledge.

Figlio, Karl (2014). Epistemological or disciplinary differences in psycho-social studies: A reply to Stephen Frosh. *Journal of Psycho-social Studies* 8.1: 170–178.

Fine, Michelle (2010). The breast and the state: An analysis of good and bad nipples by gender, race, and class. *Studies in Gender & Sexuality* 11.1: 24–32.

Fink, Bruce (2007). *Fundamentals of Psychoanalytic Technique: A Lacanian Approach for Beginners*. New York, NY and London: W.W. Norton & Company.

Fonagy, Peter, Felicitas Rost, Jo-Anne Carlyle, Susan McPherson, Rachel Thomas, R.M. Pasco Fearon, David Goldberg and David Taylor (2015). Pragmatic randomized controlled trial of long-term psychoanalytic psychotherapy for treatment-resistant depression: The Tavistock adult depression study (TADS). *World Psychiatry* 14.3: 312–321.

Forrester, John (2016). *Thinking in Cases*. Cambridge: Polity Press.

Fraiberg, Selma (1982). Pathological defenses in infancy. *Psychoanalytic Quarterly* 51.4: 612–635.

Freud, Anna (1929). Report of the eleventh psycho-analytical congress. *Bulletin of the International Psycho-Analytical Association* 10: 489–510.

——— (1946). The psychoanalytic study of infantile feeding disturbances. *Psychoanalytic Study of the Child* 2: 119–132.

——— (1967). About losing and being lost. *Psychoanalytic Study of the Child* 22: 9–19.

Freud, Sigmund (1899). Screen memories. In *Standard Edition of the Complete Psychological Works of Sigmund Freud*, vol. 3, Ed. James Strachey in collaboration with Anna Freud and assisted by Alix Strachey and Alan Tyson (pp. 303–322). London: Vintage, 2001[1953].

——— (1900–1901). The interpretation of dreams (second part). In *Standard Edition of the Complete Psychological Works of Sigmund Freud*, vol. 5, Ed. James Strachey in collaboration with Anna Freud and assisted by Alix Strachey and Alan Tyson (pp. 339–627). London: Vintage, 2001[1953].

——— (1901a). On childhood memories and screen memories. In Anthea Bell (Trans.), *The Psychopathology of Everyday Life* (pp. 45–52). London: Penguin, 2002.

——— (1901b). *The Psychopathology of Everyday Life*, trans. Anthea Bell. London: Penguin, 2002.

——— (1905). Three essays on the theory of sexuality. In *The Standard Edition of the Complete Psychological Works of Sigmund Freud*, vol. 7, Ed. James Strachey in collaboration with Anna Freud and assisted by Alix Strachey and Alan Tyson (pp. 125–243). London: Vintage, 2001[1953]).

——— (1905[1901]). Fragment of an analysis of a case of hysteria. In *The Standard Edition of the Complete Psychological Works of Sigmund Freud*, vol. 7, Ed. James Strachey in collaboration with Anna Freud and assisted by Alix Strachey and Alan Tyson (pp. 1–122). London: Vintage, 2001[1953].

——— (1907[1906]). Delusions and dreams in Jensen's *Gradiva*. In *The Standard Edition of the Complete Psychological Works of Sigmund Freud*, vol. 9, Ed. James Strachey in collaboration with Anna Freud and assisted by Alix Strachey and Alan Tyson (pp. 7–93). London: Vintage, 2001[1953].

———— (1908). On the sexual theories of children. In *The Standard Edition of the Complete Psychological Works of Sigmund Freud*, vol. 9, Ed. James Strachey in collaboration with Anna Freud and assisted by Alix Strachey and Alan Tyson (pp. 209–226). London: Vintage, 2001[1953].

———— (1908[1907]). Creative writers and day-dreaming. In *The Standard Edition of the Complete Psychological Works of Sigmund Freud*, vol. 9, Ed. James Strachey in collaboration with Anna Freud and assisted by Alix Strachey and Alan Tyson (pp. 141–153). London: Vintage, 2001[1953].

———— (1909[1908]). Family romances. In *The Standard Edition of the Complete Psychological Works of Sigmund Freud*, vol. 9, Ed. James Strachey in collaboration with Anna Freud and assisted by Alix Strachey and Alan Tyson (pp. 237–241). London: Vintage, 2001[1953].

———— (1909a). Analysis of a phobia in a five-year-old boy. In *The Standard Edition of the Complete Psychological Works of Sigmund Freud*, vol. 7, Ed. James Strachey in collaboration with Anna Freud and assisted by Alix Strachey and Alan Tyson (pp. 1–149). London: Vintage, 2001[1953].

———— (1909b). Notes upon a case of obsessional neurosis. In *The Standard Edition of the Complete Psychological Works of Sigmund Freud*, vol. 7, Ed. James Strachey in collaboration with Anna Freud and assisted by Alix Strachey and Alan Tyson (pp. 151–318). London: Vintage, 2001[1953].

———— (1910a). On "wild" psychoanalysis. In Alan Bance (Trans.), *Wild Analysis* (pp. 1–9). London: Penguin.

———— (1910b). The future prospects of psycho-analytic therapy. In *The Standard Edition of the Complete Psychological Works of Sigmund Freud*, vol. 11, Ed. James Strachey in collaboration with Anna Freud and assisted by Alix Strachey and Alan Tyson (pp. 139–152). London: Vintage, 2001[1953].

———— (1911). Psycho-analytic notes on an autobiographical account of a case of paranoia (dementia paranoides). In *The Standard Edition of the Complete Psychological Works of Sigmund Freud*, vol. 7, Ed. James Strachey in collaboration with Anna Freud and assisted by Alix Strachey and Alan Tyson (pp. 1–82). London: Vintage, 2001[1953].

———— (1912a). Recommendations to physicians practising psycho-analysis. In *The Standard Edition of the Complete Psychological Works of Sigmund Freud*, vol. 12, Ed. James Strachey in collaboration with Anna Freud and assisted by Alix Strachey and Alan Tyson (pp. 109–120). London: Vintage, 2001[1953].

———— (1912b). The dynamics of transference. In *The Standard Edition of the Complete Psychological Works of Sigmund Freud*, vol. 12, Ed. James Strachey in collaboration with Anna Freud and assisted by Alix Strachey and Alan Tyson (pp. 97–108). London: Vintage, 2001[1953].

———— (1913). Letter from Freud to Ludwig Binswanger, February 20. In Gerhard Fichtner, Arnold J. Pomerans and Thomas Roberts (Trans.), *The Sigmund Freud-Ludwig Binswanger Correspondence 1908–1938* (pp. 112–113). London: Open Gate Press, incorporating Centaur Press, 2003.

———— (1914). Remembering, repeating, and working through. In John Riddick (Trans.), *Beyond the Pleasure Principle and Other Writings* (pp. 33–42). London: Penguin, 2003.

———— (1915). The unconscious. In *The Standard Edition of the Complete Psychological Works of Sigmund Freud*, vol. 7, Ed. James Strachey in collaboration with Anna Freud and assisted by Alix Strachey and Alan Tyson (pp. 159–204). London: Vintage, 2001[1953].

———— (1915[1914]). Observations on transference-love (further recommendations on the technique of psycho-analysis III). In *The Standard Edition of the Complete Psychological Works of Sigmund Freud*, vol. 12, Ed. James Strachey in collaboration with Anna Freud and assisted by Alix Strachey and Alan Tyson (pp. 157–171). London: Vintage, 2001[1953].

———— (1916[1915]). Lecture 1: Introduction. In *The Standard Edition of the Complete Psychological Works of Sigmund Freud*, vol. 7, Ed. James Strachey in collaboration with Anna Freud and assisted by Alix Strachey and Alan Tyson (pp. 15–24). London: Vintage, 2001[1953].

———— (1916[1915–1916]). Lecture 13: The archaic features and infantilism of dreams. In *The Standard Edition of the Complete Psychological Works of Sigmund Freud*, vol. 15, Ed. James Strachey in collaboration with Anna Freud and assisted by Alix Strachey and Alan Tyson (pp. 199–212). London: Vintage, 2001[1953].

———— (1917[1915]). Mourning and melancholia. In *The Standard Edition of the Complete Psychological Works of Sigmund Freud*, vol. 14, Ed. James Strachey in collaboration with Anna Freud and assisted by Alix Strachey and Alan Tyson (pp. 243–258). London: Vintage, 2001[1953].

———— (1917[1916–1917]a). Lecture 20: The sexual life of human beings. In *The Standard Edition of the Complete Psychological Works of Sigmund Freud*, vol. 16, Ed. James Strachey in collaboration with Anna Freud and assisted by Alix Strachey and Alan Tyson (pp. 303–319). London: Vintage, 2001[1953].

———— (1917[1916–1917]b). Lecture 21: The development of the libido and the sexual organizations. In *The Standard Edition of the Complete Psychological Works of Sigmund Freud*, vol. 16, Ed. James Strachey in collaboration with Anna Freud and assisted by Alix Strachey and Alan Tyson (pp. 320–338). London: Vintage, 2001[1953].

———— (1917[1916–1917]c). Lecture 20: The sexual life of human beings. In *The Standard Edition of the Complete Psychological Works of Sigmund Freud*, vol. 16, Ed. James Strachey in collaboration with Anna Freud and assisted by Alix Strachey and Alan Tyson (pp. 303–319). London: Vintage, 2001[1953].

———— (1917[1916–1917]d). Lecture 18: Fixation to traumas – The unconscious. In *The Standard Edition of the Complete Psychological Works of Sigmund Freud*, vol. 16, Ed. James Strachey in collaboration with Anna Freud and assisted by Alix Strachey and Alan Tyson (pp. 273–285). London: Vintage, 2001[1953].

———— (1917[1916–1917e). Lecture 23: The paths to the formation of symptoms. In *The Standard Edition of the Complete Psychological Works of Sigmund Freud*, vol. 16, Ed. James Strachey in collaboration with Anna Freud and assisted by Alix Strachey and Alan Tyson (pp. 358–377). London: Vintage, 2001[1953].

———— (1918[1914]). From the history of an infantile neurosis. In *The Standard Edition of the Complete Psychological Works of Sigmund Freud*, vol. 7, Ed. James Strachey in collaboration with Anna Freud and assisted by Alix Strachey and Alan Tyson (pp. 1–122). London: Vintage, 2001[1953].

———— (1923a). The ego and the id. In *The Standard Edition of the Complete Psychological Works of Sigmund Freud*, vol. 19, Ed. James Strachey in collaboration with Anna Freud and assisted by Alix Strachey and Alan Tyson (pp. 1–59). London: Vintage, 2001[1953].

———— (1923b). The infantile genital organization (an interpolation into the theory of sexuality). In *The Standard Edition of the Complete Psychological Works of Sigmund*

Freud, vol. 19, Ed. James Strachey in collaboration with Anna Freud and assisted by Alix Strachey and Alan Tyson (pp. 139–145). London: Vintage, 2001[1953].

———— (1923[1922]). A seventeenth-century demonological neurosis. In *The Standard Edition of the Complete Psychological Works of Sigmund Freud*, vol. 19, Ed. James Strachey in collaboration with Anna Freud and assisted by Alix Strachey and Alan Tyson (pp. 67–105). London: Vintage, 2001[1953].

———— (1925). Negation. In *The Standard Edition of the Complete Psychological Works of Sigmund Freud*, vol. 19, Ed. James Strachey in collaboration with Anna Freud and assisted by Alix Strachey and Alan Tyson (pp. 233–239). London: Vintage, 2001[1953].

———— (1926). Inhibitions, symptoms and anxiety. In *The Standard Edition of the Complete Psychological Works of Sigmund Freud*, vol. 20, Ed. James Strachey in collaboration with Anna Freud and assisted by Alix Strachey and Alan Tyson (pp. 75–175). London: Vintage, 2001[1953].

———— (1930[1929]). Civilization and its discontents. In *The Standard Edition of the Complete Psychological Works of Sigmund Freud*, vol. 21, Ed. James Strachey in collaboration with Anna Freud and assisted by Alix Strachey and Alan Tyson (pp. 57–145). London: Vintage, 2001[1953].

———— (1931). Female sexuality. In *The Standard Edition of the Complete Psychological Works of Sigmund Freud*, vol. 21, Ed. James Strachey in collaboration with Anna Freud and assisted by Alix Strachey and Alan Tyson (pp. 225–243). London: Vintage, 2001[1953].

———— (1933[1932]). Femininity. In *The Standard Edition of the Complete Psychological Works of Sigmund Freud*, vol. 22, Ed. James Strachey in collaboration with Anna Freud and assisted by Alix Strachey and Alan Tyson (pp. 112–135). London: Vintage, 2001[1953].

———— (1940). An outline of psychoanalysis. In Helena Ragg-Kirkby (Trans.), *An Outline of Psychoanalysis* (pp. 173–236). London: Penguin, 2003.

Frizell, Nell (2015). All about my mother: The most Freudian exhibition ever. *The Guardian*. London, 3 September. URL www.theguardian.com/artanddesign/2015/sep/03/jennifer-rubell-mother-naked-freudian-exhibition. Accessed 14 January 2020.

Froggett, Lynn and Wendy Hollway (2010). Psychosocial research analysis and scenic understanding. *Psychoanalysis, Culture & Society* 15.3: 281–301.

————, Julian Manley and Alastair Roy (2015). The visual matrix method: Imagery and affect in group-based research setting. *Forum: Qualitative Social Research* 16.3: 1–31.

———— with the Creative and Credible Project Team (2015). Researching aesthetic experience in arts and health: The visual matrix (pp. 1–2). URL http://creativeandcredible.co.uk/wp-content/uploads/2015/07/CreativeCredible_Researching-Aesthetic-experience-The-Visual-Matrix.pdf. Accessed 19 September 2019.

Frosch, Allan (2006). The culture of psychoanalysis and the concept of analyzability. *Psychoanalytic Psychology* 23.1: 43–55.

Frosh, Stephen (2003). Psychosocial studies and psychology: Is a critical approach emerging? *Human Relations* 56.12: 1545–1567.

———— (2005). *Hate and the "Jewish Science": Anti-Semitism, Nazism and Psychoanalysis*. Basingstoke and New York, NY: Palgrave Macmillan.

———— (2008). On negative critique: A reply. *Psychoanalysis, Culture & Society* 13.4: 416–422.

———— (2010). *Psychoanalysis Outside the Clinic: Interventions in Psychosocial Studies.* Basingstoke and New York, NY: Palgrave Macmillan.

———— (2013). Transdisciplinary tensions and psychosocial studies. *Enquire* 6.1: 1–15.

———— (2014). The nature of the psychosocial: Debates from 'Studies in the Psychosocial'. *Journal of Psycho-Social Studies* 8.1: 159–169.

———— (Ed.) (2015a). *Psychosocial Imaginaries: Perspectives on Temporality, Subjectivities and Activism.* Basingstoke and New York, NY: Palgrave Macmillan.

———— (2015b). Introduction. In Stephen Frosh (Ed.), *Psychosocial Imaginaries: Perspectives on Temporality, Subjectivities and Activism* (pp. 1–20). Basingstoke and New York, NY: Palgrave Macmillan.

———— (2016). Towards a psychosocial psychoanalysis. *American Imago* 73.4: 469–482.

———— (2018). Rethinking psychoanalysis in the psychosocial. *Psychoanalysis, Culture and Society* 23.1: 5–14.

———— (2019a). Psychosocial studies with psychoanalysis. *Journal of Psychosocial Studies* 12.1–2: 101–114.

———— (2019b). New voices in psychosocial studies: Introduction. In Stephen Frosh (Ed.), *New Voices in Psychosocial Studies* (pp. 1–20). Basingstoke and New York, NY: Palgrave Macmillan.

———— and Lisa Baraitser (2008). Psychoanalysis and psychosocial studies. *Psychoanalysis, Culture & Society* 13.4: 346–365.

———— and Belinda Mandelbaum (2019). Psychosocial histories of psychoanalysis. *Revista Praxis y Culturas Psi* 1: 1–13.

Frost, Liz and Stuart McClean (2014). *Thinking about the Lifecourse: A Psychosocial Introduction.* Basingstoke and New York, NY: Palgrave Macmillan.

———— and Helen Lucey (2010). Editorial. *Journal of Psycho-Social Studies* 4.1: 1–5. URL www.psychosocial-studies-association.org/volume-4-issue-1-june-2010/. Accessed 21 March 2019.

———— and David W. Jones (2019). Editorial. *Journal of Psychosocial Studies* 12.1–2: 3–7.

Fuss, Diana (1995). Fallen women: "The psychogenesis of a case of homosexuality in a woman". In *Identification Papers: Readings on Psychoanalysis, Sexuality, and Culture* (pp. 57–82). London and New York, NY: Routledge.

Gabbard, Glen O. (Ed.) (2001a). *Psychoanalysis and Film.* London and New York, NY: Routledge.

———— (2001b). Introduction. In Glen O. Gabbard (Ed.), *Psychoanalysis and Film* (pp. 1–16). London and New York, NY: Routledge.

———— (Ed.) (2007). *Key Papers in Literature and Psychoanalysis.* London and New York, NY: Routledge.

Gehrie, Mark J. (1992). Freud's vision: Key issues in the methodology of applied psychoanalysis. *Journal of the American Psychoanalytic Association* 40.1: 239–244.

Gerald, Mark (2003–). "In the shadow of Freud's couch: Portraits of psychoanalysts in their offices". Photographic project. URL www.markgeraldphoto.com. Accessed 21 March 2019.

———— (2011). The psychoanalytic office: Past, present, and future. *Psychoanalytic Psychology* 28.3: 435–445.

———— (2016). I wish that you could stay a little longer: Seeing the image in psychoanalysis. *Psychoanalytic Inquiry: A Topical Journal for Mental Health Professionals* 36.8: 644–652.

Giffney, Noreen (2003). Que(e)rying Mongols. *Medieval Feminist Forum: A Journal of Gender and Sexuality* 36.1: 15–21.

——— (2004). *"The Age is Drowned in Blood": Reading Anti-Mongol Propaganda, 1236–55*. Unpublished. PhD diss., University College Dublin, Dublin.

——— (2012). Monstrous Mongols. *Postmedieval: A Journal of Medieval Cultural Studies* 3.2: 227–245.

——— (2013–). (Director). Psychoanalysis +. International, Interdisciplinary Initiative. Ireland.

——— (2013a). Desire in psychoanalytic psychotherapy: The writings of W.R. Bion. *Psychoanalytic Psychotherapy* 27.3: 215–227.

——— (2013b). Reading (with) Bion: An experience in reading. *American Journal of Psychoanalysis* 73.3: 288–304.

——— (2013–2014). (Convener). Film: In session – A series of conversations around psychoanalysis and film. Filmbase, Dublin, Ireland.

——— (2015a). Sex as evacuation. *Studies in Gender & Sexuality* 16.2: 103–109.

——— (2015b). (Convener). Conducting psychoanalytic research for publication workshop. University College Dublin, Ireland.

——— (2015c). (Convener). The clinical usefulness of Wilfred Bion's writings for psychotherapists clinical conference. Birkbeck, University of London, London, UK.

——— (2016a). A theory of thinking: A theory of desiring. *Studies in Gender & Sexuality* 17.3: 150–164.

——— (2016b). (Convener). Cinematic encounters with violent trauma and its aftermath symposium. Science Gallery Dublin, Ireland.

——— (2017a). Clinical encounters in sexuality: Psychoanalytic practice and queer theory. In Noreen Giffney and Eve Watson (Eds.), *Clinical Encounters in Sexuality: Psychoanalytic Practice and Queer Theory* (pp. 19–48). New York, NY: Punctum Books.

——— (2017b). (Convener). The artist/analyst is present: At the interface between creative arts practice and clinical psychoanalytic practice public screening and discussion. IMMA – The Irish Museum of Modern Art, Dublin, Ireland.

——— (2017c). Psychoanalysis in Ireland: An interview with Noreen Giffney. *Breac: A Digital Journal of Irish Studies* 7. URL https://breac.nd.edu/articles/psychoanalysis-in-ireland-an-interview-with-dr-noreen-giffney/. Accessed 26 June 2020.

——— (2019). The use of an object. *Studies in Gender & Sexuality* 20.4: 245–248.

——— and Sophie Byrne (2016). (Conveners). Sexuality, identity and the state symposium. Interdisciplinary Event. IMMA – The Irish Museum of Modern Art, Dublin, Ireland.

———, Tina Kinsella, Anne Mulhall, Emma Radley and Eve Watson (2014). (Conveners). Melancholia. Multidisciplinary Event. National Museum of Decorative Arts and History, Dublin, Ireland.

——— and Lisa Moran (2018–2019). (Conveners). Unconscious objects: A series of conversations around art and psychoanalysis. IMMA – The Irish Museum of Modern Art, Dublin, Ireland.

——— and Eve Watson (Eds.) (2017a). *Clinical Encounters in Sexuality: Psychoanalytic Practice and Queer Theory*. New York, NY: Punctum Books.

——— (2017b). (Conveners). Psychoanalysis and sexuality today clinical conference: Psychosocial influences on transference and countertransference. The National Museum of Decorative Arts and History, Dublin, Ireland.

———— (2018). (Conveners). What can psychoanalysis learn from queer theories of sexuality? Multidisciplinary conference: 113 years after Freud's "Three essays". The Freud Museum, London, UK.

———— and Philip Lance (2018). Noreen Giffney and Eve Watson in discussion with Philip Lance about *Clinical Encounters in Sexuality*. New Books in Psychoanalysis Podcast Series. URL https://newbooksnetwork.com/noreen-giffney-and-eve-watson-clinical-encounters-in-sexuality-psychoanalytic-practice-and-queer-theory-punctum-books-2017/. Accessed 20 September 2019.

Glover, Edward (1927). Lectures on technique in psycho-analysis. *International Journal of Psychoanalysis* 8: 311–338.

Golding, William (1954). *Lord of the Flies*. London: Faber and Faber, 1958.

Goldstein, Gabriela (Ed.) (2013). *Art in Psychoanalysis: A Contemporary Approach to Creativity and Analytic Practice*. London: Karnac.

Gomez, Lavinia (2017). *Developments in Object Relations: Controversies, Conflicts and Common Ground*. London and New York, NY: Routledge.

Good, Michael I. (1998). Screen reconstructions: Traumatic memory, conviction, and the problem of verification. *Journal of the American Psychoanalytic Association* 46.1: 149–183.

Goodley, Dan (2011). Social psychoanalytic disability studies. *Disability & Society* 26.6: 715–728.

Gourguechon, Prudence (2011). The citizen psychoanalyst: Psychoanalysis, social commentary, and social advocacy. *Journal of the American Psychoanalytic Association* 59.3: 445–470.

———— (2013). Typology of applied psychoanalysis. *International Journal of Applied Psychoanalytic Studies* 10.3: 192–198.

Green, André (1986). The dead mother. In *On Private Madness* (pp. 142–173). London and New York, NY: Karnac, 2005.

———— in dialogues with Gregorio Kohon (1999). The greening of psychoanalysis. In Gregorio Kohon (Ed.), *The Dead Mother: The Work of André Green* (pp. 10–58). London and New York, NY: Routledge.

Greenberg, Jay and Stephen Mitchell (1983). *Object Relations in Psychoanalytic Theory*. London and Cambridge, MA: Harvard University Press.

Greenson, Ralph R. (1967). *The Technique and Practice of Psycho-Analysis*. London: The Hogarth Press and the Institute of Psycho-Analysis, 1985.

Greenspan, Jack (1979). Oral conflict: Is there a relationship to carcinoma of the breast? *International Review of Psycho-Analysis* 6: 441–454

Grinberg, León (1994). Foreword. In Virginia Hunter (Ed.), *Psychoanalysts Talk* (pp. ix–xiv). New York, NY and London: The Guildford Press.

Gross, Jonathan (2020). Holding together loss and hope: Reflections on the need for art in times of crisis. *Journal of Psychosocial Studies* 13.2: 209–217.

Grossman, Lee (1995). A woman with a nipple fetish. *Psychoanalytic Quarterly* 64.4: 746–748.

Grosz, Stephen (2014). *The Examined Life: How We Lose and Find Ourselves*. London: Vintage.

Haga Gripsrud, Birgitta, Ellen Ramvi, Lynn Froggett, Ingvil Hellstrand and Julian Manley (2018). Psychosocial and symbolic dimensions of the breast explored through a visual matrix. *NORA – Nordic Journal of Feminist and Gender Research* 26.3: 210–229.

Hagman, George (Ed.) (2017). *Art, Creativity, and Psychoanalysis: Perspectives from Analyst-Artists.* London and New York, NY: Routledge.

Hansbury, Griffin (2017). Unthinkable anxieties: Reading transphobic countertransferences in a century of psychoanalytic writing. *TSQ: Transgender Studies Quarterly* 4.3–4: 384–404.

Harris, Adrienne and Robert Sklar (1998). Wild film theory, wild film analysis. *Psychoanalytic Inquiry* 18.2: 222–237.

Hayward, Rhodri (2012). The invention of the psychosocial: An introduction. *History of the Human Sciences* 25.5: 3–12.

Heimann, Paula (1949/50). On counter-transference. In Margret Tonnesmann (Ed.), *About Children and Children-No-Longer: Collected Papers 1942–80* (pp. 73–79). London and New York, NY: Routledge, 1989.

——— (1959/60). Counter-transference. In Margret Tonnesmann (Ed.), *About Children and Children-No-Longer: Collected Papers 1942–80* (pp. 151–160). London and New York, NY: Routledge, 1989.

Hering, Christoph (1986). The preserved nipple closeness and distance in the mothering of a baby. *British Journal of Psychotherapy* 3.2: 144–150.

Herzig, Cori (2001). Good breast/bad analyst: False dichotomies in understanding aggressive patients. *Fort Da* 7.2: 56–78.

Hinshelwood, Robert D. (1991). *A Dictionary of Kleinian Thought.* London: Free Association Books.

——— (1994). Internal objects. In *Clinical Klein* (pp. 58–77). London: Free Association Books.

——— (2013). *Research on the Couch: Single-Case Studies, Subjectivity and Psychoanalytic Knowledge.* London and New York, NY: Routledge.

——— and Tomasz Fortuna (2018). *Melanie Klein: The Basics.* London and New York, NY: Routledge.

Hobson, Peter (Ed.) (2013). *Consultations in Psychoanalytic Psychotherapy.* London: Karnac.

Hogg, Sally (2019). *Rare Jewels: Specialised Parent-Infant Relationship Teams in the UK Report.* Kettering: Parent Infant Partnership United Kingdom.

Hoggett, Paul (2008). What's in a hyphen? Reconstructing psychosocial studies. *Psychoanalysis, Culture & Society* 13: 379–384.

Hollway, Wendy (2006). Paradox in the pursuit of a critical theorization of the development of the self in family relationships. *Theory and Psychology* 16.4: 465–82.

——— (2008). Turning psychosocial? Towards a UK network? *Psychoanalysis, Culture & Society* 13: 199–204.

——— (2014). Psychosocial challenges of building psychosocial studies: A response to Sasha Roseneil. *Journal for Psycho-Social Studies* 8.1: 137–145.

——— and Tony Jefferson (2013). *Doing Qualitative Research Differently: A Psychosocial Approach*, 2nd ed. London: Sage, 1st ed. 2000.

Holmes, Jeremy (2014). *The Therapeutic Imagination: Using Literature to Deepen Psychodynamic Understanding and Enhance Empathy.* London and New York, NY: Routledge.

Holmes, Joshua (2019). *A Practical Psychoanalytic Guide to Reflexive Research: The Reverie Research Method.* London and New York, NY: Routledge.

Hook, Derek (2008). Articulating psychoanalysis and psychosocial studies: Limitations and possibilities. *Psychoanalysis, Culture & Society* 13.4: 397–405.

Hopson, Jacqueline (2019). Stigma and fear: The "psy professional" in cultural artifacts. *The British Journal of Psychotherapy* 35.2: 233–244.

Hunter, Virginia (1994a). *Psychoanalysts Talk*. New York, NY and London: The Guildford Press.

——— (1994b). Author's notes. In Virginia Hunter (Ed.), *Psychoanalysts Talk* (pp. 1–5). New York, NY and London: The Guildford Press.

——— (1994c). Personal factors subjectively influencing interpretation. In Virginia Hunter (Ed.), *Psychoanalysts Talk* (pp. 6–13). New York, NY and London: The Guildford Press.

Huskinson, Lucy and Terrie Waddell (Eds.) (2014). *Eavesdropping: The Psychotherapist in Film and Television*. London and New York, NY: Routledge.

International Journal of Applied Psychoanalytic Studies (2004–). Hoboken, NJ: Wiley. International Research Group for Psycho-Societal Analysis (2001–). URL https://psycho-societal.org Accessed 26 June 2020.

Irish Association for Creative Arts Therapies (1992–). URL www.iacat.ie. Accessed 28 November 2019.

Jacobs, Amber (2015). The demise of the analogue mind: Digital primal fantasies and the technologies of loss-less-ness. In Stephen Frosh (Ed.), *Psychosocial Imaginaries: Perspectives on Temporality, Subjectivities and Activism* (pp. 126–144). Basingstoke and New York, NY: Palgrave Macmillan.

Jaffee Nagel, Julie (2013). *Melodies of the Mind: Connections between Psychoanalysis and Music*. London and New York, NY: Routledge.

Jaques, Eilliott (1961). Foreword. In Melanie Klein, *Narrative of a Child Analysis: The Conduct of the Psycho-analysis of Children as Seen in the Treatment of a Ten-Year-Old Boy* (pp. 5–6). London: Virago, 1998.

Jefferson, Tony (2008). What is "the psychosocial"? A Response to Frosh and Baraitser. *Psychoanalysis, Culture & Society* 13.4: 366–373.

Jervis, Sue (2009). The use of self as a research tool. In Simon Clarke and Paul Hoggett (Eds.), *Researching beneath the Surface: Psycho-Social Research Methods in Practice* (pp. 145–166). London and New York, NY: Routledge.

Johns, Jennifer (2005). The facilitating environment. In Susan Budd and Richard Rusbridger (Eds.), *Introducing Psychoanalysis: Essential Themes and Topics* (pp. 81–94). London and New York, NY: Routledge.

Johnson, Katherine (2015). *Sexuality: A Psychosocial Manifesto*. Cambridge and Malden, MA: Polity Press.

Joseph, Betty (1960). Some characteristics of the psychopathic personality. *International Journal of Psychoanalysis* 41: 526–531.

——— (1966). Persecutory anxiety in a four-year-old boy. *International Journal of Psychoanalysis* 47: 184–188.

——— (1985). Transference: The total situation. In Michael Feldman and Elizabeth Bott Spillius (Eds.), *Psychic Equilibrium and Psychic Change: Selected Papers of Betty Joseph* (pp. 156–167). London and New York, NY: Routledge.

——— (1989). Projective identification: Some clinical aspects. In Michael Feldman and Elizabeth Bott Spillius (Eds.), *Psychic Equilibrium and Psychic Change: Selected Papers of Betty Joseph* (pp. 168–180). London and New York, NY: Routledge.

——— (2005). The paranoid-schizoid position. In Susan Budd and Richard Rusbridger (Eds.), *Introducing Psychoanalysis: Essential Themes and Topics* (pp. 39–46). London and New York, NY: Routledge.

———— (2011). Interviewee as part of *Encounters through Generations*. London: Institute of Psychoanalysis Audio Video Project. Documentary film.

———— (2015). Here and now: My perspective. *International Journal of Psychoanalysis* 94.1: 1–5.

Kahr, Brett (2011a). Dr Paul Weston and the blood-stained couch. *International Journal of Psychoanalysis* 92.4: 1051–1058.

———— (2011b). On painting the consulting room. *American Imago* 67.4: 669–675.

Kernberg, Otto F. (2016). *Psychoanalytic Education at the Crossroads: Reformation, Change and the Future of Psychoanalytic Training.* London and New York, NY: Routledge.

Keval, Narendra (2016). *Racist States of Mind: Understanding the Perversion of Curiosity and Concern.* London: Karnac.

Kimble Wrye, Harriet (1997). The body/mind dialectic within the psychoanalytic subject: Finding the analyst's voice. *The American Journal of Psychoanalysis* 57.4: 360–369.

King, Pearl (1989). Introductory memoir. In Paula Heimann and Margret Tonnesmann (Eds.), *About Children and Children-No-Longer: Collected Papers 1942–80* (pp. 1–9). London and New York, NY: Routledge, 1989.

———— and Riccardo Steiner (Eds.) (1991). *The Freud-Klein Controversies, 1941–45.* London and New York, NY: Routledge.

Klein, George (1973). Is psychoanalysis relevant? *Psychoanalysis and Contemporary Science* 2.1: 3–21.

Klein, Melanie (1932a). *The Psycho-Analysis of Children.* London: Vintage, 1997.

———— (1932b). The technique of early analysis. In *The Psycho-Analysis of Children* (pp. 16–34). London: Vintage, 1997.

———— (1935). A contribution to the psychogenesis of manic-depressive states. In *Love, Guild and Reparation and Other Works 1921–1945* (pp. 262–289). London: Vintage, 1997[1975].

———— (1946). Notes on some schizoid mechanisms. In *Envy and Gratitude and Other Works 1946–1963* (pp. 1–24). London: Vintage, 1997[1975].

———— (1948). On the theory of anxiety and guilt. In *Envy and Gratitude and Other Works 1946–1963* (pp. 25–42). London: Vintage, 1997[1975].

———— (1952a). On Observing the behaviour of young infants. In *Envy and Gratitude and Other Works 1946–1963* (pp. 94–121). London: Vintage, 1997[1975].

———— (1952b). Some theoretical conclusions regarding the emotional life of the infant. In *Envy and Gratitude and Other Works 1946–1963* (pp. 61–93). London: Vintage, 1997[1975].

———— (1952c). The emotional life of the infant. In *Envy and Gratitude and Other Works 1946–1963* (pp. 61–93). London: Vintage, 1997[1975].

———— (1955). On identification. In *Envy and Gratitude and Other Works 1946–1963* (pp. 141–175). London, UK: Vintage, 1997[1975].

———— (1957). Envy and gratitude. In *Envy and Gratitude and Other Works 1946–1963* (pp. 176–235). London: Vintage, 1997[1975].

———— (1960). On mental health. In *Envy and Gratitude and Other Works 1946–1963* (pp. 268–274). London: Vintage, 1997[1975].

———— (1961). *Narrative of a Child Analysis: The Conduct of the Psycho-analysis of Children as Seen in the Treatment of a Ten-Year-Old Boy.* London: Vintage, 1998.

———— (1975a). *Love, Guilt and Reparation and Other Works 1921–1945*. London: Vintage, 1998[1975].

———— (1975b). *Envy and Gratitude and Other Works 1946–1963*. London: Vintage, 1997[1975].

Kohon, Gregorio (2016). *Reflections on the Aesthetic Experience: Psychoanalysis and the Uncanny*. London and New York, NY: Routledge.

Kohut, Thomas A. (2003). Psychoanalysis as psychohistory or why psychotherapists cannot afford to ignore culture. *The Annual of Psychoanalysis* 31: 225–236.

Kuhn, Annette (Ed.) (2013a). *Little Madnesses: Winnicott, Transitional Phenomena and Cultural Experience*. London and New York, NY: I.B. Tauris.

———— (2013b). Little madnesses: An introduction. In Annette Kuhn (Ed.), *Little Madnesses: Winnicott, Transitional Phenomena and Cultural Experience* (pp. 1–10). London and New York, NY: I.B. Tauris.

LaFarge, Lucy (2012). The screen memory and the act of remembering. *The International Journal of Psychoanalysis* 93.5: 1249–1265.

Lance, Philip (2019). Welcome to the family: A queer affection for psychoanalysis. *Studies in Gender & Sexuality* 20.4: 220–225.

Laplanche, Jean and Jean-Bertrand Pontalis (1967). *The Language of Psychoanalysis*, trans. Donald Nicholson-Smith. London: Karnac, 2006.

Layton, Lynne (2008). Editor's introduction to special issue on British psycho(-)social studies. *Psychoanalysis, Culture & Society* 13.4: 339–340.

———— (2012). "You can't be neutral on a moving train": The psychosocial connection between patient and analyst. *Psychoanalysis, Culture & Society* 17.1: 58–63.

———— (2020a). Toward a social psychoanalysis: Culture, character, and normative unconscious processes. In Marianna Leavy-Sperounis (Ed.), *Toward a Social Unconscious: Culture, Character, and Normative Unconscious Processes* (pp. 34–43). London and New York, NY: Routledge.

———— (2020b). Section 1: What is social psychoanalysis? In Marianna Leavy-Sperounis (Ed.), *Toward a Social Unconscious: Culture, Character, and Normative Unconscious Processes* (pp. 1–3). London and New York, NY: Routledge.

———— (2020c). Attacks on linking: The unconscious pull to dissociate individuals from their social context. In Marianna Leavy-Sperounis (Ed.), *Toward a Social Unconscious: Culture, Character, and Normative Unconscious Processes* (pp. xxiii–xxxix). London and New York, NY: Routledge.

Leavy-Sperounis, Marianna (2020). Social psychoanalysis: Centering power dynamics and affirming our interdependence. In Lynne Layton and Marianna Leavy-Sperounis (Eds.), *Toward a Social Unconscious: Culture, Character, and Normative Unconscious Processes* (pp. xiv–xx). London and New York, NY: Routledge.

Lebeau, Vicky (2001). *Psychoanalysis and Cinema: The Play of Shadows*. London and New York, NY: Wallflower Press.

Lebovici, Serge and Evelyne Kestemberg (1993). The breast and breasts. *The Journal of Child Psychotherapy* 19.1: 5–31.

Lee, Graham (2015). The location of authenticity. In Margaret Boyle Spelman and Frances Thomson-Salo (Eds.), *The Winnicott Tradition* (pp. 273–290). London: Karnac.

Leichsenring, Falk and Susanne Klein (2014). Evidence for psychodynamic psychotherapy in specific mental disorders: A systematic review. *Psychoanalytic Psychotherapy* 28.1: 4–32.

Lemma, Alessandra (2012). Keeping envy in mind: The vicissitudes of envy in adolescent motherhood. In Paola Mariotti (Ed.), *The Maternal Lineage: Identification, Desire and Transgenerational Issues* (pp. 306–322). London and New York, NY: Routledge.

——— (2015a). *Minding the Body: The Body in Psychoanalysis and Beyond*. London and New York, NY: Routledge.

——— (2015b). Off the couch, into the toilet: Exploring the psychic uses of the analyst's toilet. In *Minding the Body: The Body in Psychoanalysis and Beyond* (pp. 143–159). London and New York, NY: Routledge.

——— (2016). *Introduction to the Practice of Psychoanalytic Psychotherapy*, 2nd ed. Oxford: Wiley Blackwell, 2003.

———, Mary Target and Peter Fonagy (2011). *Brief Dynamic Interpersonal Therapy: A Clinician's Guide*. Oxford: Oxford University Press.

Levine, Howard (2011). "The consolation which is drawn from truth": The analysis of a patient unable to suffer experience. In Chris Mawson (Ed.), *Bion Today* (pp. 188–211). London and New York, NY: Routledge.

Lewis, C.S. (1950). *The Lion, the Witch and the Wardrobe*. London: HarperCollins, 2001.

Lewis, Gail (2009). Rebirthing racial difference: Conversations with my Mother and others. *Studies in the Maternal* 1.1: 1–21.

——— (2012). Where might I find you? Objects and internal space for the father. *Psychoanalysis, Culture & Society* 17.2: 137–152.

Little, Margaret (1985). Winnicott working in areas where psychotic anxieties predominate: A personal record. *Free Associations* 1.3: 9–42.

Long, Susan (2018). The socioanalytic interview. In Kalina Stamenova and Robert D. Hinshelwood (Eds.), *Methods of Research into the Unconscious: Applying Psychoanalytic Ideas to Social Science* (pp. 43–54). London and New York, NY: Routledge.

Lopez-Corvo, Rafael E. (2006). *Wild Thoughts Searching for a Thinker: A Clinical Application of W.R. Bion's Theories*. London: Karnac.

Lubbe, Trevor (1996). Who lets go first? Some observations on the struggles around weaning. *The Journal of Child Psychotherapy* 22.2: 195–213.

Luiz, Claudia (2018). *The Making of a Psychoanalyst: Studies in Emotional Education*. London and New York, NY: Routledge.

Magnenat, Luc (2016). Psychosomatic breast and alexithymic breast: A Bionian psychosomatic perspective. *International Journal of Psychoanalysis* 97.1: 43–63.

Manley, Julian (2010). From cause and effect to effectual causes: Can we talk of a philosophical background to psycho-social studies? *Journal of Psycho-Social Studies* 4.1: 65–87.

——— (2018). *Social Dreaming, Associative Thinking and Intensities of Affect*. Basingstoke and New York, NY: Palgrave Macmillan.

——— and Alastair Roy (2016). The visual matrix: A psycho-social method for discovering unspoken complexities in social care practice. *Psychoanalysis, Culture & Society* 22.2: 132–153.

Mapping Maternal Subjectivities, Identities and Ethics (MAMSIE) Network (2007–). URL http://mamsie.org. Accessed 26 June 2020.

Masur, Corinne (2009). Parent-infant psychotherapy. *Journal of the American Psychoanalytic Association* 57.2: 467–473.

Matthis, Iréne and Imre Szecsödy (Eds.) (1998). *On Freud's Couch: Seven New Interpretations of Freud's Case Histories*. Northvale, NJ: Jason Aronson.

McDougall, Joyce (1989). *Theatres of the Body: A Psychoanalytical Approach to Psychosomatic Illness*. London: Free Association Books.

———— (2004). The psychoanalytic voyage of a breast-cancer patient. *The Annual of Psychoanalysis* 32: 9–28.

Meltzer, Donald (1967). *The Psycho-Analytical Process*. London: Karnac.

———— (1973). *Sexual States of Mind*. London: Karnac.

———— (1976a). Temperature and distance as technical dimensions of interpretation. In Meg Harris Williams (Ed.), *A Meltzer Reader: Selections from the Writings of Donald Meltzer* (pp. 22–34). London: Karnac, 2010.

———— (1976b). The delusion of the clarity of insight. In Meg Harris Williams (Ed.), *A Meltzer Reader: Selections from the Writings of Donald Meltzer* (pp. 56–68). London: Karnac, 2010.

———— (1978). Routine and inspired interpretations – Their relation to the weaning process in analysis. *Contemporary Psychoanalysis* 14: 210–225.

———— (1990). *The Claustrum: An Investigation of Claustrophobic Phenomena*. London: Karnac Books.

———— and Martha Harris (1974). From puberty to adolescence. In Meg Harris Williams (Ed.), *Adolescence: Talks and Papers by Donald Meltzer and Martha Harris* (pp. 131–142). London: Karnac, 2011.

————, Giuliana Milana, Susanna Maiello and Diomira Petrelli (1986). The conceptual distinction between projective identification (Klein) and container-contained (Bion). In Donald Meltzer et al. (Eds.), *Studies in Extended Metapsychology: Clinical Applications of Bion's Ideas* (pp. 50–69). London: Karnac.

Michels, Robert (2000). The case history. *Journal of the American Psychoanalytic Association* 48.2: 355–375.

Miller, Lynda (1987). Idealization and contempt: Dual aspects of the process of devaluation of the breast in a feeding relationship. *Journal of Child Psychotherapy* 13.1: 41–55.

Mitrani, Judith L. (2001). Changes of mind: On thinking things through in the countertransference. In *Ordinary People and Extra-Ordinary Projections: A Post-Kleinian Approach to the Treatment of Primitive Mental States* (pp. 147–156). London and New York, NY: Routledge.

Money-Kyrle, Roger (1956). Normal counter-transference and some of its deviations. In *The Collected Papers of Roger Money-Kyrle*, Ed. Donald Meltzer with the assistance of Edna O'Shaughnessy (pp. 330–342). London: Karnac, 2015.

Mordecai, Aslan and Danuta Waydenfeld (1998). The assessment consultation. In Judy Cooper and Helen Alfillé (Eds.), *Assessment in Psychotherapy* (pp. 87–106). London: Karnac.

Morgan, David (Ed.) (2019). *The Unconscious in Social and Political Life*. Bicester: Phoenix Publishing House.

———— (Ed.) (2020). *A Deeper Cut: Further Explorations of the Unconscious in Social and Political Life*. Bicester: Phoenix Publishing House.

Mulligan, Dhipthi (2017). The storied analyst: Desire and persuasion in the clinical vignette. *The Psychoanalytic Quarterly* 86.4: 811–833.

Nardone, Giorgio and Alessandro Salvini (Eds.) (2019). *International Dictionary of Psychotherapy*. London and New York, NY: Routledge.

National Alliance for Arts, Health & Wellbeing (2012–). URL www.artshealthand wellbeing.org.uk. Accessed 28 November 2019.

Negri, Romana (1994). *The Newborn in the Intensive Care Unit: A Neuropsychoanalytic Prevention Model*, ed. Meg Harris Williams, trans. Maria Pia Falcone. London: Karnac.

"New Library of Psychoanalysis 'Beyond the Couch'" book series (2010–). London and New York, NY: Routledge.

Nigianni, Chrysanthi and Angie Voela (2019). Psychoanalytic practice and queer theory: Queering the clinic. *Studies in Gender & Sexuality* 20.4: 234–237.

Northern Ireland Group for Art as Therapy (1976–). URL www.nigat.org. Accessed 28 November 2019.

Nurka, Camille (2015). Labiaplasty and the melancholic breast. *Studies in Gender and Sexuality* 16.3: 204–225.

O'Connor, Frank (1963). My Oedipus Complex. In *My Oedipus Complex and Other Stories* (pp. 12–22). London and New York, NY: Penguin.

Oelsner, Robert (Ed.) (2013). *Transference and Countertransference Today*. London and New York, NY: Routledge.

Ogden, Benjamin H. and Thomas H. Ogden (2013). *The Analyst's Ear and the Critic's Eye: Rethinking Psychoanalysis and Literature*. London and New York, NY: Routledge.

Ogden, Thomas H. (1999). *Reverie and Interpretation: Sensing Something Human*. London: Karnac.

——— (2005). On psychoanalytic writing. *International Journal of Psychoanalysis* 86.1: 15–29.

——— (2009a). On teaching psychoanalysis. In *Rediscovering Psychoanalysis: Thinking and Dreaming, Learning and Forgetting* (pp. 50–69). London and New York, NY: Routledge.

——— (2009b). On psychoanalytic supervision. In *Rediscovering Psychoanalysis: Thinking and Dreaming, Learning and Forgetting* (pp. 31–49). London and New York, NY: Routledge.

——— (2009c). Rediscovering psychoanalysis. In *Rediscovering Psychoanalysis: Thinking and Dreaming, Learning and Forgetting* (pp. 1–13). London and New York, NY: Routledge.

——— (2012a). Some thoughts on how to read this book. In *Creative Readings: Essays on Seminal Analytic Works* (pp. 1–10). London and New York, NY: Routledge.

——— (2012b). Comments on transference and countertransference in the initial analytic meeting. In Bernard Reith, Sven Lagerlöf, Penelope Crick, Mette Møller and Elisabeth Skale (Eds.), *Initiating Psychoanalysis: Perspectives* (pp. 173–188). London and New York, NY: Routledge.

——— (2015). On potential space. In Margaret Boyle Spelman and Frances Thomson-Salo (Eds.), *The Winnicott Tradition* (pp. 121–133). London: Karnac.

——— (2016). *Reclaiming Unlived Life: Experiences in Psychoanalysis*. London and New York, NY: Routledge.

——— (2018). How I talk with my patients. *The Psychoanalytic Quarterly* 87.3: 399–413.

O'Neill, Sylvia (2005). Psychoanalytic application and psychoanalytic integrity. *International Journal of Psychoanalysis* 86.1: 125–146.

Orbach, Susie (2016). *In Therapy: How Conversations with Psychotherapists Really Work*. London: Profile Books in association with Welcome Collection.

——— (2016–2017). *In Therapy*. Radio programme, 2 series. Dir. Ian Rickson. London: BBC.

——— (2018). *In Therapy: The Unfolding Story*. London: Profile Books in association with Wellcome Collection.

Parker, Ian (2018). Psychoanalytic case presentations, the case against. *Lacunae: APPI International Journal for Lacanian Psychoanalysis* 17: 6–36.

Petrov, Rumen (2009). Autobiography as a psycho-social research method. In Simon Clarke and Paul Hoggett (Eds.), *Researching beneath the Surface: Psycho-Social Research Methods in Practice* (pp. 193–213). London and New York, NY: Routledge.

Phillips, Adam (2002). *Promises, Promises: Essays on Literature and Psychoanalysis.* London: Faber and Faber.

Pick, Daniel (2015). *Psychoanalysis: A Very Short Introduction.* Oxford: Oxford University Press.

Piotrowska, Agnieszka (Ed.) (2015). *Embodied Encounters: New Approaches to Psychoanalysis and Cinema.* London and New York, NY: Routledge.

Poland, Warren S. (2002). Psychoanalysis in the culture. *The Journal of the American Psychoanalytical Society* 50.4: 1103–1108.

Psychoanalysis, Culture & Society (1996–). Basingstoke and New York, NY: Palgrave Macmillan.

"Psychoanalysis and Popular Culture" book series (2013–). London: Karnac, 2013–2018; London and New York, NY: Routledge, 2018.

Psychoanalytic Electronic Publishing (PEP) (1998–). URL www.pep-web.org. Accessed 26 June 2019.

Racker, Heinrich (1953). A contribution to the problem of counter-transference. *International Journal of Psycho-Analysis* 34: 313–324.

——— (1957). The meanings and uses of countertransference. *Psychoanalytic Quarterly* 26: 303–357.

——— (1968). *Transference and Countertransference.* London: The Hogarth Press and the Institute of Psycho-Analysis, 1988.

Ramvi, Ellen, Julian Manley, Lynn Froggett, Anne Liveng, Aase Lading, Wendy Hollway and Birgitta Haga Gripsrud (2018). The visual matrix method in a study of death and dying: Methodological reflections. *Psychoanalysis, Culture & Society* 24.1: 31–52.

Raphael-Leff, Joan (2012). The intersubjective matrix: Influences on Independents' growth from "object relations" to "subject relations". In Paul Williams, John Keene and Sira Dermen (Eds.), *Independent Psychoanalysis Today* (pp. 87–162). London: Karnac.

Redding Mersky, Rose and Burkard Sievers (2018). Social photo-matrix and social dream-drawing. In Karlina Stamenova and Robert D. Hinshelwood (Eds.), *Methods of Research into the Unconscious: Applying Psychoanalytic Ideas to Social Science* (pp. 145–168). London and New York, NY: Routledge.

Redman, Peter (2016). Once more with feeling: What is the psychosocial anyway? *Journal for Psycho-Social Studies* 9.1: 73–93.

Redmond, Mark, Rachel C. Sumner, Diane M. Crone and Samantha Hughes (2019). "Light in dark places": Exploring qualitative data from a longitudinal study using creative arts as a form of social prescribing. *Arts & Health: An International Journal for Research, Policy and Practice* 11.3: 232–245.

Reith, Bernard, Sven Lagerlöf, Penelope Crick, Mette Møller and Elisabeth Skale (2012). General introduction. In Bernard Reith, Sven Lagerlöf, Penelope Crick, Mette Møller and Elisabeth Skale (Eds.), *Initiating Psychoanalysis: Perspectives* (pp. 1–15). London and New York, NY: Routledge.

Rendell, Jane (2017). *The Architecture of Psychoanalysis: Spaces of Transition.* London and New York, NY: I.B. Tauris.

Rhode, Maria (2018). Object relations approaches to autism. *International Journal of Psychoanalysis* 99.3: 702–724.

Richards, Barry (2018). *What Holds Us Together: Popular Culture and Social Cohesion.* London: Karnac.

——— (2019a). Beyond the angers of populism: A psychosocial inquiry. *Journal of Psychosocial Studies* 12.1–2: 171–183.

——— (2019b). *The Psychology of Politics.* London and New York, NY: Routledge.

Richards, David (2019). How queer can psychoanalysis be? Reflections on the encounter between analytic practice and queer theorizing of sexuality. *Studies in Gender & Sexuality* 20.4: 231–233.

Riesenberg-Malcolm, Ruth (1994). The three WS: What, where and why – The rationale of interpretation. In Priscilla Roth (Ed.), *On Bearing Unbearable States of Mind* (pp. 168–180). London and New York, NY: Routledge, 1999.

Rifkind, Gabrielle (2018). *The Psychology of Political Extremism: What Would Sigmund Freud Have Thought about Islamic State?* London and New York, NY: Routledge.

Rinder, Irwin D. (1958). The image of breast feeding advanced by "The magazine all about babies". *American Imago* 15.4: 425–431.

Rocha Barros, Elias Mallet (2013). What does the presentation of case material tell us about what actually happened in an analysis and how does it do this? *International Journal of Psychoanalysis* 94.6: 1145–1152.

Rollin, Lucy and Mark I. West (1999). Introduction. In Lucy Rolling and Mark I. West (Eds.), *Psychoanalytic Responses to Children's Literature* (pp. 1–16). Jefferson, NC: McFarland and Company, Inc.

Rose, Gilbert J. (2004). *Between Couch and Piano: Psychoanalysis, Music, Art and Neuroscience.* London and New York, NY: Routledge.

Roseneil, Sasha (2012). Building the field: The psychosocial studies network and beyond. . . *Journal of Psycho-Social Studies* 6.1: 1–2.

——— (2014a). The psychosocial challenges of establishing the field of psychosocial studies. *Journal of Psycho-social Studies* 8.1: 105–136.

——— (2014b). On meeting Linda: An intimate encounter with (not-)belonging in the current conjecture. *Psychoanalysis, Culture & Society* 19.1: 19–28.

——— (2019a). On missed encounters: Psychoanalysis, queer theory, and the psychosocial dynamics of exclusion. *Studies in Gender & Sexuality* 20.4: 214–219.

——— (2019b). Broader (than psychoanalysis) and deeper (than sociology): The psychosocial promise of group analysis. *Psychoanalysis, Culture & Society* 24.4: 493–501.

Rosenfeld, David (2014). *The Body Speaks: Body Image Delusions and Hypochondria.* London: Karnac.

Roy, Alastair and Julian Manley (2017). Recovery and movement: Allegory and "journey" as a means of exploring recovery from substance misuse. *Journal of Social Work Practice* 31.2: 191–204.

Rubell, Jennifer interviewed by Claire Bartleman (2018). In *Then Again, Maybe I Won't* (pp. 33–39). Unpublished. MA diss. London: ON: University of Western Ontario.

Rubin, Jeffrey (1997). Fostering tolerance and creativity in the culture of psychoanalysis. *The Journal of the American Academy of Psychoanalysis* 25.1: 15–35.

Rustin, Margaret (1989). Encountering primitive anxieties. In Lisa Miller, Margaret Rustin, Michael Rustin and Judy Shuttleworth (Eds.), *Closely Observed Infants* (pp. 7–21). London: Duckworth.

Rustin, Michael (2019). *Researching the Unconscious: Principles of Psychoanalytic Method*. London and New York, NY: Routledge.

Ryan, Joanna (2017). *Class and Psychoanalysis: Landscapes of Inequality*. London and New York, NY: Routledge.

Sabbadini, Andrea (2014a). *Moving Images: Psychoanalytic Reflections on Film*. London and New York, NY: Routledge.

——— (2014b). Listening to sounds. In *Boundaries and Bridges: Perspectives on Time and Space in Psychoanalysis* (pp. 119–128). London: Karnac.

——— (2014c). On the couch. In *Boundaries and Bridges: Perspectives on Time and Space in Psychoanalysis* (pp. 79–90). London: Karnac.

Sarlin, Charles N. (1981). The role of breast-feeding in psychosexual development and the achievement of the genital phase. *Journal of the American Psychoanalytic Association* 29.3: 631–641.

Scharff, David E. (2020). Living in the object. In David E. Scharff (Ed.), *The Use of an Object in Psychoanalysis: An Object Relations Perspective on the Other* (pp. 4–16). London and New York, NY: Routledge.

Schinaia, Cosimo (2019). Respect for the environment: Psychoanalytic reflections on the ecological crisis. *International Journal of Psychoanalysis* 100.2: 272–286.

Schmidl, Fritz (1972). Problems of method in applied psychoanalysis. *Psychoanalytic Quarterly* 41.3: 402–419.

Schreiber, Sanford (1974). A filmed fairy tale as a screen memory. *The Psychoanalytic Study of the Child* 29: 389–410.

Schwarz, David (1997). *Listening Subjects: Music, Psychoanalysis, Culture*. Durham, NC: Duke University Press.

Segal, Hanna (1958). Fear of death – Notes on the analysis of an old man. *International Journal of Psychoanalysis* 39: 178–181.

——— (1987). Silence is the real crime. *International Review of Psycho-Analysis* 14: 3–12.

——— (1988). Seating it out. *Psychoanalytic Study of the Child* 43: 167–175.

Shabad, Peter and Stanley S. Selinger (1995). Bracing for disappointment and the counterphobic leap into the future. In Edward G. Corrigan and Pearl-Ellen Gordon (Eds.), *The Mind Object: Precocity and Pathology of Self-Sufficiency* (pp. 209–227). Northvale, NJ and London: Jason Aronson Inc.

Shapiro, Vivian, Selma Fraiberg and Edna Adelson (1976). Infant-parent psychotherapy on behalf of a child in a critical nutritional state. *The Psychoanalytic Study of the Child* 31.1: 461–491.

Shedler, Jonathan (2010). The efficacy of psychodynamic psychotherapy. *American Psychologist* 65.2: 98–109.

Shulman, Graham (2019). Through the lens of infant observation: Some reflections on teaching infant observation and its applications to professionals working with infants. *Infant Observation: International Journal of Infant Observation and Its Applications* 22.1: 4–20.

Single Case Archive Project (2013–). The. Colchester and Ghent: University of Essex and Ghent university. URL www.singlecasearchive.com/. Accessed 6 March 2019.

Sklar, Jonathan (2019). *Dark Times: Psychoanalytic Perspectives on Politics, History and Mourning*. Bicester and Oxford: Phoenix Publishing.

Skodstad, Wilhelm (2018). Psychoanalytic observation – The mind as research interview. In Kalina Stamenova and Robert D. Hinshelwood (Eds.), *Methods of Research into the Unconscious: Applying Psychoanalytic Ideas to Social Science* (pp. 107–125). London and New York, NY: Routledge.

Slochower, Harry (1964). Applied psychoanalysis: As a science and as an art. *American Imago* 21.1–2: 165–174.

Smadja, Eric (2015). *Freud and Culture*. London and New York, NY: Routledge.

Smyth, Ailbhe (2013). Women's studies and the disciplines (1992). In Noreen Giffney and Margrit Shildrick (Eds.), *Theory on the Edge: Irish Studies and the Politics of Sexual Difference* (pp. 9–13). Basingstoke and New York, NY: Palgrave Macmillan.

Sociology, Psychoanalysis and Psychosocial Study Group, British Sociological Association (2011). URL www.britsoc.co.uk/groups/study-groups/sociology-psychoanalysis-and-the-psychosocial-study-group/. Accessed 26 June 2020.

Sophocles (1984 [1977]). *Oedipus the king*. In Robert Fagles (Trans.), *The three Theban plays: Antigone, Oedipus the King, Oedipus at Colonus* (pp. 155–251). London: Penguin.

Spurling, Laurence (1997). Using the case study in the assessment of trainees. In Ivan Ward (Ed.), *The Presentation of Case Material in Clinical Discourse* (pp. 64–76). London: Freud Museum.

———— (2015). *The Psychoanalytic Craft: How to Develop as a Psychoanalytic Practitioner*. Basingstoke and New York, NY: Palgrave Macmillan.

———— (2019). Mapping the field of psychoanalytic psychosocial practice. *Psychoanalysis, Culture & Society* 24.2: 175–196.

Stamenova, Kalina and R.D. Hinshelwood (2018). Introduction. In Kalina Stamenova and R.D. Hinshelwood (Eds.), *Methods of Research into the Unconscious* (pp. 10–16). London and New York, NY: Routledge.

Stein, Alexander (2007). The sound of memory: Music and acoustic origins. *American Imago* 64.1: 59–85.

Stein, Martin H. (1988). Writing about psychoanalysis II: Analysts who write, patients who read. *Journal of the American Psychoanalytic Association* 36.2: 393–408.

Steiner, John (1993). *Psychic Retreats: Pathological Organizations in Psychotic, Neurotic and Borderline Patients*. London and New York, NY: Routledge.

———— (2008). The repetition compulsion, envy, and the death instinct. In Priscilla Roth and Alessandra Lemma (Eds.), *Envy and Gratitude Revisited* (pp. 137–151). London: Karnac.

———— (2011). *Seeing and Being Seen: Emerging from a Psychic Retreat*. London and New York, NY: Routledge.

———— (2020). *Illusion, Disillusion, and Irony in Psychoanalysis*. London and New York, NY: Routledge.

Stephen Friedman Gallery (2020). Profile of Jennifer Rubell. URL www.stephenfriedman.com/artists/52-jennifer-rubell/. Accessed 6 August 2020.

Sternberg, Janine (2005). *Infant Observation at the Heart of Training*. London: Karnac.

Stewart, Harold (1995). The development of mind-as-object. In Edward G. Corrigan and Pearl-Ellen Gordon (Eds.), *The Mind Object: Precocity and Pathology of Self-Sufficiency* (pp. 41–53). Northvale, NJ and London: Jason Aronson Inc.

Stone, Rebecca (2015). Can the breast feed the mother too? Tracing maternal subjectivity in Toni Morrison's *Beloved*. *British Journal of Psychotherapy* 31.3: 298–310.

Sweet, Alistair (2013). Thoughts without a thinker, mimetic fusing and the anti-container considered as primitive defensive mechanisms in the addictions. *Psychoanalytic Psychotherapy* 27.2: 140–153.

Taylor, Barbara (2015). *The Last Asylum: A Memoir of Madness in Our Times*. London: Penguin.

Thomas, Jem (2018). "As easy as you know . . .": On the tensions between psychoanalysis and psychosocial research. In Anne-Marie Cummins and Nigel Williams (Eds.), *Further Researching beneath the Surface, Volume 2: Psycho-Social Research Methods in Practice* (pp. 3–25). London and New York, NY: Routledge.

Thomson-Salo, Frances (2014). Introduction to infant observation: An infant's inner world. In Frances Thomson Salo (Ed.), *Infant Observation: Creating Transformative Relationships* (pp. 3–14). London: Karnac.

Thorpe, Harriet (2015). Jennifer Rubell: *Not alone. Studio international*, 2 October. URL www.studiointernational.com/index.php/jennifer-rubell-not-alone-review-stephen-friedman-gallery-london. Accessed 23 February 2020.

Tolan, Janet and Susan Lendrum (1995). *Case Material and Role Play in Counselling Training*. London and New York, NY: Routledge.

Townsend, Patricia (2019). *Creative States of Mind: Psychoanalysis and the Artist's Process*. London and New York, NY: Routledge.

Treacher Kabesh, Amal (2013). Soundspace. In Annette Kuhn (Ed.), *Little Madnesses: Winnicott, Transitional Phenomena and Cultural Experience* (pp. 65–76). London and New York, NY: I.B. Tauris.

Trustram, Myna (2016). Performing the psychosocial: An enquiry into forgetting. *Journal of Psycho-Social Studies* 9.1: 53–72.

Tuckett, David (1994). The conceptualisation and communication of clinical facts in psychoanalysis. *International Journal of Psychoanalysis* 75: 865–870.

Turkle, Sherry (2007). What makes an object evocative? In Sherry Turkle (Ed.), *Evocative Objects: Things We Think With* (pp. 307–326). Cambridge, MA and London: The MIT Press.

Tylim, Isaac and Adrienne Harris (2018). Introduction: The frame. In Isaac Tylim and Adrienne Harris (Eds.), *Reconsidering the Moveable Frame in Psychoanalysis: Its Function and Structure in Contemporary Psychoanalytic Theory* (pp. 1–11). London and New York, NY: Routledge.

Volkan, Vamik D. (2018). Large group identity. In Salman Akhtar and Stuart Twemlow (2018a) (Eds.), *Textbook of Applied Psychoanalysis* (pp. 45–54). London and New York, NY: Routledge.

——— (2020). *Large-Group Psychology: Racism, Societal Divisions, Narcissistic Leaders and Who We Are Now*. Bicester and Oxford: Phoenix Publishing.

Vyrgioti, Marita (2019). In the closets of Fanon and Riviere: Psychoanalysis, postcolonial theory and the psychosocial. In Stephen Frosh (Ed.), *New Voices in Psychosocial Studies* (pp. 23–37). Basingstoke and New York, NY: Palgrave Macmillan.

Walker, Carl, Orly Klein, Nick Marks and Paul Hanna (2019). Caring spaces and practices: Does social prescribing offer new possibilities for the fluid mess of "mental health"? In Laura McGrath and Paula Reavey (Eds.), *The Handbook of Mental Health and Space: Community and Clinical Applications* (pp. 149–162). Abingdon, Oxon and New York, NY: Routledge.

Walkerdine, Valerie (2008). Contextualizing debates about psychosocial studies. *Psychoanalysis, Culture & Society* 13.4: 341–345.

Ward, Ivan (1997). Introduction. In Ivan Ward (Ed.), *The Presentation of Case Material in Clinical Discourse* (pp. 5–10). London: Freud Museum.

Waska, Robert (2013). *A Practical Casebook of Time-Limited Psychoanalytic Work: A Modern Kleinian Approach*. London and New York, NY: Routledge.

——— (2015). Pushed to the limits in the counter-transference. In *A Casebook of Psychotherapy Practice with Challenging Patients: A Modern Kleinian Approach* (pp. 43–55). London and New York, NY: Routledge.

Watson, Andrea (1990). On his brother's blindness. *Journal of Child Psychotherapy* 16.1: 127–134.

Watson, Eve (2017). Afterword: Reflections on the encounters between psychoanalysis and queer theory. In Noreen Giffney and Eve Watson (Eds.), *Clinical Encounters in Sexuality: Psychoanalytic Practice and Queer Theory* (pp. 445–473). New York, NY: Punctum Books.

——— (2019). Psychoanalysis and queer theory: Towards an ethics of otherness. *Studies in Gender & Sexuality* 20.4: 242–244.

Weintrobe, Sally (Ed.) (2013). *Engaging with Climate Change: Psychoanalytic and Interdisciplinary Perspectives*. London and New York, NY: Routledge.

Wengraf, Tom (2018). Researching dated, situated, defended, and evolving subjectivities by biographic-narrative interview: Psychoanalysis, the psycho-societal unconscious, and biographic-narrative interview method and interpretation. In Kalina Stamenova and Robert D. Hinshelwood (Eds.), *Methods of Research into the Unconscious: Applying Psychoanalytic Ideas to Social Science* (pp. 211–234). London and New York, NY: Routledge.

Wille, Robbert S.J. (2011). On the capacity to ensure psychic pain. *Scandinavian Psychoanalytic Review* 34.1: 23–30.

Williams, Raymond (1985). *Keywords: A Vocabulary of Culture and Society*, revised ed. New York, NY: Oxford University Press, 1976.

Wilson, Scott (2015). *Stop Making Sense: Music from the Perspective of the Real*. London: Karnac.

Winnicott, Donald W. (1936). Appetite and emotional disorder. In *Through Pediatrics to Psychoanalysis: Collected Papers* (pp. 33–51). London: Karnac, 1984.

——— (1949a). Birth memories, birth trauma, and anxiety. In *Through Pediatrics to Psychoanalysis: Collected Papers* (pp. 174–193). London: Karnac, 1984.

——— (1949b). Mind and its relation to the psyche-soma. In *Through Pediatrics to Psychoanalysis: Collected Papers* (pp. 243–254). London: Karnac, 1984.

——— (1952). Anxiety associated with insecurity. In *Through Pediatrics to Psychoanalysis: Collected Papers* (pp. 97–100). London: Karnac, 1984.

——— (1953). Transitional objects and transitional phenomena. In *Playing and Reality* (pp. 1–34). London and New York, NY: Routledge, 1991.

——— (1960a). The theory of the parent-infant relationship. In *The Maturational Processes and the Facilitating Environment: Studies in the Theory of Emotional Development* (pp. 37–55). London: Karnac, 1990.

——— (1960b). The relationship of a mother to her baby at the beginning (pp. 21–28). In *The Family and Individual Development*. London and New York, NY: Routledge, 1989.

———— (1963). The development of the capacity for concern. In *The Maturational Processes and the Facilitating Environment: Studies in the Theory of Emotional Development* (pp. 73–82). London: Karnac, 1990.

———— (1967). The location of cultural experience. In *Playing and Reality* (pp. 128–139). London and New York, NY: Routledge.

———— (1968a). Breast-feeding as communication. In *Babies and Their Mothers* (pp. 23–33). London: Free Association Books, 1988.

———— (1968b). Communication between infant and mother, and mother and infant, compared and contrasted. In *Babies and Their Mothers* (pp. 89–103). London: Free Association Books, 1988.

———— (1971a). The use of an object and relating through identifications. In *Playing and Reality* (pp. 115–127). London and New York, NY: Routledge, 1991.

———— (1971b). Playing: A theoretical statement. In *Playing and Reality* (pp. 51–70). London and New York, NY: Routledge, 1991.

———— (1971c). Playing: Creative activity and the search for the self. In *Playing and Reality* (pp. 71–86). London and New York, NY: Routledge, 1991.

———— (1988). Establishment of relationship with external reality. In *Human Nature* (pp. 100–115). London: Free Association Books.

Wittenberg, Icsa (1975). Primal depression in autism: John. In Donald Meltzer, John Bremner, Shirley Hoxter, Doreen Weddell and Icsa Wittenberg (Eds.), *Explorations in Autism: A Psychoanalytical Study* (pp. 56–98). London: Karnac.

Wolfreys, Julian (2004). *Critical Keywords in Literary and Cultural Theory*. Basingstoke and New York, NY: Palgrave Macmillan.

Wood, Heather (2014). Working with problems of perversion. *The British Journal of Psychotherapy* 30.4: 422–437.

Woodward, Kath (2015). *Psychosocial Studies: An Introduction*. London and New York, NY: Routledge.

Yakeley, Jessica (2014). Psychodynamic psychotherapy: Developing the evidence base. *Advances in Psychiatric Treatment* 20.4: 269–279.

———— (2018). Psychoanalysis in modern mental health practice. *The Lancet Psychiatry* 5.5: 443–450.

Yates, Candida (2001). Teaching psychoanalytic studies: Towards a new culture of learning in higher education. *Psychoanalytic Studies* 3.3–4: 333–347.

———— (2008). "Video replay: Families, films and fantasy" as a transformational text: Commentary on Valerie Walkerdine's "Video replay". *Psychoanalysis, Culture & Society* 15.4: 404–411.

———— (2014). Psychoanalysis and television: Notes towards a psycho-cultural approach. In Caroline Bainbridge, Ivan Ward and Candida Yates (Eds.), *Television and Psychoanalysis: Psycho-Cultural Perspectives* (pp. 1–28). London: Karnac.

———— (2018). Reflecting on the study of psychoanalysis, culture and society: The development of a psycho-cultural approach. *Psychoanalysis, Culture & Society* 23.1: 54–67.

———— (2019). The psychodynamics of casino culture and politics. *Journal of Psychosocial Studies* 12.3: 217–230.

Yeomans, Frank E., John F. Clarkin and Otto F. Kernberg (2015). *Transference-Focused Psychotherapy for Borderline Personality Disorder: A Clinical Guide*. Arlington, VA: American Psychiatric Publishing, 2015.

Zeavin, Lynne (2018). Frame matters. In Isaac Tylim and Adrienne Harris (Eds.), *Reconsidering the Moveable Frame in Psychoanalysis: Its Function and Structure in Contemporary Psychoanalytic Theory* (pp. 57–71). London and New York, NY: Routledge.

Zittoun, Tania (2013). On the use of a film: Cultural experiences as symbolic resources. In Annette Kuhn (Ed.), *Little Madnesses: Winnicott, Transitional Phenomena and Cultural Experience* (pp. 135–147). London and New York, NY: I.B. Tauris.

Zysman, Samuel (2012). Theories as objects: A psychoanalytic inquiry into minds and theories. In Jorge Canestri (Ed.), *Putting Theory to Work: How Are Theories Actually Used in Practice?* (pp. 135–156). London: Karnac.

Artworks

Black, Karla (2011). *There Can Be No Arguments. Art sculpture*. Cologne: Galerie Gisela Capitain.

Brennan, Cecily (2005). *Melancholia. Video*, 10 minutes, 36 Seconds. Dublin: IMMA – The Irish Museum of Modern Art, purchase, 2006.

Coogan, Amanda (2014). *Oh Chocolate. Solo Art Performance*, 2 hours. Dublin: The National Museum of Decorative Arts and History.

Danby, Francis (1828). *The Opening of the Sixth Seal. Oil Painting*. Dublin: National Gallery of Ireland.

IMMA Collection: Freud Project (2018–2019). *Gaze. Art Exhibition*. Dublin: IMMA – The Irish Museum of Modern Art. URL https://imma.ie/whats-on/imma-collection-freud-project-gaze/. Accessed 26 June 2020.

Rubell, Jennifer (2012). *My Shrink's Couch. Art Installation*. New York, NY. URL http://jenniferrubell.com

——— (2013). *Portrait of the Artist. Art Installation*. New York, NY. URL http://jenniferrubell.com. Accessed 1 May 2019.

——— (2015a). *Us. Art Sculpture*. New York, NY. URL http://jenniferrubell.com/projects/8-projects/61-us. Accessed 14 January 2020.

——— (2015b). *Not Alone. Art Exhibition*. London: Stephen Friedman Gallery. URL www.stephenfriedman.com/exhibitions/past/2015/jennifer-rubell-not-alone/. Accessed 14 January 2020.

Shahroudy Farmanfarmaian, Monir (2018). *Sunset, Sunrise. Art Exhibition*. Dublin: IMMA – The Irish Museum of Modern Art. URL https://imma.ie/whats-on/monir-shahroudy-farmanfarmaian-sunset-sunrise/. Accessed 26 June 2020.

Swanzy, Mary (2018–2019). *Voyages. Art Exhibition*. Dublin: IMMA – The Irish Museum of Modern Art. URL https://imma.ie/whats-on/mary-swanzy-voyages/. Accessed 26 June 2020.

Tillmans, Wolfgang (2018–2019). *Rebuilding the Future. Art Exhibition*. Dublin: IMMA – The Irish Museum of Modern Art. URL https://imma.ie/whats-on/wolfgang-tillmans-rebuilding-the-future/. Accessed 26 June 2020.

Films and Television Series

Be'Tipul (2005–2008). Television programme, 2 seasons. Created by Levi Hagai, Ori Sivan and Nir Bergman. Israel: HOT3.

Cyrus (2010). Feature film. Dirs. Jay Duplass and Mark Duplass. Produced by Scott Free Productions, London and Los Angeles, CA.

Encounters through Generations (2011). Documentary film. Produced the Audio-Visual Project. London: Institute of Psychoanalysis.

The Incredible Hulk (1977–1982). Television show, 5 seasons. Developed by Kenneth Johnson. New York, NY and Los Angeles, CA: CBS.

In Treatment (2008–2010). Television show, 3 seasons. Developed by Rodrigo Garcia. New York, NY: HBO.

Max Richter's Sleep (2020). Documentary film. Dir. Natalie Johns. London: JA Films.

Melancholia (2011). Feature film. Dir. Lars von Trier. Denmark: Zentropa.

Morvern Callar (2002). Feature film. Dir. Lynne Ramsay. London: Company Pictures.

[Safe] (1995). Feature film. Dir. Todd Haynes. New York, NY: American Playhouse and Good Machine; London: Channel 4 Films.

Shame (2011). Feature film. Dir. Steve McQueen. Produced by See-Saw Films, London and Sydney; Film4 Productions, London, UK Film Council, London; Lipsync Productions, London; Alliance Films, Montreal; and HanWay Films, London.

Music tracks and albums

Britell, Nicholas (2016). End credits suite. In *Moonlight*. Beverly Hills, CA: Lakeshore Records.

Cage, John (2010). 4'33". In *Cage Against the Machine*. London: Wall of Sound.

Dead Can Dance (2007). Sanvean. In *Toward the Within*. London: 4AD.

De Moor, Vincent (2007). Close encounters of the second mind. In *Trance Top 100*. Amsterdam: Armada Music.

O'Neill, Perri (2006). Bass society. In *South-West Saga EP*. Amsterdam: Armada Music.

Richter, Max (2015). *Sleep*. New York, NY: Avatar Studios, London: AIR Studios, Berlin: Studio Kino.

Sepultura (1993). The hunt. In *Chaos AD*. New York, NY: The All Blacks B.V.

Sonic Youth (1991). White kross (live). In *Dirty Boots EP*. Santa Monica, CA: UMG Recordings, Inc.

Wingo, David (2011). At the beach. In *Take Shelter Original Motion Picture Soundtrack*. Paris: Grove Hill Productions LLC, under exclusive license to Editions Milan Music.

Index

Note: Page numbers in *italics* indicate a figure on the corresponding page.